THE FIRST TIME GARDENER

The Book Guild Ltd.
25 High Street,
Lewes, Sussex

First published 1992
© Barbara Kelsey 1992
Set in Baskerville
Typesetting by Acorn Bookwork,
Salisbury, Wiltshire
Printed in Great Britain by
Antony Rowe Ltd.
Chippenham, Wiltshire.

A catalogue record of this book is
available from the British Library

ISBN 0 86332 792 3

THE FIRST TIME GARDENER

Barbara Kelsey

The Book Guild Ltd.
Sussex, England

*This book is dedicated
to the 'Q' who
shared my life*

Q writes: *My thanks to Rosie Holbech who helped to get
this book into blossom.*

CONTENTS

INTRODUCTION

Another gardening book! Let us say a book for those who buy a house with a garden, window-box, balcony or roof-garden. They may not be gardeners, but are not prepared to look out at a patch of mud and bricks left behind by the builders, or a wilderness of nameless plants and bushes left by the previous owners. They are busy and not necessarily very ambitious for their garden, feeling that their wants are simple, a desire to have flowers for most of the year without too much trouble and expense. They may be retired people who have not had the leisure to garden before, perhaps have always lived abroad, have come to a town garden from the country, or even the young couple in a new home.

Such people are often told to stick to shrubs which they may not like, or to pave some sort of a concrete jungle containing only tubs, which they may not like either.

We shall try and do better than this. My purpose is to go through the months easing some difficulties and giving some advice from long experience in answering questions which are somehow not dealt with in books.

My "Q" who appears through the months is a real, though composite, Person. All the questions are ones I have been asked, some of them many times. As the reader will see, "Q" is quite ready to answer back and inclined to make statements rather than ask questions, which happens in real life more often than in books. He or she may not appear to be very bright, but the real-life questioners can be bursting with brains in other directions; it is simply that nature and growing things have up till then been the proverbial closed book.

I do not forget the young couple whose parents were keen on gardening and who long to have a garden of their own. They may find themselves in a town when their old home was in the country; the soil or the aspect of the garden is different from the one they knew; they may not have the same tastes as their

9

parents (for fashions change in gardens as well as in other things). On the other hand, they may not like modern gardens and want to make their own more like the one they remember. In any case, they will lack experience and time and money will be just as scarce, so their problems will not be so different.

In gardening, subjects overlap each other and some things will turn up in every month, in the mind if not actually in the ground. If we start in January as is logical and are talking about planning, we are bound to be looking forward to the spring months and backwards to the autumn months when so much is planted. What about the reader who has bought a house in June and will naturally turn first to that month?

We must have an Index. As you will see from the text, I have highlighted by the use of bold type, the names of plants so that they stand out from the page and are therefore easily found, having first been looked up in the index.

I wish everyone, gardeners and non-gardeners great happiness in this lovely hobby which has given me such pleasure all my life. Let us end on this note and forget Pests and Disappointments until they come!

January

January is a slack month in the garden; for the most part the plants are resting (dormant), the weather is bad and it is too early to plant anything, so that the most you are likely to do in the way of active gardening is to walk round and get some idea of the size and lay-out of your new acquisition, whether it is sunny or shady − or rather where things seem to be growing best, since there is not much sun at this time of year. You will be pretty sure to experience the cold East or Northeast wind, the commonest in our winters, and will soon see how well-sheltered or otherwise your garden is.

For the moment we are thinking of the 'new' garden which has been cultivated and planted already and what you might see in it at this season − the depths of winter. Trees and bushes (gardeners call the latter shrubs) are easily seen, anything with green leaves at this season is evergreen − possibly trees planted in a line to form a screen against the cold winds or the next-door garden. There might be a lawn with formal-shaped flower-beds. If they have roses they are easy to recognise, but if they seem to have nothing but rather straggly looking dead plants in no sort of order, the chances are that these are weeds and the beds were filled with bedding plants in the summer − the sort of thing you will have seen in window boxes and tubs, sold already in bud or flower and only meant to last the one season.

If there are any long-shaped beds or borders, often with a wall or fence behind them, they too may seem to contain nothing but a lot of dead-looking sticks or dead stalks and leaves, which look very unpromising. However much the hardy perennial or hardy border plant dies down in the winter, it will grow again in the spring. Hardy means that it can stand the winter outdoors. Some people cut down the stalks when they have died, others

11

Iris Stylosa

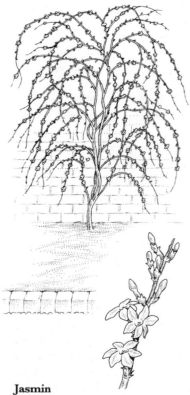

Camellias

Jasmin

leave the dead stalks on to protect the young shoots coming up from the base and they can be seen right at ground level even at this time of year in some plants. Perennial means that they go on from year to year unlike the bedding plants, though most have to be divided every so often, generally about every three or four years.

So there is no need to be discouraged if there is not much to be seen, Next month or the month after could see bulbs coming up from what looks like bare earth.

Q There is deep snow in my garden, will it hurt the plants?
A No, I should say straight away that snow is a marvellous fertilizer and should be welcomed; it also protects the plants' roots from the cold night frost. It is not so strange – one thinks of the Alpine meadows, under feet of snow all the winter and with masses of flowers in the spring.

SOME WINTER PLANTS AND QUERIES

We might be in luck and see some flowering shrubs even at this time of year. Here are some of the most likely:
winter jasmine (Jasmine nudiflorum)

Q There is a very pretty yellow flower out at the moment but it is the most fearful mess. I don't really know if it is a climber or a bush, I thought it was a forsythia, but they say it is a winter jasmine.

A The forsythia comes out later in early spring and has larger flowers which are a brighter yellow; on the whole it flowers more reliably than the jasmine, so it is very good to hear yours is doing so well. Winter flowers are a great bonus in a garden and these can be picked in bud (sometimes as early as November) and brought into the house when they will come out in the warmth of an ordinary room. Snow and heavy rain outside would spoil the flowers which had opened, though the plant comes to no harm. If you cut them in bud wait until they are showing colour, yellow in this case.

Q It's certainly worth keeping then, but how can I get it in hand? It has climbed halfway up the wall and the flower branches are hanging down like streamers on top of what looks like a lot of dead wood.

A As you have already seen, this kind of climber-shrub is not self-supporting, it sends out masses of these streamer-like stems which collapse onto each other, making the untidy mass you see. When it was younger it could have been trained laterally (sideways) along a wire on the wall, or tied to nails at intervals as it grew up, but we must cope with it as we find it now. The 'nude' part of the Latin name means that it flowers before the leaves come, the usual thing for winter-flowering shrubs. If you can get at it when the flowers have died, although there may be leaves coming out it will not really start growing for another month or so, you can cut the 'streamers' back to the main stem, even if they have not flowered all the way down, which will shape things a little. You may then be able to see what wood is really dead all the way up and that can be cut right out from the base. Overgrown shrubs and trees overhanging are so much a problem of the new garden that we do not want to get too bogged down with cutting back or pruning until the time comes in March or April.

There is one more thing worth noting about the jasmine: if any of the streamers are long enough to have reached the ground they may have rooted and be busy turning themselves into little plants of their own and thus adding to the chaos. They can be cut where they join the parent plant and 'lifted' – that is dug up – and moved to another place or given away to friends. Mild weather, with light rain, is best when lifting plants.

Q I'm never sure when the wood is dead.

A It's a matter of practise and if you get a gardening friend to show you at first you will soon get the hang of it. Dead wood feels dry and brittle and can usually be broken quite easily. It is a different colour and it will be much easier to see in springtime when the plant will be growing its leaves. You can do no harm if you just cut back the shoots which have flowered.

Q In the corner of the same wall there is another very untidy-looking plant with thick straggly leaves. It is low-growing and produces the most lovely flowers, light mauve, almost like an orchid.

A This is the **Iris unguicularis stylosa**, the winter iris. The buds can be picked and will open up almost immediately indoors so that they go very well with the jasmine. It is interesting that you have found them so near together, it means a sunny wall. The iris particularly needs sun to flower well; it likes the poor gritty soil at the base of the wall so that it needs no fertilizing, only some sulphate of potash in the spring to remind it of its native Algeria. It is a good idea to have it tucked away in a corner where it is not too conspicuous because as you say it is an untidy plant.

I should add that there is also a purple winter-flowering variety called 'Mary Barnard'.

Q I shall keep this too – should I cut the leaves back?

A Don't cut the leaves back, they are protecting the young buds from the cold. It will finish flowering near the beginning of March and you can pull gently at any dead-looking leaves when you give it its potash. If the leaves come out easily they are dead, but this is the best one can do. Put out slug bait (I use Slugdeath) to prevent the slugs eating the buds.

Q I can't see anything else out – I had rather hoped for some **Snowdrops**.

A Well, you are lucky to have two such reliable winter-flowerers already established – that is well-grown and settled in – they both are slow growers and take a little time before they flower well. You may have snowdrops as well, though not as a rule before February, and even that is early in a cold year. They come up with the white bud already showing, so they will be up and out in no time once you see them above ground.

Camellias

In my own new garden I was lucky enough to find two well-grown camellias. They are evergreens and according to variety will flower all the winter, starting as early as November and going on to the end of March or early April. There are two main kinds the first **Camellia Japonica** with its rounded very shiny, dark green leaves, held straight on the stalk. This kind keep their flowers on the branch without dropping the petals as they fade and bad weather causes them to turn an ugly brown which many people dislike. I am quite happy to take a chance with this, the flowers are so welcome in the dark winter months. The other kind, **x Williamsii**, has longer more pointed leaves which hang down and may look rather 'droopy' in bad weather, possibly because one is more anxious that they are surviving a really cold spell. Nevertheless both kinds are much more hardy than one would think from the frail appearance of their flowers. The *williamsii* drop their petals as they fade exactly like a rose, leaving a coloured carpet on the ground which is not at all unsightly.

Camellias do well in town gardens but they must have an acid to neutral soil. You can find out whether you have an acid soil by buying an inexpensive soil testing kit from a garden shop or centre. They are very easy to use. They should not be exposed to a cold wind or hot sun. The general advice is not to plant them facing East where the cold winds damage the flowers after a frosty night, particularly as this is the side which gets the early-morning sun. Common sense counts just as much in gardening as in anything else. The camellias which flower early are always in danger of being spoiled by bad weather wherever they are planted. My own two are sheltered by the house – the small garden is only a few feet across – so that they come to no harm from facing East. The double-pink *Camellia japonica* has sometimes flowered from November to March without one flower being badly spoiled, but in other years there has been one cold night in a mild spell of winter and they have all gone. There are usually two or three buds all together, when one is over the other is waiting to come on, so it is worth risking. The double-red x *williamsii* comes later in about March. This ensures that the flowers are almost never spoiled because of course they are not there in the winter. As in so many cases, the new gardener must decide for himself. Never be in too much of a hurry, live through the year in your garden and then begin to see what is worth keeping and what is simply taking up space without contributing anything.

Q I must say I thought camellias were hothouse things. Are they difficult to grow?

A You might well have seen them growing in the Temperate House at Kew, where there are some beauties, but they grow outside as well in the shelter of a wall and even came through the exceptionally cold winter of 1946–47 when the snow did not go until the end of April and the wind was said to come from the Russian Steppes – I felt it and am sure it was true! Indeed, I believe it was this winter which first convinced the professional growers that camellias were worth cultivating for gardens. Camellias are sometimes confused with gardenias, the flower of which is very similar but always double-white and scented. Camellias are mostly shades of red and pink, some white, striped white or striped pink and either single or double.

The plants like to grow in partial shade, with plenty of leafmould. They do not need much in the way of feeding (that is using manure or fertilizer) which tends to encourage leaves at the expense of flowers. Experts advise using a general fertilizer like Growmore once a year in the autumn to keep the roots healthy.

Like all evergreens, they shed their leaves gradually – the biggest leaf drop is after they have flowered and the new shoots are growing. If there is a long dry spell in summer, they should have a bucket or two of water, particularly if more leaves than usual are falling.

Q Don't people give them tea-leaves?

A Yes I had forgotten that – the tea-plant is a camellia, and tea-leaves round its roots as a mulch to keep the soil damp would be just the thing. Most plants will grow out towards the sun and so become unbalanced. However, they are very easy to keep in order, only trimming such as one might do to tidy up one's own hair is necessary. The time to trim is after the flowers have died – the new leaves will come in early summer and the buds begin to form again about July.

Q I never realised the flower-buds came so early.

A Yes, it is one of the wonders of nature that the plant should be getting ready for flowering several months in advance. Winter and early spring-flowering shrubs should be pruned (trimmed or shaped) in spring rather than autumn for this reason.

Q Are they expensive?

A They are not too bad if you only buy a small one but it is worth paying more for something bigger – say 4ft tall and already starting to flower, for camellias are slow-growing, although this is often an advantage in a town garden. My bushes are about 30 years old and have grown 8ft, upwards and outwards, making nice compact bushes.

The Witch Hazel (*Hamamellis Mollis*)

The other two suggestions for 'dead' winter are both trees; if you have room the winter-flowering witch hazel has attractive spidery yellow flowers which come out in the coldest January days and look best against a dark background – say an evergreen.

It wants space of course as it is a tree and there is nothing more frustrating than having to mutilate a tree by cutting it into an unnatural shape just when it reaches maturity and is looking its best. As a rough guide, 20–25ft is the height of the top of a first-floor window – so not to be grown in a front garden unless it extends twenty or so feet back from the road. It is not a forest tree, really large, but about the size of the smaller flowering cherry.

I must be honest with the reader though and say that this is my own preference as the Q's to whom I have recommended it all think the flowers too small and insignificant. I saw it first on a cold January day at Kew, looking so brave and cheerful with its little yellow flowers against the wintry sky, and longed to have room to grow it myself. There is a variety **Pallida** where the flowers are more bunched and make more of a show, but I think the flowers show off to better advantage growing singly. Perhaps some first-timer will agree with me.

The Winter Prunus

This is about the same sized tree and has small pinkish-white flowers, much more massed than the witch hazel and a very reliable winter flowerer – it may go on for some weeks, much longer than most flowering trees. Another advantage is that the leaves are an attractive reddish colour when the flowers fade. Prunus is the Latin name for the flowering cherries in general, but this is the one which people call a Prunus and the grower will know it under this name.

Q Do any shrubs flower twice?

A No, I'm afraid not – unless one counts a rose as a shrub (for the stems are woody) and here we have more confusion for the shrub roses only flower once. There is a movement amongst the professionals to produce new varieties which have a longer flowering period, but in any case roses are summer things. Your best bet for long flowering is the camellia or hydrangeas in the summer.

Next month we are going on to other things which flower in winter, but need mild weather to show them at their best.

ASPECT

When talking about the sunny and shady parts of a garden and where the cold winds come from, we are really discussing the 'aspect' which is very important as it cannot be changed and one might as well get a few things of this kind out of the way before the busy months come. It is a great help in planning to understand some of the reasons why a plant does well or badly. Though some plants do well in the shade, nearly all like a certain amount of sun and a South-facing garden does not have many problems but this does not mean that a North-facing one is hopeless, particularly if it is not overlooked by high walls or tall trees. When the sun is at its highest you will find that most parts of your North-facing garden will get sun. I know because my first London garden faced this way.

Q I may be dim, but I'm not sure that I know which way my garden does face. I know the points of the compass in theory, but they are very difficult to work out in a town with lots of buildings. Also, for instance is a West wall on the West side or does it face West?

A Yes it is all very well in the country where you may have a clear view all round; let's pretend for the moment that the view is clear and follow the sun through the day. The sun rises in the East and that part of your garden which gets the morning sun will face East, (the West wall); this will not last long as the sun will climb rapidly to the South and will be at its highest at midday (1pm British Summer Time – BST). In high summer the shadows hardly exist as the sun is overhead; then it will go round to the West when the shadows will lengthen and the sun eventually sets.

In a town you may well find that certain parts of the garden only get sun at certain times of year, when the days get shorter and the sun lower the garden may be in the shade of trees or tall buildings. Winter plants are much better able to cope with little sun, which is only to be expected and the trees will be leafless then for the most part.

Q If the sun only goes in a half-circle it can never get to the North side.

A Though the sun never shines from the North in our part of the world, it will be high enough in the summer to shine into a North-facing garden – we could see the Pole Star over the back garden at night so it certainly faced North. When we came there first there was a large open space to the West where three houses had been bombed and during the late spring and summer months the garden got sun for most of the day. It was a different story when the houses were re-built, but one just had to grow different things.

Here is a plan of our first garden – a very typical town garden facing, most conveniently for a diagram, exactly North as one looks down the garden from the house – the way maps always face.

SHADE-LOVING PLANTS

Q You say that some plants do like the shade but I have never had much success with them, even though they were supposed to be shade-loving. Some died and some never flowered at all, just grew leaves.
A The trouble with so-called shade-loving plants is that often they only tolerate shade really preferring sun, anyhow for part of the day and the lack of sun is probably what is stopping them flowering. The plants which dislike full sun are often almost water plants and must have moisture as well as shade. (The astilbe looks very like the meadowsweet one sees growing in water-meadows in the summer and it will grow up against the North side of the house and flower well). They need a soil which retains moisture, or one can add plenty of leaf-mould or peat to help keep it in. Not many things will grow in deep shade under trees and if you should see plants flourishing in what looks like an awkward corner I advise you to leave them there for the moment. It might be some sort of a ground cover plant sold for just this kind of thing.

The garden compost heap is a great help too for retaining moisture.

COMPOST

Q I rather dread the idea of a compost heap it always sounds so complicated.
A It need not be and I would scarcely have dared to write down my own amateur 'composting' (even though it produced excellent results) had I not met by chance no less a person than the daughter of Harry Wheatcroft, the famous rose grower, who does exactly the same thing in her own country garden and who thought she had invented her method.

When I told her I was writing this book, she not only said that I

North facing

East facing

West facing

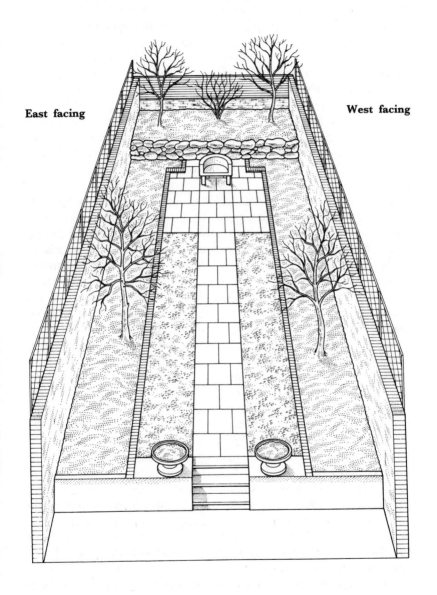

Our first garden

could quote her, but implored me to pass on her message "DO tell them how important it is" so here goes!

First of all, it is not necessary to have anything elaborate in the way of a container. A wooden or metal frame, about 3ft all ways is all that you will need, to keep the leaves from blowing about. The metal container is made up of four squares, looking rather like metal trellis work and held in the corners with plastic clips. The whole thing can be folded flat and put away in the toolshed. As the container arrives in four pieces and has to be assembled, it is useful to know that the plastic clips can be made more pliable by putting them in hot water. This saves much struggling, particularly as one or two clips may come off when it is being folded or opened up again.

I have never found that any of the 'accelerators' which are sold make any difference. What speeds things up most is a mild winter and warm spring, not to be bought alas. I used to follow the instructions on the packet religiously, first a layer of weeds or leaves or whatever I had put in, then a layer of earth, then the accelerator, then more layers, then the tiring heavy business of turning the material in the heap every so often. In the spring I looked eagerly at the heap with its careful layers and saw the leaves looking exactly the same as they had when I put them there the autumn before. It seemed to be nearly the next autumn before one could use the stuff – I can't remember how long this went on. One spring I must have got tired of waiting and when the weather started to warm up I opened up the boards of the compost bin – the one I was using then had wooden boards which fitted into grooves – raked the whole thing out and left it to dry for a week or so, then put it straight onto the beds without bothering whether it had rotted down or not. The result was that I had compost when I wanted it to help keep in moisture throughout the dry weather. At first I did make some effort to dig it in, now I don't bother even to do that and it rots away in no time at all, turning itself into a leafy compost.

Q How about when you make the compost, do you still put earth in between the layers?

A I sometimes put some earth over the leaves to weight them down, but I never use an accelerator.

Q You do cheer me up. What about weeds though?

A One of the advantages of a town garden is that very few weeds grow in winter. Those there are can go in with the leaves and in summer they rot down very quickly. My wooden bin was permanent – I grew a yucca to hide it – but my present garden is too small and the metal container would look ugly in the summer, so I remove it and bury the weeds where it stands in winter.

Q What about grass cuttings?

A Older readers will remember how haystacks caught fire if the hay was not completely dry when it was stacked. A small quantity of grass cuttings from grass strips (such as we had) will do no harm and will warm up the compost and help it to rot down but anything larger will swamp the bin and will need a heap on its own which you turn occasionally – no risk of fire here – rotted grass (when it has turned brown) makes a useful mulch to keep the moisture in. At one time it was much used for roses, but my mother, a great gardener, thought it encouraged disease like Black Spot whose spores lurk in the ground. In any case, never put green cuttings down as they will grow and you will have a lawn!

Q Some people use all kinds of household refuse.

A I know they do, but with my method one would not risk smelly cabbage leaves or orange peel not properly rotted down. The reader should beware of wasps. Even with an enclosed compostor such material attracts them. I know of one wasp's nest in such circumstances which resulted in a nasty sting.

Q What about rose cuttings or shrub prunings?

A Never put rose cuttings in for fear of disease – burn them if possible. Small trimmings as the year goes on from shrubs will not hurt, the leaves will rot and the stems prevent the heap becoming too dense and matted. When the garden is being cleared for the first time arrange with the firm to take the rubbish away. If the small town garden is too small for a bonfire you can get rid of anything awkward in discreet quantities, as luckily many towns have dustvans which grind up the refuse on the spot.

Q What is the difference between humus and compost?

A Humus is the name for rich dark material formed from decayed organic matter and I suppose peat, compost and the leafmould we have been speaking of are the best known. Composted manure, that is farmyard manure rotted down by a similar process, is especially valuable as it feeds the plants as well as improving the soil. The word compost also refers to the mixes of peat, or loam and fertilizer sold for seed sowing, potting and taking cuttings.

Q I've no leaves in my garden, perhaps a few leaves but that's all.

A It is possible to buy peat and leaf-mould, but if you offer to clear the leaves for someone who is not a gardener he will be only too pleased to let you have as many as you like. He may think you slightly mad, but you know better!

Q What is black spot? You mentioned that roses could get it.

A It is a fungal disease of roses. The danger time is in winter when the mulch can preserve the spores in the ground. In the spring the large black spots on the leaves give it away and they can be sprayed – the leaves should be burned as we said. Bought peat and composted manure will have been sterilised so it cannot of itself bring any disease, it has to be in the ground already. I was planning to deal with this when the time for spraying comes so let us leave 'Pests and Diseases' until then.

Before I finish my amateur description, I could mention a television programme on a New Zealand garden in South Island, which has a climate much nearer to ours, where the owner was asked what she did with the truckload of weeds shown in the picture. "Put them back under the bushes" she answered! That's 'REAL' compost.

For a larger garden, one can now buy 'shredders' which are fairly expensive but they deal with shrub prunings. The compost bin should be 4ft by 4ft minimum.

DIFFERENT KINDS OF SOIL

As well as aspect we ought to be thinking about different kinds of soil before the planting time comes.

Q I didn't know there were different kinds. I'm afraid I shall never make a gardener.

A We needn't make it too complicated and like sun and shade, soil is important for the different plants which like different kinds of soil.

Q I have heard people talk about acid soil and I never know what it means, but it sounds as if nothing would grow.

A Doesn't it, like an acid bath and the opposite, which is alkali, doesn't sound much better. Chalk and cheese, though less elegant, give one a better idea. The chalk, like the White Cliffs of Dover, against the 'cheesy' acid of the peaty bog and heathlands where the heather and rhododendron grow wild.

In between come the clay and gravel of so many town gardens and these incline towards the chalky end though one would not think so. Strangely, pink hydrangeas refusing to turn blue are a sign of alkaline soil, which is just the opposite to litmus paper. Sand, often found near heathland and in river valleys is very poor soil, inclining towards the acid.

Nowadays one can send a sample of soil to be analyzed and they will tell you how to get a good balance and what you should add to it or you can buy the simple kit that was mentioned earlier.

I still think one of the best methods is to see what is growing well in the neighbours' gardens and one soon learns from experience; for instance, I could have told the 'experts' not to plant rhododendrons at Hyde Park Corner of all places, where they promptly died from traffic pollution and dust of all kinds. Rhododendrons are particularly sensitive to lime or mortar dust on their leaves. Even the cement used when having your garden paved, will upset them. All evergreens are sensitive to pollution and should not be planted in front gardens where they are subject to the exhaust fumes of passing cars.

GRAVEL

I will start with town soil for this is what I know best and it is the most difficult. My first garden had gravel – mostly stones and what was in those days a topsoil which was frankly pure soot. The gravel extended for about two feet, then came clay. Gravel drains easily after heavy rain, which is about all you can say in its favour, except that it is not as heavy to dig as clay. If the garden has been neglected, however, you will find a hard stony crust which is not easy to work. Ordinary builder's sand, such as is used for mixing with cement, is a great help. There might be builders about in your new house and they nearly always have sand to spare. Prevail upon them to move it near where you want it for it is heavy and simply scatter it over the soil and after it has rained dig it in with a big fork.

Gravel is a very poor soil on its own and needs plenty of feeding with manure, fertilizer and all the compost you can manage; the latter makes a tremendous difference.

There are some plants which do well in poor soil and positively dislike manure. If you are offered any **Lupin** plants, as I was, they do wonderfully well. Plant them about the end of March (they will be little plants, not seeds) and they will flower in June. The Perennials will last for five or six years at least, but if they are annuals which only last the year they are still useful, because they can be dug back into the soil with good results as they 'sweeten' sour or neglected soil. Farmers used to grow crops of annual lupins for this purpose.

CLAY

Your town soil or indeed country soil for that matter may be all clay. Clay is the heavy sticky stuff, very obvious if you try to dig it after rain. It is good for retaining moisture and anything, notably roses, which likes it cool and damp round the roots will do well. Sand makes it lighter to work but digging clay soil for the first time is a formidable task. You can welcome the frost and snow at this time of year for they help to soften and break up the soil ready for the spring digging. Do not worry too much about weeds, when they come out eventually the tough ones will bring a lot of soil with them and it all helps in breaking up the surface.

There are many clay-soil 'improvers' on the market, I have not myself found them much more use than the compost accelerator. I would recommend an all-purpose compost from "Cuttings", a firm I have dealt with for over 40 years ever since I have had a garden of my own. They will deliver to your door and if you combine their clay soil crumbler with a traditional compost such as well rotted farmyard manure which is not smelly you will get a good mixture. The texture will improve with working. The ideal is known as 'friable' and the best way of imagining this is to think of the soil they can be seen 'digging' in television gardening programmes – unkind persons have been heard to say that they buy it from Harrods – still it is good to know what one is aiming for.

[Cuttings address: Cuttings Compost Ltd, Wem, Nr. Shrewsbury, Shropshire SY4 5QA]

Primroses and their relatives the garden polyanthus and the coloured winter primrose do well in clay soil.

CHALK

A chalk soil makes one think of cliffs and downs in the country and is easy enough to recognise, but is not commonly found in towns. It drains very quickly which is a great advantage if your chalk garden is a second home and perhaps only visited at week-ends as one can get quickly down to gardening after rain.

This soil can also be stony and difficult to work and for the bigger country garden it is worth mentioning here that there is a wonderful machine called a rotovator, which can be hired by the day and which will do the job of digging mechanically and save much back-breaking work. Once dug, add manure and humus as we have said before.

Q People tell me that nothing will grow in chalk.

A People will say anything particularly if it is depressing. Many books have been written about wonderful chalk gardens, though perhaps even these are written with the idea of saying what can be done under what are felt to be difficult conditions. Why not go for a walk and see what grows – dogwood is everywhere in the hedges and the wild clematis or 'Old Man's Beard'. Here are two plants, already one a shrub and one a climber which have many cultivated varieties. A very choice **Anemone**, the **Pasque Flower**, grows wild on the Berkshire Downs and I have found the wild Bee Orchid on the Downs at Kearsney, above Dover. Besides the Pasque Flower, the woods are a mass of wood anemones in the spring and their garden equivalent the coloured **Anemone Blanda** grows well under trees or in a wild garden.

There are certain flowers known for their dislike of chalk. **Rhododendrons** and **Azaleas** are the best known and as we have seen belong to the acid or cheesy end of soils. Luckily if one likes them particularly, rhododendrons have 'ball roots', that is the roots don't spread out in the way of other plants and in fact the more tightly the soil is packed round them the better they like it. One can therefore dig a hole and fill it with the soil they do like, leaf-mould and peat ('acid' humus in fact) and a bit of rotted manure and potash to encourage flowers. Experts say that the leaf-mould should be carefully chosen in case the trees had grown on chalk. I am sure this is logical and so pass the tip on to the reader, but I have never heard of plants being affected with 'chalky' leaf-mould. If the holes are dug a reasonable size, as though one was planting in a tub, the roots will not spread beyond the prepared soil and they will flourish, provided the nurseryman is consulted as to the best kinds to buy for these circumstances.

The **Madonna Lily** does well in chalk, also the old-fashioned red **Peony** – both need sun and can be difficult to grow elsewhere.

Q   I call it the St Joseph's Lily.

A   The *Lilium Candidum*, the one we are talking about, has the English name of Madonna Lily, but it is the one more often depicted being carried by St Joseph which makes it confusing. The other lily so often seen in Church, particularly at Easter is the **Arum** its Latin name is *Zantedeschia aethiopica* and it is not strictly a lily, because it comes from a different family. These grow wild in the West of Ireland so would be very much at the cheesy end of the scale, but luckily they do very well in pots; keep them there if you want them for your chalky garden.

All the **Viburnums** like chalk and **Cowslips** grow wild on the chalk downs – the latter would do for the wild garden.

I have expanded a little on chalk soil and its possibilities because although I have never had a chalk garden of my own, I know a very successful one belonging to my sister and brother-in-law. Though they have a gardener they do a tremendous amount themselves, in spite of only being there for the most part at week-ends and have led as busy a life with politics and a family as anyone could imagine and their lovely garden is a tribute to them both and shows what can be done. **Daffodils** have been 'naturalised' (that is planted in grass) very successfully and **Tulips** also do well. They are left in the ground which is usually fatal since Tulips get diseased if not lifted, but perhaps the chalky ground acts as a kind of disinfectant. The borders are planted more or less regardless, that is the plants are left to "sink or swim". The combination of a busy life and 'difficult' soil has only meant that a lot of things flourish which are not supposed to, notably lupins the great lime-haters. The remedy seemed to be farmyard manure which somehow neutralised the chalk and suited them, although they usually dislike that as well. I feel this should encourage new gardeners not to worry overmuch; nature has not read any gardening books, as a Q rightly pointed out to me. Let the reader just pick up a hint here and there, much as one does in any other reference book.

PEATY SOIL

By this I mean soil found in heathland and pinewood gardens, for example my old school at Ascot was in this kind of country and had wonderful grounds filled with rhododendrons. Much the best way to overcome the difficulty of an acid soil of this kind is not to worry about flower beds but to have trees and flowering shrubs of all kinds, all of which do well in this kind of soil. Azaleas, of the taller kind, make a wonderful show. There were some flower beds but I believe they had had to have special soil brought in from outside the area which is a terrible business nowadays.

Needless to say, a heather garden, so much in fashion, would do well.

Less well known for this kind of soil is the **Calico Bush** (*Kalmia Latifolia*), which is particularly pretty with its pink cup-shaped flowers and the double **Guelder Rose**, with its white balls of flowers. Though not so much seen nowadays it is very attractive to children and I remember it well.

A BOG GARDEN

To make a bog garden is outside our scope, but the reader might have the luck to find a pond or stream in his garden. So many attractive wild plants grow at the edge of streams that you may well find them there already in which case do not bother to plant anything else. The yellow flag iris is as good as any cultivated garden plant.

At this time of year you will still be able to see leaves, mostly the long grassy-looking leaves of rushes and reeds. We shall have to wait until the spring and early summer for the flowers. For the first year wait until you see what comes out, if you want to add to the plants then there are specialist growers who will help you. Meanwhile here are some ideas of what might bloom.

Two **Irises**: *Iris pseudacorus* – yellow – the water iris. *Iris foetidissima* – dull purple or occasionally yellow – Gladwyn iris.

Yellow and purple **Loosestrife** – the former is used as a garden plant and it is very useful to fill a gap after the late spring or early summer things. They are not the same family. The purple L. looks very like the willow herb which was such a

feature of the bomb sites in London as it likes the potash from the
burnt soil. The **Willow herb** you are most likely to find is the
hairy willow herb (*Epilobium hirsutum*). Later on comes the
Comfrey with drooping bell-like flowers.

Reeds and Rushes: These are pretty tough things as you will
soon find; you might have to get someone in to cut them back
if they are encroaching on the water itself.

Most people know **Bulrushes** and it is generally accepted that
the **Typha latifolia** (large) and **Typha minima** (small) after
years of having been called reedmace by flower books are the
true bulrushes or bullrushes – the former seems to be the
modern spelling. There is such a fashion at the time of writing
for preserving and growing wild flowers that firms which specialise show at the Chelsea Flower Show. I therefore add one or
two plants which can probably be bought if they have not planted
themselves. The mimulus or **Monkey Flower** is often sold as a
garden plant though it prefers the rather colder northern climate
and is seen in Scotland. The **Water forget-me-not** grows in
mud or very shallow water and will flower throughout the
summer. The **Marsh marigold** or kingcup has rounded, dark
green leaves and bears bright golden-yellow flowers in spring.

The Himalayan balsam (*Impatiens glandulifera*).

This sounds exotic and it is; this is a plant which seeded itself
along the river banks of the Thames and Wey. Most first-timers
will know the cultivated relation the little bedding plant *Impatiens*
or busy Lizzie. The flower is quite unmistakable and two smaller
balsams, *Impatiens Noli-Tangere* ("not to touch" the flying seeds!) and
parviflora (rather small), might be there already.

The spectacular pink and red flowers of the Himalayan balsam
used to grow on the Wey Canal near Addlestone in Surrey and I
am told it also grows on the Avon near Salisbury. The garden
busy Lizzie is so easy to take cuttings from that the wild ones
should not be difficult to grow and an approach to the specialist
might be successful, though I have not as yet seen any for sale
it is worth looking into. I should like to think of some reader growing this lovely plant round their pond, lake or by a stream.

Q How did it get there in the first place?

A The theory is that the seeds were in the bags of cement used to strengthen the river banks. These bags were made of jute which comes from India.

Two **Water-lilies**, the small yellow and larger white are both natives of this country and are obtainable.

The Bog itself: A strange fashion has grown up for the insect-eating plants. The best known wild ones are the **Sundews**, which are round and long-leaved and can be found in the New Forest. If there is a boggy bit at the fringe of your water-garden you might like to try them. We must not forget the **Meadow-sweet** which is very much a plant of the water-meadows and will flower twice if it is cut down after the first flowering in the early summer.

SANDY SOIL

Sandy soil is often found in a river valley and of course in a seaside garden. My old home was in the Thames Valley and the light sandy soil grew almost anything given the addition of manure. In those days it was farmyard manure arriving by the cartload from the farm which had to be rotted down before it could be used. Nowadays the reader may have to use compost of all kinds and chemical fertilizer.

My parents were both great gardeners; my Father took charge of the lawn and my Mother master-minded the flower garden with the aid of a gardener, who also looked after the kitchen garden − for younger readers, vegetables and flowers mixed. There was usually a wide border down either side of the garden bordering the vegetables and fruit grew against walls in a walled garden. My Mother was particularly successful with herbaceous border plants. Herbaceous means that the plants have soft not woody stems. No shrubs were included as they might be nowadays; the exception was the occasional rose of the old-fashioned shrub variety.

As we have seen these border plants are perennial, that is they go on year after year. They are so useful for picking for the house and making a 'permanent' background for the annual bedding plants or plants raised from seed − which are the kind one sows straight onto the bed where they are to flower.

As we go through the year we will try and go into a little more detail as to names and times of flowering. My guess is that many

of the flowers the reader remembers and would like to grow himself will be found in the old-fashioned border.

Sandy soil is very easy to work and drains well, hence the
number of golf courses made out of sand dunes.

THE SEASIDE GARDEN

The seaside garden might be a small patch round your second
home, bought principally for the family to have easy access to
the seaside. The nearer the sea the sandier and windier it is and
most people settle for a lawn and hedges, planted chiefly as windbreaks. The **Tamarisk** (that feathery shrub seen frequently in
coastal regions) is a great standby at the seaside particularly in
the West Country.

Q I can't bear it, with that other evergreen thing, it reminds me
of Bognor as a child.

A I must admit that I don't like the **Griselinia** (well-named) the
usual evergreen, but the poor tamarisk is rather under-rated as it
seems to grow in pure sand, has quite pretty pink flowers too and I
would prefer it as a fence.

There is a variegated evergreen, **Euonymus japonicus**
'**Ovatus Aureas**' which is slightly less grisly than the griselinia.
It's unlikely cousin is the pretty wild spindleberry.

If one moves a little inland, away from the salt winds, or to a
walled garden one can grow more or less what other sandy gardens will grow. **Carnations** and **Pinks** which are difficult in
many other soils do very well. Fuchsias also do well a little
inland and the hardy **Fuchsia magellenica** grows almost wild
in the West Country and will make a hedge. **Hydrangeas** do
well by the seaside and as iron in the soil is frequently found
near sand and heathland, for those who like blue hydrangeas
they will be as blue as anyone could desire – rather an ugly
colour to my mind, I prefer the soft blues and mauves of the halfway soils.

Q Sand is terribly poor soil really.

A Yet some flowers which you take for granted are seldom seen
elsewhere. There is a small border plant with woolly leaves and
red flowers which no one ever knows the name of – we notice
it at the beginning of summer before most things are out. It is
called **Lychnis** and is a useful plant for the front of the border.

The **Acanthus**, a beautiful tall border plant does well in sand and can prove difficult elsewhere. It needs shelter so is not for the seaside. **Monkshood (Aconitum)** is another border plant not often found elsewhere.

LOAM

I have left this to the last because it is the very best kind of soil, is easy to work and rich, so that the plants grow themselves. Our gardener at my old home was lucky enough to have a garden and allotment of loam (lower down and nearer the river than our sandy garden) and I learnt of its merits from him. I congratulate the reader who is so fortunate as virtually anything will grow except the things which actually like poor soil such as lupins or nasturtiums.

The first-timer might turn to the general notes on Planting, Planning and Clearing, otherwise he will do very well without too much detailed advice if he plants what he sees in other gardens.

Q I'm sure I shouldn't succeed, everything I plant seems to die.
A Do not be discouraged, as we said before nature writes her own gardening book and will look after your plants. Much the most likely reason was that you were trying the impossible such as planting things in a difficult soil or situation, or perhaps the plant was not much good in the first place. It takes a bit of practise to pick out good plants and a year or so before you find what your garden will or won't grow. We have made a start on 'Aspect' and 'Soil' and are going on to 'Planting, Cutting and Planning'.

The new gardener must not blame himself for everything that dies, nature can be very awkward as well as helpful and there is such a thing as beginner's luck. Here is a word of encouragement to end the first month; I can think of one instance in particular:-

An American neighbour from Texas, on her first visit to this country, bought a plant from a barrow; having been told that it would flower winter and summer she planted it in her front garden, where it did just that, producing flower after flower all through the year. It was actually a house-plant, a kind of primula and should never have been planted outdoors in the first place, but nature provided an exceptionally mild winter and hot summer and it flourished .

COMPOST BINS

Q   I have a plastic bin which I bought from an "ad" in the paper and it works beautifully.

A   If you have room these are very good but beware of wasps! I particularly like the wooden kind with removable slats because they are easy to get at. I should also say that I am not 'knocking' those who go to the trouble of making real sieved compost and leaf-mould. I am the grateful receiver of leaf-mould made in this way and my lilies flourish in it. I am merely pointing out to those who have little time or energy, that it is not strictly necessary.

As we have already noted, the weather this month is not likely to be such as to tempt the first-time gardener, or any gardener, out of doors; February is a cold, wet month in most of Britain and snow and sleet are quite normal, with bitter winds thrown in. However, there might be a few dry days on which one could start a bit of clearing, even if it is only sweeping leaves from the flower-beds or lawn. It is never too early to start planning and getting together necessary things like tools, fertilizers and sprays against pests. If a friend has any garden catalogues, it is fun to go through them and see the sort of thing you would like to have in your own garden, all ready for when the spring comes.

Q When does it come?

A Spring comes officially on March 25th and it will do quite well as an average; of course the spring is just as variable as any other season in our climate, but nothing can stop the sun getting warmer and the days longer. As far as this month goes, we can forget about planting for the moment.

Q I only asked because several friends have offered me 'bits' from their gardens when the spring comes.

A I am very glad to hear it, for even a small garden can need a lot of plants if one is starting from scratch as I was after the war in my bombed garden. Very few things had survived and I relied heavily on plants given to me by kind friends and relations. The most successful were the ones from London itself, they were used to the heady mixture of soot, broken glass, stones and rubble which was the 'soil' of those days. Even if one lives further out or right in the country, the plants to go for are those from the same soil and roughly the same aspect as the garden they are coming to.

Most people are likely to give the hardy border plants which we were speaking of in January. They should really be divided in the autumn, but gardeners can cope when the weather is mild for a day or two if they want something for a friend. At this time of year appearances can be very deceptive. Someone may present you with a miserable-looking spiky thing, but look at its roots and if they are strong and healthy it may grow into a tall bushy plant which you will want at the back of the border. Don't forget they are more or less 'permanents' so find out how they are going to develop. Some plants are really only edging, or low 'spreaders' to cover awkward bits and you do not want them swamped by taller things, nor do you want a 'spreader' romping away in the middle of a bed where you can't get at it.

HEELING IN

Q What if he weather is bad when the plants come?
A As I have said, this is not really planting time so we must assume that the weather has been unusually mild and you will be quite safe to 'heel them in'. Dig a hole in a sheltered but not too dry a spot and do not aim the spade straight but dig slantwise and lay the plants with the stalks and leaves (if any) lying on the slope and the roots resting on the bottom. Cover lightly with earth as far as it has been covered when they were growing. This puts no pressure on the roots when they are moved to their permanent place.
Q What if it's pouring with rain?
A Presumably your friend would have lifted them for you (I mean in the gardener's sense of 'dug up' of course) the same day, or possibly the day before, having waited for good weather, but if you are unlucky and are worried that you might not be able to get out for a day or two, protect the roots by wrapping them in several layers of damp newspaper and put in a cool place – it should be frost-proof but not heated. Remember that these hardy plants have been used to roughing it outside and will find even a cold garden shed quite warm and comfortable. Put them on a shelf in a shallow tray or box to keep them out of the draughts on the floor, or place them on a bench away from the window.

HARDY AND HALF-HARDY PLANTS

Q I never understand what plants are called hardy and what are half-hardy.
A Roughly speaking, plants which survive the winter outdoors are called hardy, but there are a great many plants which were originally introduced from warmer climates which have settled down so well that we take them for granted! Nevertheless they can succumb to an exceptionally cold winter.
Q Are they what they call half-hardy?
A No not exactly, here is another confusion for the beginner, There is nothing wrong in describing such plants as half-hardy, but generally speaking the plants which are called half-hardy are the ones we are going to use as bedding-out plants in the summer (spring is too early as the frosts must be over). Already the professional growers will have sown their seeds ready to bring them on in the cool greenhouse. Hardy seeds can be sown where they are to grow in late April or early May. You may remember sowing candytuft in your garden as a child.

When buying seeds the term is HA (hardy annual) or HHA (half-hardy annual). The latter need a sunny window-sill or the protection of a frost-proof greenhouse or a little heat to bring them on.
Q Do these last only the one year then?
A Yes, the vast majority of 'bedders' are only intended to see the summer and early autumn through. If geraniums – the kind used for bedding – are left in their pots they can be brought in to a sheltered balcony, or a veranda. The modern conservatory would provide just the place for them.
Q I am not keen on anything likely to die in the winter, I think I would like something really permanent.
A Most of us know that geraniums are tender or half-hardy, whichever one prefers. As for the outdoor plants, it would be clearer to stick to 'tender' or 'inclined to be tender' according to how well they cope. It would be a pity, particularly if one's garden is in a town or warm and sheltered part of Britain, to worry too much about the exceptionally cold winter.

The winter of 1984–85 was unusually cold in Southern England and on the Continent, notably the South of France and Italy and this was followed by another cold winter in 1986–87. The second winter was made worse by a freakishly warm January after a mild early winter; the plants were tempted to start their spring growth too soon and when the very cold weather came in February it finished many things which might have survived the one bad winter. Very bad luck, but exceptional.

Sadly, a neighbour lost a lace-cap hydrangea and a well-grown white lilac; these do come into the 'inclined to be tender' group but survive most winters quite happily. It was the exceptional warmth of the autumn, followed by only one cold snap in November which was not enough really to stop growth and then the contrast of the very cold winds and low night temperatures which did the damage. It is always a help if a plant is well established – that is, settled in. On the other hand one can lose an older plant for the same reason as we go out ourselves when elderly in a cold winter.

The main casualties in our London neighbourhood were bay trees grown in tubs. In the ground, plants will recover in an amazing way, so do not give up hope unless the are not showing signs of growth by the next autumn. The little maple tree in our own patio garden, sheltered enough normally, was badly cut by the North East winds.

Obvious exotics like the yucca also fared badly, although those in Holland Park, near where I live in London survived due to the shelter of a bamboo plantation. The latter though also obvious "foreigners" will be cut back by such winters and look dreadful all the summer, but it will not be long before the fresh green appears at the base and they start recovering as if by a miracle.

Q I never thought of something like a bamboo coming through a cold winter, do you reckon most plants will survive in the end.
A Yes, many more than one would suppose. After a cold winter in the 60's when we were driving to Poole in Dorset for the sailing season, I was horrified to see the numbers of dead looking plants and trees in the gardens as we passed. As the summer went on it was most heartening to see everything recovering gradually – I had supposed they were gone for ever. All tender plants must be a bit of a gamble but the garden would be sadly depleted without them.

There are some tender plants which have a bad reputation of seeming to be quite established and healthy then along comes the cold winter and they go, leaving a sad gap. The **Cypress** *Cupressus macrocarpa* is one of the chief offenders because it is so often used as a hedge or row of trees to hide an ugly view and its going is doubly annoying because often others in the row have survived.

This has given it a bad name and the *Leyland* cypress (x *Cupresso-cyparis leylandii* is the favourite now; it is more hardy, I think a prettier green and growth in general is more pleasing. It has to be kept trimmed, though, it is fast growing and can reach 120 feet. I have seen some beautiful examples in the gardens of stately homes and from what I have seen so far, all have come through the recent winters.

Three more that the reader should be careful where they plant are: the **Choisya**, also called the Mexican Orange Bush, an evergreen shrub with white flowers; **Pieris**, the Forest Flame with its red leaves in the spring and white lily-of-the-valley flowers; and a wall shrub the **Ceanothus**, with clusters of blue flowers. All three are beautiful plants and much grown, and all three got through the cold winters in the gardens of my sheltered part of London, but alas, are not to be recommended for more exposed positions.

As a footnote to those two cold winters on the Continent, sad descriptions came in of dead olive trees on the hills above Naples and dead palm trees along the Promenade des Anglais in Nice, followed by more cheerful news some months later; the Palm trees were already sprouting as were some of the vines, but farmers in Tuscany had lost half their crop. Those who had to translate Virgil in their schooldays will remember from the Georgics that the same thing happened in classical times, but it did not deter the farmers from re-planting. Incidentally, the palm trees in the South of France are no more natives than are those in Torquay or other favoured spots. They come from North Africa. We are establishing a point of general interest as you are not likely to want to grow palm trees or vines.

Q   Not yet anyway, though I was very impressed when I visited an English vineyard.

A   Perhaps you will be like a great many Qs who have romped ahead of me and have much bigger and better gardens than anything I could produce.

SOME MORE WINTER FLOWERS

There are one or two winter-flowering plants which need a warm winter to show them at their best. Though they are quite hardy the new gardener must decide if sunny winters come often enough to make them worth growing.

Q I only have a small garden and I don't want it filled up with winter things, particularly if they don't do well. My grandparents had a boring evergreen with white flowers which I used to hate as a child, it never seemed to come to anything.

A It sounds very much like the **Laurustinus** which was looked down on and thought Victorian in the days of my childhood but is now making a comeback.

Q I like them, I should love to grow one.

A We have already noted how fashions come and go in gardens, and the poor laurustinus suffered from its own reliability, being about the only plant which flowered throughout the winter in spite of what was then the soot and dirt of towns. It will grow in awkward, indeed rather dreary, places and this has affected its image.

The laurustinus too is a native of a warmer climate. When I first saw it growing on the slopes of the hills above Naples on the way to Amalfi in early October, with its glossy green leaves and large white flowers (pink in the bud) just coming into their best, it was hardly recognisable as the rather sad plant of the London garden. The mild winter of 1987–88 caused my own plant to blossom freely all the winter, a beautiful sight and much admired. In any case, with the cleaner air, the leaves are much more attractive and the flowers are always useful for winter picking.

The first-timer should be warned that it is a big bush, about 8ft each way. There is a variety, '**Eve Price**', which is more compact, that I am trying in a tub where the bay tree died and so far it is very successful and should stay neat.

Another winter viburnum is the old **V. fragrans**, the Latin name speaks for itself and many people grew it for its scent in the winter and remember it just as viburnum. It is not an evergreen, being one of those winter flowerers with a bunch of flowers at the end of a long bare stalk, which are not great favourites of mine. However, it is difficult to find in the modern catalogues (although L.R. Russell of Windlesham do stock it). According to its picture the nearest is *V. x bodnantense* 'Dawn' which I have never grown. Maybe it is an improved variety of *fragrans*, for it seems to have the flowers rather more gracefully arranged.

Another scented viburnum I have grown is **V. x burkwoodii** but it will not be out until March. It keeps some of its leaves in winter but they are not up to much and the real leaf-growth comes with the flowers. It grows to quite a big bush, about 6ft

Laurel

each way, but is easy to trim and keep in order. The branches are inclined to grow lengthways as well as upwards which makes them suitable for a screen by a fence.

V. davidii is much grown for its attractive leaves which are oval with a marked pattern of veins. The male and female plants are separate, so that one must have both for the female to bear attractive blue berries, like sealing-wax. It is a nice compact plant, say 4ft each way and looks well bordering a sloping path or steps.

We have written the names as they might be in the catalogue – it will start off with VIBURNUM then shorten to V. + the special name.

Garrya elliptica

I include this shrub which is another tall one, about 8ft each way – because it is so often written up at this time of year.

Q I can't understand why, it is the most boring thing ever. One could go past it even when its catkins are out and never notice them.

A The male plant has the large catkins, so perhaps the invisible ones are the smaller female. This is another winter flowering shrub which needs a little shelter or a warm winter to show up well. Seen planted in the corner of a wall it is a change from the more usual winter plants. It is evergreen, with pretty grey-green leaves, provided they are not exposed to cold winds which mark them. The catkins, even the larger ones are still rather the same colour as the bush which one could consider dull but have a look at it first and then see how you feel. I would leave it alone for a year or two if I found one planted in my garden.

Japonica – Chaenomeles

What everyone calls 'Japonica' used to have *Pyrus japonica* (i.e. the Japanese Quince) as its Latin name, now the name is *Chaenomeles japonica*.

It is usually trained against a wall though not a climber and one cuts it back to the main branches in the late spring after it has flowered. At this time of year the buds may be showing colour and they will come out in the warmth of a room, usually on very short stems as they appear to be growing straight out of the wood at the angle of a branch. If the weather is kind and the main flowering is not too early for the bees to pollinate, fruit will appear in September which can be treated as a quince (not eaten raw but made into a jelly or puree). The old word for the latter was 'cheese' but I think younger readers would not recognise it under that title. As for the flowers they can make a good show, but they too need a mild winter.

Bergenia

Q   What is that thing with the huge ugly leaves and has some kind of pink flower like a primula? I call it Elephant's Ears. The mild winter of 1987–88 has absolutely transformed it – I didn't know it could do so well.
A   Of all the plants which like a mild winter to show at their best I should name the poor Bergenia. Because it is so adaptable and will grow almost anywhere it has suffered rather the same fate as the laurustinus. We associate bergenia, unfairly of course, with seaside rockeries usually seen in the summer when the flowers are over and we are left with the ugly leaves.
Q   I have one growing over a stone in my front garden. I feel nothing much else would grow because it is right in the shade of a hedge.
A   Why not leave it for the moment unless you really hate it – always my motto with a new garden. It doesn't sound as if it would be very noticeable, unless the miracle of a mild and sunny winter occurs, when it is transformed into a really handsome plant with its big pink flowers. Incidentally, it is no trouble and requires minimum attention which says a lot for a plant in a busy household.
Q   What about **Winter Pansies**? Mine never seem to flower.
A   I have never had any luck with them either, they only come into flower about the end of March when there are plenty of other things coming on. They seem to need a big open garden or a sunny raised front garden and again a mild winter to flower really well. I have seen them at Kew, where the yellow and blue which are their colours make a very effective combination. Even amongst such experts there was one mistake, a hybrid show-

ing a mixture of both colours looking particularly healthy and pleased with itself as it spoiled the display.

Q   I don't feel I am that expert.

A   Nor am I, but perhaps I should add that the growers tell me that the variety of winter flowering pansy, the **Universal** is much more reliable.

Winter Primroses

I would much sooner recommend the coloured primroses, blue, pink, red and yellow which have been developed in recent years. They come on sale about October to flower through the winter. I grew them on a South facing balcony with a little protection (a glass panel about 3ft high) and they flowered without ceasing the winter through. Planted outside in a sunny spot they may be affected by a frost, but soon pick up.

Q   Are they the same as polyanthus?

A   They are the same family. When you were picking primroses as a child, someone may have shown you how the flowers of the wild primrose are all joined at the root level but the stem isn't seen. The polyanthus has a long stalk and is not a winter but an early spring bedder. They can be seen outdoors in winter in places like the South of France, where they are much favoured. Even there, umbrellas have to be hastily put over the beds when the occasional flurry of snow or sleet comes. The modern strains have beautiful colours and being taller and more showy than the primroses may be preferred in a larger flower-bed, for instance the sort of place one might plant the wallflowers which we will discuss a bit later – they come out at much the same time. Most people buy them as bedders already in flower and they will flower all the winter. If grown in the open frost will affect the flowers but they will recover. Any winter-flowering plant should have as much sun as possible; that is to say where the sun is likely to come on the short winter days. Facing South or West is best.

Heathers

Heathers are much recommended these days as winter-flowerers. We have already noted that they are plants of the acid peaty

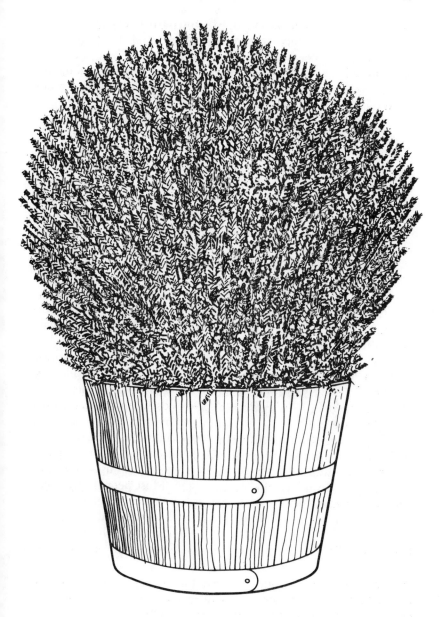

Heather
Heather can easily be grown in a container

heathlands and somehow to me look wrong in a garden. It is a
difficult plant to mix with other things and often does not
flower well in a town garden. My roof garden was an exception
as I was able to grow heathers in containers where they flourished
and the exposed position suited them. The new 'gold' and 'silver'
varieties are very suitable for all kinds of containers and their
leaves are always pretty, even when out of season, unlike so
many kinds of heather.

Wallflowers

Like the summer bedders, wallflowers are brought on in gentle
heat and then transplanted when the frosts are over to make
nice bushy plants outdoors. They will be on sale in the autumn,
to winter outside in your garden and flower in the early spring.
They do not always come through a cold winter and the dangerous time is when a sharp early frost comes before they have had
time to settle in their new home. Buy strong bushy plants as soon
as you see them and do not go for the cheap bundles, looking half-
dead already, which I suspect have not been properly transplanted
from their seed beds. Give them some sort of shelter, a low wall is
ideal – I have seen them survive a really hard winter frost in the
shelter of a wall not more than three bricks high, when some
others planted in a raised container had all gone under to the
same January frost.

Q Is that why they are called wallflowers?
A I have always supposed it was because the wild wallflower
grows in old walls, but the name is a good reminder that they
like lime, as found in the crevices of old walls and that they
need protection.

BIENNIALS

We have had annuals (one year, like the bedders), perennials (like
the border plants) and here is a third kind, biennial (bringing a
plant on one year to flower the next). Wallflowers are one such
biennial.

Q I think that I have some wallflowers in my front garden which
is not very big. Will they be there all the year as I should like to

have room for something else?

A Well it is good news that they have survived until now, the hardest frosts are usually in January and they will soon flower if we get a sunny spell in March. Some at any rate would survive if left in the ground and become bigger and hardier, but most people feel as you do and want them out of the way before the summer. They will be over, as far as flowers go, well before the summer bedders are on sale and you will have a big choice then.

Forget-me-not

The plant most often treated in the same way is the forget-me-not. If treated as a bedder and left alone in their corner of the garden to seed themselves which they do very satisfactorily, one need not keep the old plants when they have flowered. Besides they often don't get through even the best winter. If used as biennials, they can be bought in the autumn like wallflowers and like them need a fairly sheltered spot. A front garden is good because it is usually in the shelter of the wall of the house. Forget-me-nots are often grown with tulips and I'm glad to see that my Mother's old arrangement of "Clara Butt" tulips, a lovely pink and deep blue forget-me-nots is back in fashion. The seeds she used were Sutton's Royal Blue and the firm is still going strong I am glad to say.

LATIN AND 'POP' NAMES

Q Does one really need to know the Latin names, they seem so complicated?

A Since I am writing for first-timers I had made up my mind to be as non-technical as possible, but already we have been obliged to give the Latin names so as to be sure of pin-pointing the right plant. Those who learnt botany at school will have no great difficulty and there is no need to use them all the time; the important thing when ordering a plant is to give its first name (like a surname) and then the second name which will give you the exact plant you want.

We have had a good example with viburnum, which to many people means the scented plant of winter; if we want the laurustinus we shall have to order *Viburnum tinus*. If I tell the reader that even the Latin names have been altered he must not worry as most of the growers still call them by the names they have been familiar with through the years.

The reader may have noted that the euonymus (this was the less grisly seaside shrub) had four bits to its name; probably 'the gold variegated Euonymus' would have been enough, it is the one most widely grown, but it makes a point. *E. japonicus* is an evergreen (not all the euonymus's are) and we want the more interesting variety – 'Ovatus Aureus'.

Q I am a bit muddled, I thought viburnum was the Latin name.
A It is part of the Latin name – as we have seen the 'surname' comes first and is very often enough. In this case we have got tied up with the 'pop' name, the one which most people call the plant but which will be different in the catalogue. There are one or two traps like this and the grower is familiar with most of them; for instance the Latin name for lilac is *Syringa*.
Q Is it really, I thought that was the mock orange.
A So do most of us as the bush is always called a syringa, but of course if you want one you do not want to end up with a lilac. The mock orange's real name is *Philadelphus*.

The nurseryman will use the Latin names, partly because he is used to them and partly to be sure of giving you what you want. It is as well to look your plant up before you go, so you will know an *Acer* is a maple tree and that flowering cherries have the Latin first name of *Prunus*.

When buying bedding plants from the garden centre you will not have to trouble with names as there they are all spread out before one and mostly labelled with their familiar English names – I say mostly because one or two like *Ageratum* have never managed a 'pop' name.

Geraniums

If we are in the garden centre the geraniums will be the plant of the window-boxes and formal displays. It may be a bit surprising in a nursery, or looking through a list of border plants, to find that the true geranium is a garden cranesbill and grows quite different-ly. It is hardy and can be treated like any border plant. The bedding geranium is a zonal pelargonium; the 'zones' are the bands on its leaves.

Q I have bought a pelargonium but it isn't a bit like an ordinary geranium.

A No, they have different leaves and the flowers which make up the flower-head are much bigger. They are rather more green-house or conservatory plants and will not succeed outside unless the summer is sunny, so are rather a gamble. They make good pot-plants but still need sun to keep them in flower and this kind is called the Regal pelargonium.

If we are thinking of a wild garden, any good wildflower book will have a list of English names with their Latin ones. If the first-timer gets hooked on his plants he will get a great deal of interest from the Latin names and even some warnings. We saw the Latin name of the wild mauve iris was *Iris foetidissima*, bad enough but the English is even more explicit: stinking. Such plants do not smell unpleasantly outside, but should not be brought into the house where their name will be only too appropriate.

Q Isn't the Latin name more correct then?

A I think not for us amateurs; we should keep them for ordering and speaking to the expert – though one, Tradescant, who writes the leading article for the Royal Horticultural Society's own maga-zine, says that to use botanical names is to stray into a minefield! Who are we to contradict him; we will stray as little as possible.

GARDEN TOOLS

We need not spend too much time on these. As I write I realise the rather strange fact that I have never been asked a single ques-tion on tools, so obviously the reader can look after himself in this respect. Now is the time to buy them before the weather improves and one is dying to get out and start clearing and planting.

Enough to say we shall want a small weeding fork and trowel (red handles are a good idea as they are renowned for disappear-ing as one weeds and digs); a large spade and fork for digging; a rake and a dutch hoe – this latter is very useful for 'roughing up' the earth and removing weeds from large spaces in the garden, say in a shrubbery. For the flower-beds I prefer to use the little weed-ing fork as I like to see what I am doing and if the earth comes up caked it can be crumbled in the other hand. It is when the tele-phone or the front door bell rings that the little fork does its disappearing act, but hopefully the red handle will show up.

A pair of stainless steel secateurs, stainless because they too are apt to disappear and get left out in the rain. A pair of shears of whatever size suits you, if you need to clip anything such as grass or hedges and a long-handled pruner for trees, a luxury but very useful.

If you have a lawn, a lawn rake – the other garden rake was for the flower-beds to tidy up and leave a smooth even finish to the earth and to get at weeds when you have hoed them. The specially made lawn rakes are a great boon when the leaves begin to fall; for grass and paths a broom or a brush, whichever you prefer and I always have a garden dustpan and brush such as one uses in the house. For watering in the summer we need a watering-can with a detachable 'rose' (sprinkler) and if the garden is any size, a garden hose. The modern plastic hose is much lighter but it kinks more easily. One needs a reel to wind it onto but these can be a bit cumbersome in a small space. Best of all is the new 'flat' hose, which takes up very little room.

THE GARDEN SHED

We need somewhere to keep the garden things of course and the best is a garden shed. Though my present garden is so small, it accommodates one very nicely and is the first of my three gardens where I have been able to have a proper one. My first garden was quite big enough, but there was nowhere to hide a shed, it would have been an eyesore and annoyed the neighbours. We had to make do with the little pantry (for younger readers this was the domain of the parlourmaid, the cook reigned in the kitchen). The little room led straight out into the garden and had a small cupboard and its own sink under which the hose and its reel could go. For the roof garden we would not have been allowed to build anything even if it had been a possibility and luckily I was able to make do with the entrance to the roof garden which was an extended platform for the lift mechanism. The reader may be able to adapt something of the kind, otherwise the best thing would be a waterproof box. The Country Garden catalogue advertises one at rather a high price but I think it would be worth the money, since it must be rot proof and it is a boon to get the things quickly and easily out of the way once they are finished with for the day.

The shed came from Silver Mist Buildings, Betchworth, Surrey, bought from an "ad" in the *Daily Telegraph* (most newspapers have a column of garden advertisements on a Saturday). The shed arrives flat and the driver will carry it to where it is wanted. The D.I.Y. skill needed is about the same as for a bedroom cupboard and needs two people, one a reasonably skilled carpenter. The instructions are not very clear so avoid for instance mistaking the roof for the floor, but once this is sorted out there is no great difficulty and no concrete floor is needed. It is beautifully waterproof, showing no signs of damp after eight years. The wood comes ready-treated, but an extra coat of brown Wood Preserver is advisable. The construction is what would be called clinker-built in a boat, overlapping wooden planks which gives a nice effect. The little sloping roof has weather-proofing material supplied.

Q Isn't it better to have a concrete base?

A Ideally yes, but it adds to the time and expense. Ours has done well without one and the floor is slightly raised which seems to keep it dry.

SPRAYS, FERTILIZERS AND MANURE

We shall need something to keep the pests at bay and a spray to spray them with.

Q I hate spraying, there is nothing more tedious and I always get soaking wet.

A The modern plastic spray is a great improvement on the old brass syringe or squirt. The old syringes had leather washers which took ages to 'take up' at the beginning of the season, causing the water to run down one's arm. The plastic sprays are small and tubby and work on the pumping principle so once primed, simply press on the lever and the spray comes out without the tiring arm movement of the old syringe. They are very clearly marked on the outside and usually hold half a gallon or two litres. [When calculating quantities, remember 2 pints = 1 quart, 4 quarts = 1 gallon]. To get the pressure up you will have to pump up and down about a dozen times, but you will know when it is ready because it becomes more and more difficult to pump. If the pressure doesn't seem to be coming after five or six goes, check that the neck is screwed up tightly.

To start with a general pest control, for greenfly and the like, "Sybol" is one product I have used for years and also the useful puffer pack of Derris powder, which is very handy if one has no spray mixed. Murphy's Fungicide is a copper spray for use against leaf diseases in roses, such as rust, black spot and mildew. I hear good reports of "Roseclear", a pest control and fungicide combined.

Q Is an insecticide the same as a pesticide?

A No, and this is important. The 'insects' in the case of insecticides are things like wasps, bluebottles and ants – the sprays are out to kill and will also kill your plant if you use them against greenfly. Look on the bottle as there are usually very graphic pictures of the pests they are designed to get rid of. Slugdeath is a powder, or pellets, prepared against slugs and snails and is the one that seems most effective.

Material from the compost heap with bonemeal added, makes a good substitute for farmyard or compost manure (such as Cuttings). Peat and lime come into the category of soil improvers and both are useful for town soil, but go easy with the lime.

We have not said anything about quantities, because so much depends on the size of the garden and the amount of storage space. The bottles of spray go a long way and the first-time gardener is always surprised at the small quantity required for a gallon or half-gallon of water.

Fungicides, weed-killers and liquid fertilizers are sold in bottles. Garden lime (not builders') is sold in bags and three pounds lasts for ever, so be careful that it is in at least two plastic bags as well as its own, as it can work its way through anything. Powdered fertilizers are sold in packets or bags. Bonemeal is a safe fertilizer, also Toprose which is specially prepared for roses. Many people swear by Growmore, an all-purpose chemical fertilizer. Dried Blood, in spite of its gruesome name is a very useful pick-me-up when a plant is in bud. Keep all the packets dry by putting them in plastic bags.

We shall have more to say about how and when to apply as we go through the year. The thing is to be prepared and not get caught out by a batch of plants or fine weather as I so often have. Somehow the extra effort of having to go out to buy the fertilizers etc. makes the whole thing much more wearisome than it need be.

Q I should have no idea of what quantities to order.

A A medium-sized bottle of liquid fertiliser does the small garden for a season. Bonemeal 3−7 lbs. In general, you will use less spray (or powder) and chemical fertilizer and more peat and other bulky stuff (which comes in sacks) than you expect.

Q What size are the sacks?

A The size nowadays is 25 kg. (55 lbs), more or less the old half cwt sack. I make no pretence as whatever kind of weight measurement one uses it adds up to a heavy sack, but the little folding trolleys bought for moving heavy luggage are a great help. Get the sack as near as possible to the bed and then shovel it out with the coal-shovel − it is the most labour-saving way I have been able to devise.

Q Is it worth it? I dread the day the compost comes.

A Yes, it is well worth it and goes quite a nice long way though not as far as one would like. The best method is to give it to special plants such as roses and not to try and spread it too thinly all over, but more about this later. I should hasten to reassure the reader in one respect, composted manure does not smell at all and hop manure only has a slight smell of the brewery as one would expect. Made from spent hops, it is acid and is not so easy to get nowadays, but it is useful as a fertilizer, safe for your plants which hate lime and very good in a 'second-home' garden as it holds the moisture and helps prevent drying out.

Q What are organic fertilizers?

A The natural manures we have just mentioned. Being bulky for the most part they also help to improve the texture of the soil. Bonemeal is natural, made from crushed bones. Dried blood is organic, from the slaughter-houses presumably. Growmore, pellet-like powder, is made from a chemical formula which includes the substances found naturally in the organic ones, but of course it is less hit and miss − being concentrated you can overdo it so use only as directed. Toprose has a most complicated formula. Potash (ashes from the bonfire are a great organic source of potash) is useful because it encourages flowers. Sulphate of potash made to a chemical formula can be bought in powdered form in a packet and should be used "as directed". I have found it very good. All chemical fertilizers should only be used "as directed". As for mixing quantities with water, keep to the directions − you will find few gardeners bother to be too exact and most use things stronger than directed, but it is well to be on the cautious side at first. Always keep absolutely to the directions with weedkiller and start off with expert advice.

Q   But isn't organic best? Everyone recommends it.

A   Yes, there is a great fashion, particularly for vegetables about which I know very little. The fact is, people like myself who learnt gardening from their parents or other gardeners find themselves more or less organic gardeners – that is we use a lot of compost from the heap, manure from the compostor and anything like peat or leaf-mould we can lay our hands on. I believe real organic gardeners or farmers do not use weedkiller or sprays. I cannot see any reason why specially balanced chemical formulas in a tried and trusted form such as Growmore should be inferior, except that it does not improve the soil at the same time.

OUR POLICY

The reader will want something practical so I give him the practical results of my own and other people's experience.

1. Get rid of weeds. Dig them out if you have plants you want to save and do not use weedkiller. With some weedkillers you have to leave the ground for three months before planting.

2. Improve the texture of the soil by adding peat and compost from the heap if available. Use composted manure when planting and leave to settle for a week or so.

3. When planting, a handful of bonemeal under the bulb or plant is safe and effective.

4. In autumn and spring dig in composted manure or bonemeal (the latter is always available). For special plants such as roses, use Top-rose twice a year as directed. When plants are safely in, keep them weeded – they should not need more feeding if given a good start.

5. For flagging plants – bud dropping particularly – use dried blood which should be sprinkled round the plant and watered in well. The feeding roots are a little away, say three or four inches, from the holding roots.

6. For good general growth Growmore is just what it says. Use it twice a year as directed, but if your soil is rich by a lucky chance you will not have to bother.

7. Later on, when the garden is more established, you may like to think of growing some special plants and keeping them going through the season. You should use some form of liquid

manure, the best being diluted farmyard manure, the natural stuff, but town-gardeners and even country ones will not find this practical and will have to use a liquid chemical fertilizer. The one I have always used is Liquinure, it is very well-known and can be bought at any garden centre. Use it for things like sweet peas which need nourishment and for your bedding plants to keep them in flower through the summer. I hear that there is a very good new Liquinure intended for tomatoes which can be used for flowers as well. The bottle will recommend you to use it fortnightly and as the plants will need watering anyhow through most summers, this is no great hardship – simply add it to the watering can.

Q How soon should I start?

A We are moving on to March and will hope to make a start to clearing and planting. The liquid feeding starts in early summer, when the bedding plants are in flower.

We have already noted that spring comes officially at the end of this month and with any luck the weather will improve. It tends to be sunnier and one often gets a kind of false spring right at the beginning of the month when the sun feels really warm and for a day or two at least you will be tempted into the garden. We will get down to as much cutting and clearing, with or without help, as is practicable, but it is still a little early to start digging.

Q Why is that?

A After a cold winter the ground will be too hard to dig and after a wet one too wet; as most winters are a combination of the two the ground may be both hard and water-logged. The March winds should dry things up for you and frosts followed by a sunny day help to break up the surface. I should not start digging a large neglected area until April and hope for some good weather then. I am thinking mostly of hard clay, gravel or other stony soil, but with a lighter sandier one you might be able to start a week or two earlier. If all this sounds a bit depressing, I should point out that only the first 'dig' is really hard work and once the soil is dug and worked regularly it becomes much easier.

A START TO CLEARING AND PLANNING

Q We have just moved into a bigger house to give the children more space inside and outside. It is not really the country, but all the same it is surrounded by trees which overhang the walls. Everything has gone wild and I simply don't know where to start.

A You must get "on the spot" advice; a gardening friend or neighbour who will come and identify plants and shrubs for

56

you. At this time of year too, you should be able to see the tips of bulbs showing and some will be in flower.

It is astonishing how some plants will survive and even flourish on complete neglect; particularly the ones which like plenty of leaf-mould as they have had the benefit of their own leaves over a number of years. Equally, it is astonishing how short a time it takes for a garden to become overgrown, so things may not be as bad as you think.

You will be busy enough in the house, so I suggest you get a gardening firm to send someone to do the heavy work for you. These firms charge by the hour so you will know the cost of a day's work; they can do in days what would take you as many weeks. A neighbour's advice is helpful here too as to who to contact, as the gardener must know his stuff.

Q I think there is a garden centre here that will supply people for this kind of work, but I shouldn't know what to tell them to do.

A If you can't persuade your gardening friend to be with you when they come, here are a few ideas. Tell them to clear paths, remove any dead plants or shrubs and trim the trees which are overhanging your garden or house. A day or two should be enough for you to see how the garden was laid out originally and you will have the whole of spring and summer before you to see what comes up and will have time to make your own plans before the autumn planting.

Q I don't know much about gardening and if there are any things which have survived this wilderness I am inclined to let them go on growing. I don't really want to do any more than I can help.

A I very much sympathise, for so many people say this kind of thing. There are quite a number of trees and shrubs which more or less grow themselves, but if you have to remove dead or dying ones they can be replaced in the autumn which is the planting time. Meanwhile, if what is left has been well planted in the first place it will form the framework for your garden which you can leave, except perhaps for yearly pruning or trimming.

If the garden has been allowed to grow wild, then once you have the trees and shrubs in order, you may be faced with unattractive undergrowth comprising perhaps a mixture of dead grass, the more intractable weeds such as nettles and probably ivy and brambles. In a more 'towny' situation you could have bare hard earth which has never, or seemingly never, been cultivated.

Your gardener will probably advise weedkiller for the worst of the undergrowth and this is perfectly safe in skilled hands, but leave it to the experts. The undergrowth will take one to three months to die and it should be safe to plant after that time. Depending on how much was left to clear, you either have the firm back again or perhaps the children could be bribed with extra pocket-money (what about those long summer holidays) – I know of many keen gardeners who started off in this way as children.

If you can spare the time to hoe regularly in between the shrubs and small trees where there may be nothing but hard earth, you can have no idea how it changes the look of things. At the same time it aerates the soil which is a good thing for it encourages worms which are great cultivators.

Q I don't mind earth in between things, what I can't bear is a lot of weedy-looking creeping plants that always look untidy.

A The things you see are known as 'ground cover' and even special roses are sold for this purpose (mostly to keep down weeds). I share your dislike and one thing one can say in favour of the town garden is that the weeds are not such a problem as in the country, so keep it tidy and hoed and it will look right.

We should not overlook the fact that at this time of year something might be coming up in between your shrubs, but in a neglected garden they are not likely to be anything but weeds and if they look 'weedy' what is the point of keeping them? Your gardener will be able to tell you what is worth keeping, but a word of warning here; in the effort to 'make a good job of it' they love to cut everything back hard, including old plants which may still be flowering well. Do not listen to tales of how they will be the same again in no time, they will take at least two years before they are really flowering again and an old plant will never quite recover.

CUTTING BACK HARD

Q I never know what cutting back hard means.

A No, it's not very exact is it. Shrubs and trees particularly have main structures of boughs and branches which have remained from seedlings to full-grown plants; "Great Oaks from little acorns grow". Cutting back hard implies not just trimming, as one would one's hair, but cutting back to the main branch or bough, or with some shrubs even cutting to near ground level.

Q But doesn't it kill the plants? I should be terrified.

A Yes it can but is more likely to spoil their shape if badly done, which is another reason for making sure that the gardening firm knows its stuff.

To touch briefly on aspect, which was mentioned in January, look out for the sunny bits of your garden and make sure they are not too much shaded by trees. You may have some which you want to keep as a screen, so will just have to weigh one advantage against another.

A real country garden would probably have open spaces and fields around it so one can afford to have trees as a windbreak. The town gardener has to put up more or less with what his neighbour chooses to grow, but you are entitled to cut back what overhangs your side. Be tactful though, but there again a professional is a help, for if the neighbour sees that his trees are being expertly pruned he will not be so likely to object and you may enjoy his tree while it's not getting in the way of your own plants.

My present garden was very overgrown when we arrived and in some cases we did have to cut back very hard – here are some of the plants in our own garden and the neighbourhood, that needed sorting out:

A japonica which should have been cut back regularly so that it grew neatly against a wall.

A poplar tree growing over an apple tree so that the apple tree has grown as though blown by the wind.

A beautiful, flowering cherry had to be sacrificed because it had grown too big for the front garden.

A flowering broom which was beginning to die back in places had to be cut right down and killed.

A forsythia which had overgrown a front window was cut back into an 'umbrella' shape.

Two well-grown camellia bushes, probably about 20 years old, with no dead wood, but a few 'stragglers' needed tidying up. Both plants had grown towards the sun and needed shaping.

A beautiful little Japanese maple had been planted rather too close to one of the Camellias which needed cutting back.

A *Clematis montana*, also about 20 years old which had been left to grow as it liked and was all over the next-door garden and climbing onto the maple tree had to be removed.

Also a *Hydrangea petiolaris* (climbing) which had gone wild in a similar manner.

The rockery had also gone wild with little sycamore trees, brambles and buttercups growing in it. The experts used a weed-killer which encourages plants to overgrow and die of exhaustion. We were then advised to leave it for three months before planting again. When we removed the dead plants it appeared bare except for one Sycamore which had survived and which I pulled out time after time – it died eventually. Buttercups survived in places, wild violets seemed to come back and flourish as never before and rather to my surprise, the brambles went completely.

PRUNING

Q Is there any difference between pruning and cutting back?
A Pruning only really means trimming the plant to keep it healthy and in good shape. Nearly all shrubs grow a bit lop-sided as they reach for the sun and can be trimmed so that they do not get out of hand. Pruning includes cutting out dead wood and cutting away weak shoots or ones which are growing the wrong way and spoil the appearance.

Many flowering shrubs (we have already come across the winter jasmine) should be cut back after flowering and this should keep them a good shape without further bother.

Cutting back hard applies more to neglected gardens and to plants where not enough room was allowed when they were planted originally. Some shrubs are pruned regularly and are cut much harder; roses are the best known example. The ones grown for show purposes will be pruned each year almost to the ground, the idea being to encourage a healthy compact bush and large flowers. Ordinarily a grower will not usually be as drastic as this (the exception is if your rose has leaf disease). Pruning, particularly of roses, will be found in greater detail next month.

Your garden firm will bring its own tools and also anything needed for tying up or staking. It would be worthwhile to ask them to leave you some stout stakes, garden string and a sort of attachment (not exactly a nail) which is very useful for things climbing up a wall. We shall have more to say about staking

Pruning a shrub
Opening up the centre to let light and air through

plants in good time, border plants as well as trees, as nothing pays off better, though they may look a bit unsightly at first.

GARDEN CENTRES AND NURSERIES

Q What is the difference between a garden centre and a nursery?

A Garden centres are not growers, they are supplied by the big nurseries with the idea of catering mainly for the town and suburban gardens, including window boxes and roof gardens. This is the place to go if you are in a hurry and want an 'instant garden'. Besides bedding plants, which come and go according to the season, you will see a permanent display of rock plants, shrubs and climbers which have been grown in pots. It is very handy sometimes to be able to fill in a blank space quickly and pot-grown plants can go into the ground with very little root disturbance, so that one is not so tied down by the seasons as one was in the old days. For all that, in this book I am keeping to the right seasons as I think it is clearer and easier to follow; the plants do better too.

Q People say garden centres are expensive.

A They are indeed more expensive than similar plants bought further out of the big city or in the country and this applies also to their sundries such as manure, fertilizer, peat and so on. Tools too are more expensive there than at the ironmongers.

As so often in towns, we are paying for the convenience of having the garden centre on the spot. Also those of us buying for window boxes roof gardens and balconies, will want the flowers already in bud so as to make a display straightaway. Bringing plants into flower for the early market – say April to mid May – is expensive, particularly if the winter has been cold; it will not have been sufficient to keep the frost at bay on cold nights, heat is needed in the day as well to bring them on. Some plants will be lost in a very cold winter however experienced the grower and those that survive will be correspondingly dear. However, when the spring comes and we long for some flowers, I doubt if many readers who have a window box will bother too much about the price.

Still thinking of towns, including country towns, street markets sell plants and they will be much less expensive. There you can buy bedding plants in strips – small plastic boxes – which are much smaller and can be grown on in tubs. Small plants like **Lobelias** do very well and **Petunias**. The only drawback for the first-timer is that he will not be able to see exactly what he is buying as the plants may not yet be in bud. They are suitable for tubs or containers not just under the window so that they can come on in their own time.

NURSERIES

Many nursery gardens have garden centres as well. They have a much bigger selection and if you are buying for a large garden, this is the place to go. If you want roses, go to a nursery which specialises in them and similarly with trees. You can pick out the tree of your choice on the spot and it will be sent at the appropriate season. Growers and nurserymen are very helpful and will advise as to the best kinds for your garden. Never forget though that it is *your* garden, so however expert the advice if you don't like the look of something you have only to say so!

Nurseries give excellent value in extras like potting composts which can be expensive in large quantities at garden centres. It is always worth calling in at one of the centres and nurseries, often to be found on the outskirts of big towns, as they have sales at the end of the spring and summer seasons.

GARDEN FURNITURE

Q What about garden furniture?
A Some garden centres specialise in furniture (there is one in Chelsea that does) and most big stores sell it, particularly as the summer comes along. It can be very expensive and the advantage of the big store is the summer sale where garden furniture is often marked right down.

A roof garden benefits particularly. You will really need the sun-umbrella fixed to the table – it may be your only shade as it was on ours. Roof gardens tend to be windy and the sun-umbrella will have to be wedged to stop its maddening habit of twirling round in even a light breeze. We used the wedge sold to stop sash-windows rattling.

THE ROYAL HORTICULTURAL SOCIETY

Q What a lot there is to learn, I'm sure I shall never know it all.
A Nor will I, nor will anyone perhaps, for the experts tend to specialise. A good idea for a first-timer who would like to learn a bit more about his plants is to join the RHS or Royal Horticultural Society.
Q But aren't they all experts?
A The people who run it are and no doubt many of the Members (we are not called Fellows now), but "anyone can join" is their motto and there are a great many advantages for the new gardener.
Q Are they the same people that run the Chelsea Flower Show?
A Yes, they have their headquarters in Vincent Square, London SW1, where they hold monthly flower shows, which are very much less crowded than Chelsea and where one can talk to the stall holders (usually from specialist nurseries) and ask their advice. It is a great advantage to have them under one roof without having to travel about the country to the actual nursery. They sell plants too and there are stalls which sell sundries like gardening gloves, books and small tools. The shows are very enjoyable as a spectacle and it is a very good way of getting ideas when you are planning your garden. There is an RHS "Enquiries" table and it goes without saying that any firm they recommend would be safe to use.

Members get free admission to the Vincent Square shows, the RHS Gardens at Wisley in Surrey, the Botanic Gardens at Ness, near Liverpool, Harlow Carr Gardens in Yorkshire and the new garden at Rosemoor in Devon. Nowadays tickets have to be bought and applied for to get to Chelsea; the Show was becoming impossibly crowded and this was brought in to regulate numbers. Tickets to members are limited to two and sold at a reduced price.
Q It's all very well if you live in or near London.
A Yes it's true it started in the South of England people belong from all over the world but more and more things are happening in the regions and we must not forget the excellent magazine "The Garden" which comes free to Members. The subscription at the time of writing is £21 which is excellent value. The address to write to for full details is: The Secretary, The Royal Horticultural Society, London SW1P 2PE.

BALCONIES, ROOF GARDENS AND WINDOW-BOXES

The first-timer who begins with one of these will not have the scope of a 'real' garden, but will have the advantage of simplicity, one planting in the autumn for the spring (bulbs like **Hyacinths**, **Tulips** and **Crocuses**) and one for the summer (bedding plants such as **Geraniums**) and you are settled for the year. If your roof-garden is fairly large, you will want one or two 'permanents' in the containers as a background. It is an excellent way to practise looking after plants and they are much easier to see and get at if they are showing signs of greenfly or similar pests. If friends give you 'bits' there is no reason why you should not try them in a tub.

There are very experienced gardeners who have had country or big town gardens coming to this type of garden for the first time and they may find a bit of difficulty in adjusting to the smaller scale at first.

Q I missed my garden so much I had to try a balcony, but it is like having a new puppy after one's dog dies, you feel it can never be the same.

A My heart goes out to you, for I know what it is to lose a garden one has worked on for years and a 'concrete jungle' seems a poor exchange. Just like the new puppy it will never take the place of the old, but will acquire its own character and interest and there are compensations. The sailing gardener could think that he has gone from a swinging mooring to a marina with its many advantages. The fact is we tend to make these changes when we become elderly – what do we want with digging, mowing lawns and massive weeding at our age? Think of coming back from holiday and in half an hour your 'garden' is tidy and cared for once more! What is a pleasure when one is young becomes a bit much as one gets older, but enough of looking back, we must get on with the doing.

WINDOW-BOXES

Q I don't know much about gardening but I think I could manage a window-box. There are two at the front of the house but they don't look in very good condition.

A A window-box shouldn't be much trouble once it is planted up. If the window is recessed it will not get much rain unless it faces the prevailing wind. Light rain may not reach it at all and it will need some watering. Use a small can with a 'rose' (sprinkler) which will wet the leaves as well as the earth. The leaves need keeping clean in this way because the dust which blows about is frankly dirt as we have said before.

Q The whole thing looks dirty, box and all.

A One should never leave old dried-up earth in a window-box, it looks awful and the plants will not do well. Once the box is clear you can see what sort of condition it is in. If the corners have gone it will not be worth saving, but if they seem strong and particularly if you have the luck to inherit one which is lined in some way, probably with zinc, it is certainly worth keeping. Check that the drainage holes are not blocked. Paint the outside, or weatherproof it, but do not use anything like paint or wood-preserver inside as it should not come into contact with the roots of your plants. I am told that there are special wood-preservers sold which do not harm plants but I have not tried them. You will not need anything inside if your box is lined.

Re-fill with a good compost such as "Levington Compost" which may seem expensive but it lasts. I filled two tubs on a balcony with it and had marvellous results; it was still going strong when we left six years later.

Q The boxes do look a bit dilapidated so I was thinking of getting the whole thing done by a firm – is it very expensive?

A The window-boxes themselves are not particularly cheap, but having bought them the extra cost of filling them with compost and plants is not very great and you are saved a great deal of trouble. If you have no particular plants in mind for your window-box but only want it to look bright and pretty, I think it is a good idea to leave it all to a firm. I have always been impressed by the high quality of plants supplied in this way, often better than ones one sees for sale in the nursery or garden centre. If you buy your own box, the fibre-glass ones made to look like stone are nice and light and look attractive; their only drawback is that they are not as frost-proof as thicker materials like wood and metal. In a town, where most window-boxes are to be found, this would not be a drawback as the shelter from the window helps with frost as well as keeping off the rain, so the danger is not great.

Q Have you any ideas of an arrangement which would last all the year or would it look too dull?

A Quite near to our present house are two window-boxes which have been going winter and summer and still look very well. They were planted up with the mini-conifers, which are grown so much now for the rockery and similar sites and in between is a small green and white ivy – anything which hangs down in this way is good in such a box as it softens the hard outline. All you would have to do is to pick out the occasional weed, keep the ivy trimmed and water the little trees in dry weather. If you wanted a touch of spring, you could make room for something like three or four hyacinth bulbs in between the permanent plants. There would not be a great deal to be bought at this time of year but look out for the ones often sold from outside flower shops. They should be just opening so that you can see the bud clearly and as they come on and out so quickly in a warm spell you do not want them any further on.

Q It seems cheating to buy the bulbs half out.

A Well, it is too late to plant them now, they should have been in by the end of October at the latest. As for cheating, I don't know why one should feel like that, we are most of us living in a house designed and built by someone else, we haven't the time to do otherwise so why should you not take advantage of the expert's time and knowledge?

In our present house we have a window-box of metal, joined on to a balcony railing on the first floor. It was when I cleared this one that I found the drainage hole had become blocked up. I have put in a few extra 'crocks' – broken bits of flower-pots and large stones – in the hopes it will not happen again.

Q What do you grow in your box?

A At the moment I have ivy-leaved **Geraniums**, mixed with the silver **Cineraria**. The latter are related to the coloured cineraria with the daisy-like flowers which one sees so much in the windows of posh hotels, even as early as March. These are really greenhouse plants though they survive a certain amount of cold weather. The silver cineraria is amazingly hardy and comes through the coldest winter. My box faces East, and gets the cold winds of winter and early spring so that the geraniums do not always survive. If we have a warm winter they are at least in leaf in March, sometimes one can even see tiny buds. After a cold winter they look dead and have to go as it would take too long for them to recover. That is the way of these rather artificial 'gardens', we rely heavily on the expert grower for instant replacements. Perhaps I would buy **Winter Primroses** though it is a bit late, or **Polyanthus** or perhaps wait until I see the ivy-leaved geraniums coming back into the shops. I like their soft mauve and pink colours and the graceful way they hang down and ramble over the box, softening its stiffness. Incidentally, our neighbour's box opposite, facing North but on ground level and sheltered by our house, has geraniums (the zonal or bedding kind) which survive and flower most of the winter.

ROOF GARDENS AND BALCONIES

Q I don't know whether you would call my balcony a roof-garden, it is the flat bit over the front door and is surrounded by a balustrade, so that it is quite well sheltered – the railing is much higher than one would think from below.

A I know exactly what you mean, many Victorian town houses have them and I have fond memories of one attached to a flat in which my Father lived just after the war. If a first-timer coming from the country or bigger garden had a choice, I would recommend this type of roomy balcony (or roof).

If a balcony is too narrow, or if one makes the mistake as I did of filling it too full, balcony gardening can be very tedious. It is maddening not to be able to move freely without breaking off a bit of some plant and it is always the ones with the buds which go, as they are the most brittle. Watering and tending the plants becomes a real pain instead of a pleasure.

I remember a beautiful show of hyacinths in the spring on a roof balcony such as this and only the other day I came across a letter from my Father, to tell me that he had picked a bunch of sweet peas from one of his tubs which I had planted. He was an orthodox gardener of the old school and sweet peas had to have deep trenches dug for them, with plenty of manure, to suit their deep roots; they were not things one bought in a little pot and shoved into a tub, hoping for the best. I was younger then and no doubt beginner's luck was on my side.

Always give yourself plenty of room and if there are French windows which open onto the balcony/roof garden, take note of which way they open, not forgetting the window-cleaner either, who will need some room for his bucket and ladder. Not only was my balcony narrow, but I had not tried the sliding doors properly and had assumed they opened from both sides. A tub either side would have been quite sufficient.

The excellent geraniums supplied by the nursery, flourished thanks to the shelter of the glass panel, as they do in Italy and the South of France flowering all the winter and climbing up the trellis-work. The balcony faced South, which was a great help and it was here that the winter primroses (though terribly in the way in their container) flowered so successfully all the winter.

The other balcony was East-facing, wider and had plenty of room for two square containers with bay trees in them which were a present to the flat from my sister, she of the chalk garden; the other sister 'joined' me to the RHS; both a great help in making the transition from a real garden. I hope other first-timers will have had similar consolation presents when they left their own gardens to come to what can be just as rewarding in its own way. While the bay trees were small, there was plenty of room to plant something in the way of a colourful annual and at the suggestion of the nursery I chose the bedding **Impatiens**.

Q I'm glad you didn't say busy Lizzie, it's a dreadful name.

A Yes, but you must not let it put you off the useful little plant, particularly the modern varieties, which manage to flower and do well in dreadful sunless summers such as we had in the mid-1980's, anyhow in the South of England – perhaps others have fared better. There is no flower more likely to please the Q's who want colour all the summer, no matter what the conditions, than this bedding plant.

When the bay trees began to take up more room, I planted crocuses for the early spring, and looked for something to take over in the summer. I bought two slightly decorated terracotta pots, which are an ornament in themselves, so that they do not look dull when the plants are coming on. The lilies planted in them were the *speciosum rubrum* type with a flower like a pink tiger-lily and often seen in florists. With two small pots of ornamental ivy – the Latin name is *Hedera* – which made a background as it climbed a little frame and so onto the trellis, my display was complete.

Most variegated 'fancy' ivies are rather tender, but will do in sheltered gardens, balconies or even indoors. They can be planted out from those bowl 'gardens' which one buys as a pre-

Baytree

sent to the sick. The ivy is often the only plant to survive! The lilies did wonderfully well – the morning sun, shade in the day and shelter in winter is just what suits them. Use leaf-mould if you can get it and top up with compost manure. If you want to plant the pink speciosum lily, look for **speciosum rubrum**. There are various names even amongst the *rubrum*; the '**Grand Commander**' is a darker pink, almost red, but best of all I would choose '**Lucy Wilson**' which is pink with pink spots. Not a very poetic description, but I am sure no one could be disappointed with this lovely lily and it is easy to grow but be sure to use an acid compost. The other one often recommended for pots and easy to grow is the regal lily, **Lilium regale**. It has a lovely scent and trumpet-shaped flowers which are pure white in colour. Lilies are rather late summer flowers on the whole and these are two earlier ones; on a balcony the *regale* might be in bud by the end of May and the *speciosum* comes about a fortnight later.

I should not trouble about the ivies' special names, but choose one you like the look of. They are slow starters and not altogether hardy, but the balcony will be protection enough. The ones with small leaves, green and white or gold (yellow) and white are the most suitable and will be on sale in flower shops as well as garden centres. A South or West facing balcony would be too hot for ivy; they would do better in the partial shade of the East balcony.

Q What about a North-facing one?

A The houses near our flat had South-facing patios and North-facing wide balconies, very much recessed and wide enough to be called a small terrace. They were well-protected from the North winds and their owners found there were no particular difficulties. It would probably be wise though to move any tubs containing evergreens nearer the house to give them more protection in a cold winter. In the summer nearly all the bedding plants, particularly geraniums, did well, proving again that they do not need direct sun – indeed the hot summer of 1979 was rather too hot for the ones in my South facing balcony, they did not do as well as usual.

If the reader would like the name of a geranium for window-boxes or bedding, the red '**Paul Crampel**', one of the old 'zonals', must be one of the best ever raised, its leaves are attractive and it is a very reliable flowerer and a strong grower.

ROOF GARDENS

The same flat with the two balconies also had a roof-garden. The flat roof of the building had been partly paved over near the exit from the lift platform and the passage way between the lift machinery and the garden door made a beautiful little garden shed, as I said when we were discussing where to keep the tools etc.

On the North side the roof-garden was protected by wooden palings and a little shed which housed the water tanks, otherwise the roof was surrounded by ornamental railings which gave no protection from the wind. It was quite a large area, facing South so with plenty of sun.

The builders had somehow managed to haul up some very large tubs and had planted them out with good quality plants, unfortunately with no thought at all as to whether they were suited to their exposed position. There can be too much sun as well as too little for some things.

Three of the biggest tubs had been planted with trees, one with a ginkgo or maidenhair tree; readers may have seen the marvellous specimen at Kew Gardens, a full-sized forest tree, so to say that the poor *ginkgo biloba* was unsuited to its new home was an understatement. It was the first to die after putting out a few feeble shoots, then came the silver birch tree which lasted a little longer, then the ornamental cherry which I don't think ever had any flowers but it did manage a leaf or two. I subsequently discovered that everyone had been allocated more or less the same plants, whether they were destined for a South facing sheltered patio, or for a windy roof!

A great many other plants in the smaller tubs died after the first dry spring and I decided we must have some sort of protection. Woven fencing put up on the open South side made a vast difference, the only mistake here was not getting good enough quality fencing, it can be expensive but it would have been worth it. Very soon the fencing began to break away and leave ugly holes and there is very little one can do about it then.

What is the first-timer to do when faced with this kind of thing? If his roof is windy and unprotected he can't go wrong by putting up protective fencing, or by growing a climber such as a rambler rose which does well, is pretty and acts as a screen as well. Make sure that there is an easy way of watering as your tubs will want watering twice a day in a dry spell. You may be advised to add peat to whatever compost the plants were planted in, but if you do this remember to soak the peat first or it can act as a mat and stop the water penetrating. The last thing you want is for your plants in tubs to be encouraged to send up spongy surface roots which means they will need even more watering. Always water thoroughly – you need a tap, with a hose if possible if your roof garden is any size.

As for what is likely to survive and what isn't, I still say "wait and see". A lot of things I would have thought tender survived after a shaky start and did well.

Q My builders seem to have used every plant I most dislike when I see them in front of other people's flats. I should like to get the whole lot out and have done with it.

A It occurred to me, too late, that had I got someone along from the nursery concerned (who made a very good job of planting the balconies), I might have made some sort of a deal with them. The tragedy of these good quality plants and trees, doomed because they were in the wrong place, could have been averted perhaps by taking them away and planting them somewhere else where the nursery had a similar contract; preferably at ground level! It might be worth trying if you are willing to buy again from the same nursery, the plants you want could be supplied at a reduction at least.

The season is still rather early even for the 'instant' garden – some early tulips might be on sale if the weather has been mild and the small early daffodil. Do not buy anything too expensive, it is a sure sign that it has been forced on with heat which is costly and will not do well out of doors.

Q I thought things would be much further on.

A We all have that feeling at this time of year, March is an impatient month as a Q said to me, but never fear it will all come in the end and be all the more welcome.

PATIOS

Q My new house has a minuscule patio at the back. I think it is almost too protected, being closed in by high buildings.

A If you have a chance, before you move in any plants, white-wash the walls or get the builder to use an emulsion paint as the reflected light will be very helpful. We are moving into the longer days so keep a look-out for the sunny bits as we did in the 'real' garden.

I know an enormously successful patio tended by an experienced gardener. She simply moved all her favourite plants into pots and brought them with her and though of course they have expert tending, it shows what can be done. There are a great many house plants which can be put out in the summer, for example your Christmas **Poinsettia**, which will keep its coloured leaves or bracts much longer than one would expect and things usually seen indoors or in the conservatory, like the scented geranium, do well. Here again we are not so tied down to seasons, it is just a question of moving pots or containers in as the opportunity comes.

KEEPING THE PATIO CLEAN

Q My patio has a flower-bed as well as paving, with some shrubs already planted and there are two empty urns. My time is very limited and I am quite happy to leave it as it is so long as it doesn't become an eyesore.

A Sweeping the paving clean of leaves or anything else which might blow in, including the dirty dust of the town, is all you need to do in the winter. In the summer a hose down every now and then makes a tremendous difference.

Q Should I fill the urns now?

A Get them clear and clean and fill with new compost and if there are only the two, Levington or Bio would not come too expensive. If you are not a keen gardener, you will not mind waiting till May when the bedding plants will all be coming out for you to choose from.

Meanwhile, for the stone or composition container and for the stone edging round your flower-bed, here is an excellent way of cleaning devised and carried out by the Q who shares my life.

CLEANING STONE

Brush the loose dirt off with a stiff brush, getting into cracks etc. as much as possible. Then paint over with household bleach (Parazone or Domestos) used full strength. Leave to dry, you will see the stone whitening almost as you look, but it is best to leave a day or so to make sure it is really dry before putting on a sealer. We use BP Aquaseal, which may seem expensive, but it goes a long way and spreads very easily.

Q Do you use an ordinary paintbrush?

A Yes, a three inch bristle paintbrush does very well and can be used, after washing, for both liquids. The sealer should go on thinly and once done the stone will stay clean for a year at least.

Attaching the brush to a long handle and binding it firmly on will save a lot of back-breaking stooping.

Give yourself room to move around as before and remember in this type of container gardening, whatever form it takes, you are going to be looking at your plants more closely than in a normal garden, so 'dead-heading' and even removing dead leaves is very important.

SOME PLANTS AND QUERIES

Q What is the difference between a **Daffodil** and a **Narcissus**?

A Narcissus is the family name for both of them, they can all be found in the book or bulb catalogue under *Narcissi*. However, we all know what we call a daffodil, the one with the long trumpet and mainly yellow; the narcissus is the sweet-scented one with the white petals and short orange frill, hardly a trumpet at all and comes later in the season.

Q I'm sure I've bought some early sweet-scented Narcissi.

A Yes, here is another complication, we were speaking of single flowers on a stem; the bunch-flowered narcissi as they are called are very early, sold in the streets in February and coming from the South of France or the Scilly Isles. They are often sold as bulbs to force for Christmas.

Very soon the spring flower shows will be coming, with a great opportunity to see daffodils in particular at their best. The ones most favoured by exhibitors are the large-cupped narcissi, with a longer frill or shorter trumpet, but with the laid-back petals of the typical narcissus. They are a beautiful regular shape and one can see why they appeal to the show gardener.

Q I would never grow anything like that would I?

A Speaking for myself and I daresay many other amateur gardeners, it is cheering to look back and be able to say that of all the things I have tried, bulbs have been the most successful and the easiest. Buy them from a good bulb grower and they will not let you down.

We shall have more to say when the planting time comes, meanwhile, find a show if you can and enjoy it.

We can plant bulbs anywhere from window-box to stately home, but there are some things we must look for outside the container world, if we want them to do well.

Q My daffodils are outside but they seem to be just leaves, I can't see any buds.

A Daffodils can do this after their first planting or if left in soil which has been neglected. Bulbs which have given a wonderful show their first year can be disappointing the next and I cannot help feeling that they have been brought on too much to produce large flowers and that they need a rest for a year or so. The best thing to do is to feed them with bonemeal, a long-term fertilizer, as they die down, but this is supposing they are staying in the same place. If you lift them to make room for other things they can be heeled-in in a spare bit of the garden and when the leaves have died down, put somewhere like a shelf in the shed where they will be warm and dry.

Q It sounds rather a performance.

A It is and one can never be quite sure that they will flower well; the professionals all say that they would never risk second-year bulbs if they want to make a formal show. 'Naturalising' the bulbs by growing them in grass is much the best way of keeping them going, but if you decide to keep them in an odd corner they are useful for picking, otherwise give them away to friends in the country!

Q I am not sure I want all this chopping and changing. I would be quite happy with some early plant, not necessarily a shrub and some small bulbs.

A A sunny part of the garden would be very suitable for the smaller bulbs such as **Crocus** or **Grape Hyacinths** and as their leaves are so much smaller and die down quite quickly one can leave them in the ground.

For a shadier part of the garden, the **Hellebore orientalis** would be out now, possibly earlier and their leaves are quite pretty through the summer. The flowers are like a large Anemone and go papery when they fade, so that they are really very good value. I have always been warned against cutting off their leaves; in a hot summer they put out large rather untidy leaves at ground level to protect their roots from scorching. Nowadays, the experts cut their leaves in the spring to show off the flowers better. I still think it is best not to be too drastic; the flowers can be spoiled by a spring frost rather more likely than a scorching summer, but I believe I would keep the leaves anyhow.

In our mind's eye we have a sunny corner with the little spring bulbs and the shady one with the hellebores. They come in pastel shades of pink, mauve and white so we do not want a bright red or yellow flowered shrub to take away from them. A pink or white **Camellia** for the background, if there is nothing planted already, would be good and we could make this into a spring corner – the later camellias go on into April. Later on still if there is room, it might be a good place for **Lilies**. They flower in summer and should have been planted earlier, but if the first-timer is specially fond of them they can be bought growing in pots as soon as the frosts are over, but remember to say they are for a shady corner.

Small evergreen **Azaleas** which do not like too much sun (the tall yellow and red are not evergreen) are lime-haters as we have seen and not recommended for the first-timer, unless the soil is naturally acid and peaty – they need a lot of attention to keep them going in other soils.

For our sunny corner we might plant **Flag Irises**, which come on with the late bulbs in April, or the later **Bearded Irises** (the superior version) which come on at a very good time, after the late spring things and before the summer ones are out, a useful time to have something flowering.

Forsythia

Q You haven't said anything about forsythia.
A Yes, how could I have forgotten this lovely yellow mass which can be seen everywhere at this time of year, in wasteland as well as gardens. It seems a part of spring and a hope that summer will come eventually. It is a deeper yellow and more showy than the winter jasmine, which will just be going over. Forsythia too needs keeping in hand so prune after it has flowered.
Q My forsythia grows much more like a jasmine, the flowers

hang down in sprays and are growing over each other but there doesn't seem a great deal of dead wood.

A There are basically two kinds: yours is the *F. suspensa*, which speaks for itself and is not so much grown these days; the other kind, *F. x intermedia*, grows upwards and outwards. It has a very good variety, *F. x intermedia 'spectabilis'* which lives up to its name when in flower and grows so easily that it is no wonder that most garden centres and nurseries sell this variety.

F. suspensa can be left to grow itself provided there is plenty of room. The one found in our present garden appeared as an example in 'Cutting Back'. We had to cut it hard because it was growing across a bay window and taking light from the room.

F. x intermedia can be used as a hedge and will still flower well.

If your 'Spectabilis' is growing with other things you may have to cut it rather more than just removing dead flower shoots and there may be some dead wood as well, particularly at the first-time pruning. With a forsythia, be very careful not to remove old wood which is sheltering new shoots which may have formed after the old shoots have flowered. In other words, do not cut out old wood as one would a rose – I killed my forsythia this way, the young shoots were injured in a spring frost and never recovered.

Q Something has happened to my forsythia, it looks healthy enough but it has hardly any flowers. The new shoots are quite straight and do not seem to be going to branch off and make proper flowering shoots.

A I am afraid your plant has gone back to its wild self. If you look at the shoots which are taking over you will see that they are coming up from below the flowering branches; the suckers which come up in this way are below the graft (where the cultivated plant takes over from the wild one) and it sounds too late to do anything about it. Replace it with another shrub but if you want another forsythia, it is not wise to plant it in exactly the same place. I had always supposed, for this is a general rule not just forsythias, that the old plant had taken all the good out of the ground that that particular plant needed, but the experts say no one really knows the reason – it is just not a good thing to plant the same kind in the same place.

Q How strange, one would have thought just the opposite. Look at the way wild plants seed themselves and come up in the same place year after year.

A   I suppose that is why the experts say it is a mystery, but we have already seen how nature will manage without any gardening rules. One of the camellias I inherited also has branches which are coming up from below the graft. In this case, the parent plant must have had pinkish-red flowers with the same leaves, for the bush is a beautiful shape and the mixture of reddish and pink flowers which it produces give an attractive "Alice in Wonderland" look. Of course, nearly all our cultivated garden plants are in a sense artificial; perfected and altered from the wild, whereas nature is concerned with wild plants which have adapted and evolved themselves so that they suit their environment. As gardeners, we are sometimes trying to force plants to live outside their preferred environment, a thing I am trying to avoid for the first-timer.

Magnolia Soulangeana

Q   I've always wanted a magnolia, or tulip tree, how big do they grow?
A   They are classed as trees rather than shrubs, so be prepared for it to grow tall, say 10ft–12ft and not much less round. We have some magnificent specimens in our London neighbourhood. They do well with some shelter from the cold winds as they are such early flowerers, coming out with the forsythia. The two together make a wonderful sight but one needs plenty of room.

The real tulip tree in the magnolia family is a forest tree, an exotic and distant relative. What we want is a magnolia hybrid (mixed breeding), *soulangeana*. I expect you are thinking of the pink one, with its tulip-shaped flowers and everyone will warn you that the cold winds can ruin it but it is such a lovely thing you may be prepared to risk it. There is a white variety, 'Alba Superba', and a deep mauve one, its name seems to vary with the grower but the last I saw was called 'Lennei' and was very fine indeed. These two are not so early and therefore not so vulnerable. However, no one could ask for a better sight after a long winter than the pink *soulangeana* and 'Spectabilis' flowering side by side.

With all the warnings about spring frosts and cold winds at this time of year the owner of a small garden would be wise not to put too many eggs in the spring basket. Besides the risk of bad weather and partly because of it, the early spring things have a short season which is no reason for not planting any but one must plan accordingly. At the end of the year, when we have gone over the plants month by month the reader will find "Colour over a long Period", when I have shown how I coped as best I could in my own first garden. I was greatly helped by a church's garden on the opposite side of the road – it faced North like my own back garden and I always looked each month to see what was coming on there, particularly if I had a gap in my own.

MOSS ON THE LAWN

Q My lawn is full of moss, is it too early to do anything about it?
A One can put down lawnsand which kills and fertilizes; the moss will die and one can rake it out after about a fortnight. Lawnsand is also sold under a trade name, but the garden centre will know what you mean.
Q I used it last year and burned the grass, what did I do wrong?
A One has to be careful not to use it too thickly, for first-timers it should be explained that it is a powder, as the name implies. When sprinkling it over the grass it is easy to let it drop in patches instead of spreading it evenly all over; the best way if one does get a thick patch by mistake is to brush it away lightly. Avoid hot dry weather, which should be easy enough at this time of year.
Q All that measuring out is such a bore, I'm afraid I do rather guess the right amount.
A You need only measure out the first square yard, then the amount recommended per square yard and you will then be able to see how thickly it is meant to be spread. When the moss is raked out the grass should grow again and be all the better for it.
Q What about the bare patches?
A As we are writing for busy people and the growing time of year for grass is just starting, I should leave it for at least six weeks to see what happens. It will not be too late to sow then if necessary and the birds will have something else to eat by this stage. The warmer the soil the quicker the seed will sprout or germinate and that is a help with the sparrows too, they are chiefly interested in seeds and will leave them alone once they have

started to grow. A few strands of nylon thread above the newly seeded area is always a good idea.

Q My grass is like a hayfield, most of it seems to be dead.

A There are many different kinds of grass, the short town grass gives no trouble in this way and is evergreen. I put weed-killer on two strips of gravel in my first garden and the grass just appeared; I was told by the local nursery that this is more or less wild grass which has adapted itself to big towns, in this case London.

If your garden has been part of a field on which the house was built, the grass will indeed be something like a hayfield. In the country it is still possible to keep it scythed down once or twice a year and there are the modern mechanical aids. I have never used them in my small gardens but am told they are efficient and not too difficult to use. It could of course be a 'wild garden' with naturalised daffodils.

Q Mine is quite small, I think it would always look untidy.

A Turfing with finer grass seems the only answer and now is the time.

The first-timer may be familiar with the rolled up squares of grass looking for all the world like a chocolate sponge roll with green filling. They are laid directly onto the ground, which should be prepared and flattened beforehand, then firmed down, with a roller if possible, to get a good grip on the soil underneath. Of course, if necessary, the firm who sells you the turf will lay it as well. Grass of this kind will be superior to the one which 'just grows' – the most expensive in the old days was Cumberland turf, the fine springy grass of those parts.

Q I just want something green to look at rather than paving.

A The local nursery would supply turves lifted from somewhere locally – say a large house with a lawn which is being developed – bought in this way turf need not be expensive.

Q What about sowing a lawn, would it be difficult?

A Yes, much more tricky than turfing. It is for the experts, such as those who tend the Centre Court at Wimbledon.

Once the turf is laid, the first-timer should not have to do more than mow his lawn and give the occasional treatment with lawn-sand to nourish it and keep the weeds down. For large weeds like plantains, daisies and dandelions, dig them out by hand with an ordinary kitchen fork (kept for the purpose) before they have a chance to spread or seed themselves.

Many people use composted manure in the autumn, but wait until all the leaves are down, so as not to rake off manure with the leaves. Sprinkle it over thinly and leave to soak in during the winter and your lawn will awake refreshed in the spring.

We are at the end of March in our mind's eye, spring has come as far as it ever does nowadays in our changing climate and we must get on to April and start some real gardening.

Here is spring at last and the sooner we get on with things the better. The weather is notoriously changeable and we shall hope that the scattered showers will not turn out to be steady rain, or a return to winter with sleet or snow. The cynics are fond of pointing out that the poet who wanted to be in England when April came was living abroad at the time, but it is a very cold winter indeed which has not produced daffodils and hyacinths by the end of the month, not to mention crocuses and snowdrops. The spring flowers are a great deal tougher than we are, for all their frail looks.

A GARDEN DIARY

I keep a garden diary, it is surprising what tricks one's memory can play even after fifty years of gardening! I too invariably expect everything to be further on than it is and the entries are reassuring with dates varying surprisingly little – it is all in the mind!

Q What do you put in your diary, is it like the Edwardian Lady's?

A No I am afraid not, no flowery thoughts, I keep notes of how well things have done and particularly what did well in what kind of weather. For times of flowering it pays to give the exact date, not just the month. I write down thoughts for the next year and if something has died, what I have tried in its place.

Here is an entry for March: "2.3.85 Weather mild and rainy again. Snowdrops out, japonica coming, pink camellia coming on fast, winter jasmine just over. 'Wanda' primroses out and winter cyclamen still in bud".

Q Those last two must have been out last month and you never mentioned them.

A Yes, doesn't it prove the worth of the diary! We shall be coming to the primrose when we consider the rockery; the winter cyclamen is the **Cyclamen coum** but is not recommended as an easy 'sure-fire' plant. It is the small cousin of the familiar pot plant, likes leaf-mould, a certain amount of shade and a sunny summer which cannot come to order and as a result it tends to disappear. If the reader particularly likes these attractive little flowers, the easiest one is the **C. hederifolium** the autumn cyclamen, which I saw happily growing on the hills above Naples, along with the laurustinus.

Alas, I cannot do beautiful paintings of the plants either, but I can cut pictures out and stick them into the diary, together with helpful hints from articles on gardening.

The best way to buy any cyclamen is already growing in a pot. Buy the winter ones about October and the autumn ones in late summer. All cyclamen are difficult to raise from bulbs (or corms) – the ones we buy have been raised from seed, not difficult if one has a greenhouse, but not for the first-timer.

THE ROCKERY

Many small bulbs which we shall see flowering this month are listed "for the rockery". They do equally well planted along the edge of beds or borders and will mix in with the later flowering edging plants, which will hide the leaves as they die down.

Many gardens have little walls with a space at the top for plants which are the subject of much complaint, as the holes are often made only one brick deep and the choice of plants is very limited; like the shallow containers they dry out too easily. Small bulbs with shallow roots are ideal. The **Scilla**, the small blue *Scilla siberica* is one of the earliest and very reliable, but if the winter has been severe beware of sparrows as they will go for anything. One or two strands of nylon thread will put a stop to this. The **Chionodoxa**, a similar flower, rather bigger and with a white centre, is more unusual and just as easy to grow. I have found that they increase more readily than the scillas.

The **Crocus**, both the early and larger later ones always flower well, but the species, which are the small early ones need a sunny position to open fully. Given this sunny spot, they are rightly described as "floriferous" in the catalogue.

I am particularly fond of the **Grape Hyacinths (*Muscari*)** for the rockery because they can be planted in a ribbon running down in between the rocks. I first saw this, on a much grander scale of course, in the famous Keukenhof Garden in Holland. The best muscari for the first-timer is **'Heavenly Blue'**. It has a bigger bulb than the others we mentioned, so is not so suitable for small pockets in the rockery or the shallow wall.

Q Grape hyacinths have such messy leaves though.

A I don't think the leaves are too bad in themselves, they do have an untidy habit of sending up leaves long before they flower and a lot of people object to this. One can plant them an inch or so deeper than is necessary in the hopes that this will stop the leaves coming up too soon, but it is not so easy on a rockery. It seems mostly the mild unseasonable winter weather which tempts them to come up early. About this time of year, you will see the flower bud low down at ground level, they should soon be growing stalks and their clusters of grape-like flowers will put the leaves into perspective.

We have already noted two early bunch-flowered **Narcissi**, but for the rockery we need something rather smaller – **'Tete-a-Tete'** or **'Minnow'** are two very attractive dwarf narcissi. 'Tete-a-Tete' is a miniature daffodil with curved cyclamen-shaped petals. 'Minnow' is a miniature narcissus with several flowers on a stalk and is "one of the sweetest little things" as the catalogue says. The bulbs though small are a little bigger than the muscari and would need to be planted three or four inches down, so your rockery pockets would have to be fairly deep. You can see them in flower shops where they are often sold in bowls to give as presents. The planting time will not come until the autumn.

The early **Tulips** come in this month and are smaller than the taller Darwin or cottage tulips, which come later. Of all the early kinds, particularly for a rockery, or anything like a window-box or container which one can see from the house, I recommend the **'Red Riding Hood'** – usually classed a species tulip, these have striped leaves and of course red flowers. They are very reliable and easy to grow and can be lifted or left in the ground and will flower again the following year. Not all bulbs can be relied on as we have seen with daffodils.

Q Shouldn't one always lift tulips? People say they get diseased.

A It is unwise to leave Tulips more than a year or so in the same place. They get 'fire', so called because the leaves come up looking as if they have been burned and they fail to flower. The ground has to be left a year or two before planting tulips again. Very often the question doesn't arise because the tulips are lifted anyway to make room for summer plants. It was when I left the 'Red Riding Hood' in the rockery by mistake that I discovered they came up and flowered the next year without any trouble. In my rockery anyway, nothing lasts a great deal longer than three or four years, either they rot with the wet summers and winters we had in the late 80's, or something eats them – I suspect slugs or snails. Luckily, small bulbs are not expensive to replace.

Q What about the **Rock Irises**?

A I have known them come up 'blind', that is just leaves and no flowers, the first year after planting and any bulb that can do that is not for the first-timer. If you want to try them all the same, I recommend **Iris danfordiae** (Species) which is early, about now, or the **Iris reticulata**, a bit later. I am rather horrified to see how they have gone up in price, presumably they are tricky to propagate (increase) as well as to grow!

ROCK PLANTS

Q Is there any difference between alpine and rock plants?

A Sometimes rockery plants are referred to as 'alpines' which does make for confusion. In general, the ones which come from the high Alps do need a special house where their native mountain climate can be imitated. This is not for us obviously, though there is one unexpected exception, the famous **Edelweiss**, a plant of the high mountains if ever there was one, which flourished on my roof-garden, evidently liking the height as it failed in my ground-level rockery.

Q I can't think what all the fuss is about, I think they are rather ugly flowers, I should like to try a gentian.

A The more one gets into gardening, the more people's likes and dislikes will surface as we will see, particularly with border plants. Some people dislike any kind of daisy-like plant, to them they aren't proper flowers. This botanically is perfectly true, for the 'flower' is the bit in the middle, the coloured outside petals are just to attract the bees. However colourful the outside 'ray' petals are, somehow this doesn't make up for the general look. Daisies are weeds which come up on the lawn, spoiling its looks.

For myself, the edelweiss is the flower of the dangerous high rocks, not the cultivated one of the alpine house and garden centre. I can see one now, with the dew still on it, as it had come down from a trip to one of the high peaks near the Jungfrau. I still have it pressed in the alpine flower book.

As for the **Gentians**, the little spring one the **Gentiana verna**, was the one which sprung up unwanted when one took a late skiing holiday and the snow was deficient. Nowadays, the runs are so much higher that our old runs would probably almost seem to be in the valleys.

Q But they are such lovely flowers, not many are a true blue in the way they are.

A If you want to try one, the one most generally recommended for a lime free soil is the *Gentiana sino-ornata*. The experts will tell one it is 'easy', I suppose they mean as gentians go. Remember the Alpine meadows are very rich – not only do they get snow all the winter and the hot sun, but with the help of cows pasturing there in the summer, there is the extra manure. This last item is beginning to be sadly lacking, as the hardships of herding cattle so high up in the mountains makes this unpopular nowadays and we may have seen the best of the flowers. Give your gentians plenty of peat or loam or the equivalent which can be bought, usually as a John Innes mixture of some kind.

Reserve a small flat piece of your rockery and use plenty of peat, together with whatever else you have managed to get in the place of loam and add to that compost manure if possible. The gentians will disappear in the summer and appear in the early autumn, hopefully covered in buds, as a friend found who had forgotten all about them. Luckily she had kept them well-watered for the benefit of some other moisture-loving plant.

Q They are late-flowering then?

A Yes, I know we are in the spring in spirit, but these are the easiest, the *Gentiana verna* is much more difficult. At one time it grew wild in the Lake District, so perhaps a more northerly garden could grow it. Not for us in the South or the polluted air of a town.

Gentian
ideal for the rockery

If the reader should ever see the *Gentiana pneumonanthe*, this the native marsh gentian, on sale, – I found it years ago growing right in the heart of a dried-up marsh one hot summer – it would be a lovely bogside plant for the water garden. They have large flowers and as beautiful a true deep blue as anyone could wish.

But enough of things which are difficult to grow, here are some thoughts for the sunny rockery or little wall.

Aubrieta

There can be few people who have not seen this plant in their friends' rockeries. It is the mauve, purple or sometimes red 'spreader' which should be coming out already if the weather has been at all kind. Though everyone including the growers will call it aubrieta, the book is determined, come what may, to give it a true English name and it appears as purple rock-cress. I mention this as anything described as 'cress' comes from the wallflower family and will like sun and good drainage. The Latin is interesting, *cruciferae* for the whole cress family, because they always have four petals, arranged in a cross; "The sign of the Cross" as small children in convent schools used to be told.

Q   There is some on the rockery but it is really only flowering at the ends. I was told to cut it after flowering, but there will be nothing left if I do.

A   Aubretia is known for straggling, though the new kinds are much better in this respect. The only thing you can do now is to leave it to flower and then watch very carefully to see if you can see any signs of new growth coming further back, preferably right from the shoots as they come out of the ground. Let the new shoots develop and cut back to there. If the plant does not grow well after cutting, it may just be that it has gone too far and should be replaced. If the plant looks healthy but all its leaves look bunched together on the lower shoots, it simply means that it was not cut back in good time and has gone straggly, but if the whole thing looks miserable even at this time of year, it is time to replace it. As before, the advice is to find out what you can of what grows on other people's rockeries. A plant as easy as aubrieta should grow like the proverbial weed, but in common with other plants of its type it likes certain conditions only. It does not do well in the damp, foggy air of a town.

Q Is it all right to plant now?

A Yes, I would much sooner plant up a rockery in the spring which is its best time and there is no problem as all the plants will be sold in pots. We are talking of plants of course, bulbs go in in the autumn.

If you do re-plant, remember to cut it back in good time after flowering, so that it doesn't get the wrong shape.

Alysson or Alyssum

White Alyssum (this seems to be the more usual spelling) is an annual which can be sown now. It has small flowers smelling of honey and is often grown with lobelia, the small blue annual (the trailing variety is greatly used in window boxes). It is useful for the rockery and next month when the bedding plants start to come out in full force, it will be on sale in a strip as a little plant. The white alyssum will often seed itself and the little plants come up before the end of the summer. Look out for them in spring, the tiny seedlings come up with their flowers 'at the ready' so they are easy to recognise. It spreads very well, with no straggling and flowers all the time, which makes it valuable for the rockery as well as for bedding.

Yellow Alyssum is not a spreader, but an upright yellow perennial and is very often a companion to the Aubrieta. Given the same dry sunny situation, it will go on for years with no trouble.

Arabis

Here is another favourite for the rockery which used always to be white and was rather despised for the easy way in which it grew. Nowadays it has been transformed, with mauve and rose-pink varieties. One of the best is the *A. caucasica rosea*. All the modern rock plants are more compact than the old friends of my youth, but one should always treat them in the same way, keeping them tidy and well-trimmed. If your plant still straggles, the chances are it is simply not happy and the most likely cause is lack of sun or too heavy a soil.

Candytuft (Iberis)

Perennial candytuft is always white, unlike the mauves and pinks of the little annual you might have planted in your garden as a child. It likes a flat sunny stone to 'lean' on as do many rock plants and given plenty of sun it will make a spectacular show in the late spring. The candytuft's Latin name is *Iberis* and the rock plants are specially cultivated iberis species. I don't suppose the garden centre will worry about this, but this sort of classification is important when looking up a plant; one searches in vain amongst iberis only to find the rock garden ones coming under species. A good variety is *I. sempervirens*, it is evergreen and nice and compact.

Sedum

The succulent plant *Sedum*, or stonecrop, likes sunny dry places. They have fleshy leaves and you may have seen them growing along the edge of a cliff in the West Country.

Thrift

Anyone who knows Cornwall will have seen this growing on the cliffs. They will stand a certain amount of damp but really prefer the sunny rockery. The Greek or Attic thrift is more tender, but I can well understand why they are preferred by those who have seen the bare Greek rocks transformed in the spring by these plants.

Saxifrage

Also a native of the British Isles, the rock garden variety most grown is a deep pink or light red, whichever one prefers. Its cousin, the London pride grows wild in the hills above the lakes of Killarney.

The reader whose rockery is suited to any of these plants is almost certain to be given 'bits' from neighbouring rockeries, usually with the caution that they will "take over" if not watched. All

the same they are dismal failures if tried in the wrong place, so if
you find none in your rockery, or none growing round about, I
should leave it at that. Your soil may be too heavy as well as
the rockery having the wrong aspect. We can find other things
when we come to the "Shady Rockery".

SHRUBS FOR THE SUNNY ROCK GARDEN

Unless your rock garden is really large, there are not many compact shrubs to recommend. At the sunny end of my North garden
I grew a mini-lilac on the corner of a stone-edged bed. It arrived
as a miniature from an RHS show and grew very rapidly, before
settling down as a nice compact bush, about 2ft each way. It
should be cut well back after flowering to keep it neat and prevent it growing out of hand. I specially recommend it as it was
the one so many friends remembered when we left our first
garden. Its attractive flowers, altogether like a lilac bush in
miniature were the reason I imagine.

If your sunny rockery is dry and sandy or dry and stony, it will
not suit the lilac so well and will need added leaf-mould, topped
up each autumn.

The Latin name is *Syringa microphylla* and there is a variety with
long sprays of scented flowers which is also extremely attractive
and if cut back after flowering will flower a second time. It
seems to be called S. microphylla 'Superba', but is frequently
labelled *S. microphylla*. If you buy one by mistake as I did, keep
it because it is well worth growing.

The Cistus or Rock Rose

The rock rose is another plant I have seen growing in sunnier
climates, on the hills of N. Africa in the early spring and in
early summer on the Greek Islands, where the temperature was
already in the 80's F. and so it is not surprising that the old
books classed them as half-hardy, or as we have decided to call
them 'inclined to be tender'. They do well in sheltered spots
and can be left alone. For instance they are growing on the central flower-bed of the little estate on which I live. Most people buy
them simply by saying which colour they want – pink or white –

there are some purple listed but I have not seen them growing. As far as I know all in our neighbourhood survived the cold winter of 86–87.

It is worth mentioning that the *Cytisus* is a broom, that is to say the cultivated cousin of the wild plant similar to the gorse but without thorns. The spelling in the older garden books was cytisisus; however, as it was pronounced, it always sounded like 'Cistus' and the new version is certainly an improvement.

The broom flower is one of the pea family and like the rest of the family it has two 'lips' and has been cultivated so that the bigger wing-shaped lip is a different colour from the smaller lip; some mauve with deeper mauve, some pink with red and even some yellow with red. The larger bushes must be carefully cut back to the old wood after flowering, or they will grow leggy and resemble their name only too closely and once this happens it is too late to do anything.

Along with the rock rose in the island flower-beds in our close, two more Mediterranean plants have been tried which do very well without any attention. One is the **Phlomis** – called in books the Jerusalem sage – with very striking yellow heads which, when examined closely, still have the pea-shaped yellow flowers but in a more showy cluster or whorl (when the flower stalks are arranged all round the main stalk). The other is the **Genista** and this variety is the compact cushion-shaped plant, again with the yellow pea-shaped flowers, is very 'spiny' but needs no maintenance to speak of. Florists sell a cousin of the genista which is more of a house or conservatory plant. All these are only suitable for a large rockery.

There are special brooms sold for rockeries which spread out flat instead of growing up into a bush; the one I found most successful was a variety **Cornish Cream**. There are not many suitable smaller shrubs. There is a rock veronica or hebe, but even in the sun these can be disappointing and fail to flower, or fail to flower so that they make a good show.

Fuchsias do well in sun or partial shade. There is a '**Tom Thumb**' variety for the rockery which does not stay really small, growing to about 18ins either way. It will be very late flowering in some years, not much before mid-July, so don't depend on it as part of the early summer display. Fuchsias die right down in the winter and are not all hardy, so always ask before buying.

PLANTS FOR THE SHADY ROCKERY

I viewed my present rockery with dread when I saw it for the first time. It was entirely overgrown with brambles and one or two seedling sycamore trees, a terrible pest in a neglected garden, since the winged seeds have had time to find plenty of resting places and worse still they can lodge under stone edgings or rocks. The garden firm we employed treated the whole rockery with weed-killer in the late summer and rather to my surprise by the following spring it was covered with little plants which looked like wild **Violets**. I was not quite sure but left them to see what would happen and they were indeed violets, which flowered away and have been a great success ever since. As well as the rockery which faces north, the violets have prospered under the camellias. They must be one of the few flowers which will flower in real shade but they do like a bit of nourishment in the soil.

Q   How did you know and how is one to tell they weren't weeds?
A   We had already removed a lot of dead weeds and brambles and done our best to root out quite a fair-sized sycamore tree, leaving the rockery seemingly quite bare, then this multitude of little plants sprang up. They looked pretty with attractive leaves so I left them. If coarse ugly grass had survived, or docks or nettles (which you may remember from childhood picnics) it would have been a different thing. As for what are wild flowers and what are weeds, you can choose for yourself. I would have been quite happy to keep the buttercup which appeared at the same time, but its creeping roots proved impossible to control; we should have had a rockery of buttercups if I had left it and anyway it appears quite enough as it is.

On the other hand, the lesser **Celandine** which came up in the bed where the japonica was growing was very welcome, coming as early if not earlier than the snowdrops in the same bed. It disappears completely in the summer, returning in the coldest spring weather to gladden the eye with its yellow starry flowers; they would not be noticed in the summer, but have chosen the right time of year and one feels they cannot be classed as a weed.

In spite of the violets I might have done away with the rockery had not the rocks been so heavy, but the same garden firm did a marvellous job by lifting some of them up (they had all been lying flat and rather untidily) and thus making a "mini-mountainscape" as it was described. At the foot of the 'mountain' I have planted two little pencil-shaped mini-juniper, one rather more blue in shade than the other; they have hardly grown at all in six years. Filling up the shadiest corner I have planted hardy ferns, ivy and Solomon's seal.

HARDY FERNS

The chief thing to remember about these is to make sure they are hardy (outdoor) ferns. There are a great many very pretty ferns sold as houseplants and you must look for yours in the outside section of the garden centre.

Do not be put off by their fearsome Latin names, all you want to look for is how big they are likely to grow. Mine started off very shakily, by bad luck their first winter was very cold, but now they are established they have settled down into quite large plants, about 3ft each way – bigger than I had meant, but I am glad they have done so well as the shady corner is most attractive.

There is a fern, **Phyllitis scolopendrium**, which is a total contrast to the kind of fern I have been describing which are prettier, smaller and more lacy versions of the bracken we see on heaths. The *Phyllitis scolopendrium* has leaves more like the wild hart's-tongue which grows in the South and South West, often appearing on the gratings of old houses which were placed to give light to the cellars. The leaves of the phyllitis are a different green and the plant does not grow as quickly, so be careful it is not overgrown by ivy or any other creeping rock plants.

Ivy

We have already discussed ivies for window-boxes. On the rockery, keep to the same rules and choose the ones with small pretty leaves; they will take a little time to establish themselves. I bought an upright ivy, it had no other name, at the garden centre. It is dark green with small leaves, grows upright and then creeps, partly overground and partly underground, to appear suddenly in some spot which it thinks suitable. You will have to keep an eye on this habit and just cut it back now and then, but anything upright is most useful to break up the monotony of all the rock spreaders.

Solomon's Seal

In general and not only in the rockery, the policy is to recommend
easy plants which the first-timer can be sure of, provided the soil
and aspect are right. He might well like to know of one or two
which are more unusual and still easy. The Solomon's seal is an
old-fashioned plant coming back into fashion and though not
seen much in garden centres, can very easily be obtained from
friends. Once established and left alone in the shady leaf-
mouldy corners which it likes, it will increase and can be divided
in the autumn. It comes a little after the spring show of bulbs
which is useful. The flower is like a large lily-of-the-valley bent
into an arch and lasts very well in water, coming into the house
when there is not much else in the garden to pick. It will die
down gradually in the summer when one should look out for
the cabbage white butterfly laying its eggs, which will result in caterpillars eating the leaves.

Q   Should one kill the caterpillars?

A   Derris powder will do the trick. The Cabbage White is one of
the commonest butterflies, but nowadays we think twice about killing the caterpillars, as the butterflies which were so much a part of
the summer are diminishing fast, at least in the town gardens.
Look for the eggs under the leaves and let them grow on one
or two, the result will be caterpillars in a quantity one can cope
with. They used to eat most of my leaves in my first garden
and I can't truly say it seemed to harm the plant, only made it
look unsightly. They come well after the flowers are over.

The bud which comes up after the winter is quite unmistakable
– a large blunt nose which will make your friends say "what's
that?" Keep an eye open where the Solomon's Seal was planted
and you will be able to tell them.

Auricula

The auricula primula is another old favourite which has been re-
vived. It likes shade, but can stand a little sun and grows at the
sunny end of my North rockery with the 'Wanda' primroses.
Do not buy the 'show' auriculas, but try an easier one – I have
had success with a yellow, white eyed one with good strong
leaves, which rockery pests don't eat.

SHADE AND SUN

The sunny end of a North garden or the sunny end of an East facing rockery like mine, particularly if the rockery is in an open position, will be very favourable for such plants as the **Wanda primrose**, which is one of the earliest to appear. It is purple in colour and there is a reddish-purple variety, said to be difficult, which has succeeded in my own rockery. The little spring bulbs will do just as well as in full sun, even the small species crocus will open if it gets the morning sun.

Q Is it too early to plant things in a new rockery?

A The weather will be quite suitable and unless we are experiencing an unusually wintry April, we should not see frosts lasting for more than a night or two. Do not plant if there has been a frost in the night.

Q How can you tell if there has been a frost?

A We all know the kind of frost one gets in the dead of winter, with crisp unmelted snow on the ground, ice in the puddles and on the ponds and where lawns stay white for an hour or two. At this time of year after a cold night, the air feels extra fresh and keen (one can almost smell the frost) and the earth feels hard and cold to the touch. Leave a day or two for it to warm up before planting.

As far as rock plants are concerned, the best time to buy will be next month, when the growers who specialise in miniatures will have them all on display. If you have a new rockery to fill, you need only ask if they like sun or shade and buy some of the tempting little flowers when you see them. **Rock Pansies** or **Violas** are a very good 'shade with some sun' plant and like some compost in the ground before planting.

Q What about miniature roses?

A I have one or two in the lower part of my rockery and as the soil is clay they do fairly well, but on the whole the aspect is not sunny enough for them. Roses need moisture round their roots, which is why the town clay suits them, but on a rockery they would be inclined to dry out too much and need deep pockets too for their roots. They look so well contrasted with a dark rock in the background that it is tempting to try them.

Q The other thing is there is nothing once the spring show is over.

A If you are making a new one it could be partly out of sight as mine is. There are plants which will take over such as the small **Campanula**, the bell-flower, which most people receive as 'bits' from friends. It will do in sun or shade and flower through the summer right into the autumn, when it often has a second flowering.

This is also where the ferns and evergreens are so useful. Besides the pencil slim **Junipers**, there are the rather thicker but still very attractive **mini-cypresses**, as well as the low-spreading evergreens which are very slow growing. The **Thuja** is more feathery, but still a little tree and the golden variety has beautiful foliage in spring. Making a design with these helps to keep the rockery from looking 'over' once the spring has gone.

As the sunny aubrieta-type rockery is so spectacular in its prime in the spring, most owners settle for one good burst, tidy up and concentrate on the rest of the garden.

As for weeding, another bugbear for it must be done by hand, leave plenty of room all round your rockery if you can – my own has a path at the back which isn't noticeable from the front.

A START TO REAL GARDENING

Q The weather, which hasn't been up to much so far, is lovely and I am dying to get a move-on.

A Yes, the sooner the better, for if I know April we could be having snow this time next week, but that won't last either. Have you anything already growing as it ought to be showing signs of life by now?

Q No, it seems to be an expanse of mud, but the soil doesn't look too heavy. Would I do any harm by digging?

A If your time is limited there is no time like the present, so why not start off and see; it may not be all that wet underneath. After long neglect, you will never have a better chance of digging and giving the soil the nourishment it will need. 'Virgin soil', as it used to be called, needs only a little encouragement to produce splendid results, as there have been no plants to take the goodness out of the earth. Once they start growing though, they will be needing the extra 'food' you have provided for them.

Q What is double digging and ought I to do it?

A It is a fearful confession to have to make on the printed page, but I have never been able to follow the diagrams in the books, nor have I ever tried it myself, even in my old home I never saw the gardener doing it. I must get out of it by saying that the busy first-timer I am writing for is very unlikely to do more than I have done myself, seemingly with good results.

DIGGING

Start first of all with the big fork, that will break up the surface and make it easier to dig with the spade later on. Discard any big stones and crumble any lumps of earth with your hand. If the builders have been about, you are likely to come across dumps of anything they wanted to get rid of, so it is advisable to wear gloves (broken glass and the like are only too probable).

DIGGING A TRENCH

The idea of digging a trench, even if you are not planning to plant anything for the moment, is to put the manure, compost or any other feeding stuff at the bottom of the trench. As the roots grow they will go downwards into the earth, where they will be glad to find something to feed on and to keep them cool and moist in the summer.

Q How far should I dig down?

A A 'spit' is the depth of the spade and it is remarkable how deep this can seem. You stand in the trench as you dig, putting all the earth on one side, thus leaving the other clear for any material you have, such as compost manure, leaf-mould or the leaves themselves, even weeds, until you want it.

DO NOT USE ANY MATERIAL THAT HAS HAD WEED-KILLER ON IT.

If you want to get on with digging and have nothing handy in the way of manure, I have heard of gardeners who use shredded news paper, with the idea that it rots down to the wood-pulp from which it was made. Only recently a reader wrote to *The Independent* newspaper to say their newsprint had produced a wonderful crop of peas. If peas, why not sweet-peas or similar plants which like nourishment for their long roots? It is worth trying.

TOPSOIL

Bonemeal is a long-term fertilizer which brings out the good in the soil. Peat is very good as a top dressing, it makes the soil easier to work and as we have seen, ordinary builders' sand will stop the topsoil going into a hard crust. All this preparation is partly to nourish the soil and partly to make it easier to work. The sooner one can get rid of weeds by hoeing or using the little hand fork, the better.

In my bombed garden it was obvious that the ground was 'sour', (that is so neglected that nothing would grow) and I came across unpleasant surprises, such as a nest, if that is the right word, of houseflies; goodness knows what had caused them to breed there, even the gardener I consulted was baffled, but suggested using lime. This is the kind specially used for gardens, not quicklime. Use it sparingly and your new soil will benefit. I am thinking mainly of the sort of town soil I was battling with, but judging by the new building I have seen, all first-timers will have something of the same struggle.

When your trench is dug it will be about the width of the spade; the material you have been able to gather is at the bottom, the loose earth is back and that is it for the moment. When you come to the actual planting, digging a spit will be much easier. If you feel energetic you can dig a little deeper, where it was not dug before and put in any more material from the compost heap which has accumulated in the meantime. Tread it down well in this case and cover with a layer of earth. Your plant roots will probably reach about halfway down but do not let the roots come into direct contact with manure or unrotted compost.

Plant to the mark on the stem where you see the earth has been before; usually a swelling where the graft is in a shrub, or in a herbaceous non-woody plant, where the stems come clear from the root. Put in a handful of bonemeal if you like as you plant (bonemeal is always safe).

Q I should want more than one trench.

A Depending on the shape of your garden, it is rather like fitting or unrolling a carpet, you arrange things as best you can so that you are not always treading on the new carpet (i.e. the newly dug earth) as you go along. If you have time, you can add your bonemeal or peat to the topsoil straightaway, so as to get it all done, or it can be added later when you plant.

This is my rather rough and ready way of preparation, a bit like my compost making, but it seems to have worked in my own gardens. The fact is, if one is trying to live in the real world of would-be and more or less non-gardeners, a busy Q is not likely to do much more than this. Even if it sounds too much as it is, he must not feel guilty and give it all up as a bad job.

One forking with the big fork – beware of the roots of any plants already growing which you want to keep – at the same time digging in any of the numerous composts on the market, will be very much better than nothing and will improve the look of your garden. Thereafter, we are depending on plants which don't need too much attention, of which we have already come across some in quite a satisfactory manner.

A START TO PLANTING

Q Is April too early to start planting?
A It will seem strange, but it is a little late, the sap (the plant's lifeblood) will have risen and things will be starting to shoot or bud. The best time is in the autumn when the plant is beginning its winter rest. Contrariwise, if one is thinking of bedding plants it is a little early, the height of that season is from the middle of May onwards. So many things are raised in pots nowadays, that it would be possible to buy almost anything at any time of year and plant them out. Developers seem to get away with it, judging by what one sees of new estates and a lot of plants do survive. This may be because of the town's special climate, with its mild winters and rainy summers, almost the same for seven or eight months of the year.

If the new garden should have say, a rose bed where some need replacing, it is possible to find pot-grown roses (NOT the kind sold by florists as indoor plants), grown by specialist nurseries. The garden centre will know where to go. I bought one for my roof-garden which succeeded very well.

As we have been thinking of digging and fertilizing, it is not a great step therefore to go on to planting, for the rules are much the same for any plant, provided the weather is suitable. Never plant if the weather is hot and dry or if the ground is water-logged, particularly if the soil is heavy.

Dig the hole as we have described, with its nourishment well covered over with soil. The roots must lie easily without having to be forced to fit the shape of the hole and this applies particularly to shrubs. If a long root is sticking out in an awkward way, it is better to shorten it with clean secateurs than to bend it into place. This quite often happens where the root has been reaching out to some favoured place (probably towards some manure you have put down for something else).

Q Whatever I do, I can't make the plants go the way I want. I moved a rose last year because it was growing lop-sided and now it is just as bad as before.

A The rose will have been planted out in the nursery (pot-grown ones are the exception) and it will have acquired a way of growing that nothing will alter. One can shorten a root to even it up, say because it was growing out too much to the right, but if you try and turn it round as I have done myself, it will overbalance and not sit down properly in its new site. One has to "offer it up" as the old plumbers used to say. If it is possible to move the bush so that the strong-growing side was pointing away from the sun, it might be the only way of getting a better balance.

Q My garden has been planted up for me in exactly the way you described and is full of 'developers' plants'. All the ones I most dislike which I see all over the place in front of flats and hotels. I am tired of them already and though it seems rather drastic, I frankly should like an instant garden of my own choosing and design. Is there a firm who would do the whole thing?

A If there is no problem over what used to be called the 'ready' – if the cash flows satisfactorily – there are firms which will design you a garden and bring everything along, even trees if you want them and they also have designs and pictures to choose from. The only suggestion I have to make over this excellent idea, is to tell them if you want the garden to be trouble-free. Possibly they will send someone every so often to do the minimum amount of maintenance which is necessary in any garden. A really well-designed garden is an asset to any house and will add to its value.

PRUNING ROSES

Q What about pruning the roses? Is this the time of year? They look very straggly and untidy but I don't like cutting off the new shoots, though people say I should.

A   April was always the month for pruning roses in the old days, so you are perfectly safe to cut them now. Beware though if it has been a mild winter for I would never cut back a rose which had come on as far as showing flower buds. At this time of year one sees beautiful fat shoots beginning to develop and it is indeed hard to cut them away, but you are right to want to keep your roses in good shape. I take it we are talking of bush roses.

Q   Yes, I have what I think is a rambler climbing all over a fence. Bits do look a bit dead but it is rather hard to see and I am told that the autumn is the right time to prune.

A   Yes, that is correct and just as much to the point is that the rose may well be holding up the fence which was originally holding it up – you don't want that collapsing just as you are busy with other things. The rose will come to no harm if you leave it until the autumn.

Q   My roses look nothing like the ones in the book. For one thing all the buds are at the top, one cannot "leave three buds" when there only seem to be about three altogether. Cutting them off would not shape the bush and would leave nothing else in the way of a bud as far as I can see. Would some more come later?

A   First of all, the excellent pictures in the gardening book are really only to be thought of as diagrams or examples, rather like an 'average' person. They are explaining the theory of pruning to shape the rose and cause it to produce better flowers. I daresay the roses in the RHS gardens would look like the diagrams, but not the ones in a neglected rose bed.

The reason one wants to get on with the pruning is that the roses will have a setback, not in the sense that it will do them any real harm, simply that they will obviously have to produce more shoots in the place of those you have cut off and this will mean they will flower a little later than if left alone. Roses are sold in the autumn ready pruned and if you see any signs of this having been done, leave them alone.

SOME EXAMPLES

Q   The rose seems to have gone wild, with one or two straggly shoots which are green instead of reddish.

A   The thick stems are the original rose and the long things are suckers from the briar. Later on in the summer, look out for anything which comes up from below the swollen stem (the graft) and has leaves with seven leaflets instead of five, these are suckers. Deal with them by cutting them off as deep down as possible.

The straggly type you describe almost certainly does not have enough light and perhaps something can be removed or cut back which is shading it from the sunny side (the South or West).

If there are straggly roses in a bed which seems to have plenty of light and where some roses are doing well, look carefully for black spot – a huge black spot on the old leaves. Otherwise, if the others look well the poor specimens may just have been varieties which are less robust or more prone to leaf disease. You can prune them if you do not want a gap and hope for the best, then replace them if necessary in the autumn. If you are satisfied that a rose is dying from black spot remove it at once, it will just give it to the others. As we shall see sprays can be used against this disease, but where leaves have been left to drop and infect the ground one has to be rather more drastic.

Q Some of the roses are doing well and looking reasonably like the pictures.

A At the bottom of the bush you will see small 'weedy' bits which are going to come to nothing, cut them away and any thin stems which are crossing over others in the middle of the bush. Left with the thick stems, if they seem strong growers, cut them about a third of the way down, finishing at a bud. Cut the way the bud is growing from the stem leaving as little as possible of the stem, as it is the bit left behind which gets diseased. I have always given my roses a little Toprose after pruning – scatter a handful round the plant an inch or two from the stem and water in if the weather is dry.

If after pruning the rose simply grows from where you have cut it and seems disinclined to make shoots, not suckers, from the base it probably needs a little more feeding. My parents used woodash from the bonfire, but it can't go straight on. Let it rot over the winter.

When you are putting down your compost in the autumn give the roses something extra. Dig it in, do not let it lie for fear of encouraging disease. Roses like plenty of moisture at their roots, which is why the clay soil of the town suits them, but they should not be too enclosed and so large gardens or front gardens which are usually open are the best. It is astonishing to see how even a little way out of town, for instance Kew Gardens or the

Royal Parks, roses will grow as well or even better than in the country. The chief cause of the spindly diseased rose is lack of air and light.

SPRAYING ROSES

Q Is there a special time of year for spraying roses?
A It is not too early for greenfly or blackfly, the first ones may arrive at any moment. Roses usually get greenfly rather than blackfly, both are aphids and have no wings. They appear on the bush as if by magic and once there, the sooner they are discouraged the better, as they increase so rapidly.

I read once in a Sunday paper that a greenfly born on the Sunday could be a grandmother by the following Wednesday. That should make us realise that "prevention is better than cure", as the old copybooks used to say, likewise that the time to spray is "no time like the present".

If the roses have been found to have diseased leaves lying around or still on the bushes, they should be sprayed after pruning with a fungicide and pest killer combined, such as 'Roseclear'.

As for the weather, it is not wise to spray if it looks likely to pour with rain and the general rule is that the spray will take about two hours to dry and be effective. Spray can burn the leaves in hot sun, but this really applies later in the year. Also do not choose a windy day when the spray will be blown about.

It is not all that easy to get a dry still day which is not sunny as well and the evening tends to be the best time. Even so, one has only to go out armed with the spray for the evening breeze to spring up. Be prepared by wearing something to protect the eyes and hands – sunglasses are a good idea as they are usually rather big and snow goggles are good too; rubber gloves do for the hands.

There are some systemic all-purpose sprays (it will be printed on the bottle), which are unusually strong so be specially careful with them.

Q Are they the ones which get into the plant and keep them free of disease?
A Yes, although as far as keeping roses free from disease or greenfly, depending on what the label says, I have not found it much different from the usual kind in its long-term effects. I

tried one, on the advice of a knowledgeable cousin, on a rose which seemed pretty well done for; a 'Garnette' rose, a type unfortunately susceptible to black spot. On her advice I used an extra strong mixture, but I felt it to be rather 'kill or cure'. The rose recovered one season then was badly affected the next, so I got rid of it. It is sad, but wise, to do this if the rose does not respond to treatment as it will only infect the others.

As the systemic spray is so strong I feel inclined not to use it as a general rule. I am told that something like Roseclear used at the beginning of the season will keep your bushes free of mildew or rust later on in the season. Mildew is a powdery white substance which comes from excessive rain as well as a long dry spell. Besides looking unsightly it will often lead to rust, the other leaf disease, which is also a virus and like them all difficult to get rid of.

Q It sounds a bit alarming, how often would I have to spray?
A Once at this time of year and again after a fortnight – always leave a fortnight in between. You might be lucky and that might be it, but keep a look-out later in the season for any diseased-looking leaves or greenfly and if found one more treatment should be enough. If one thinks back again to childhood picnics in the summer holidays, some years were much worse for wasps and the same applies to all pests.

If your rose is in the right place and healthy you should not have much trouble.

IMPORTANT: Do not spray ladybirds as they eat both black and greenfly in their early stages – occasionally there are little swarms of them in the bushes, but usually they come in ones or twos.

Rescue them if they come into the house by letting them crawl onto a sheet of white paper, when they can be carried outside and will fly away.

TENDING THE NEW GARDEN

We have made a good start with pruning and spraying the roses. Anything which is not a rose in the rose bed is pretty certain to be a weed, as people do not usually mix other plants with roses, unless there are some bulbs or little edging plants.

If the small bulbs have strayed about the garden through having seeded themselves, collect them together when the flowers are over. Choose a day after rain when the ground is soft but not soggy and dig the trowel under the little bulb, taking up plenty of earth so as not to disturb the root. Then dig the same sized hole where you want it to go and the chances are it will not realise anything has happened.

Q Is it all right to cut the bigger plants down? The ones in the border have a lot of dead stuff, but there is fresh growth from the bottom. Will the dead-looking bits sprout again?

A It would be safest to get someone to look at them, but if they are herbaceous and not woody, you can cut down all last year's dead stalks and leaves.

If you can identify a fuchsia, this is the kind which *will* flower on the wood from last year. The only way to tell which bits are going to sprout is to wait until they do it which should be any moment now unless the winter has been unusually cold.

It is a bit tricky, in cutting the old wood, not to damage the new shoots so do it as soon as possible.

Q The weather turned cold in the autumn and I hadn't a chance to finish pruning my **Hydrangeas**. Is it too late now?

A April is rather like March, it seems to stand still or even go back to winter for a week or so and one feels the spring is never coming. The difference now is that one warm sunny week will bring everything on with a rush and suddenly spring is here – very pleasant when this coincides with the Easter holiday.

The hydrangeas will be ready to take off, so if you can get at them at once do so, but be very careful if you have to cut away dead branchlets inside the bush, not to break off the little shoots which contain the flower buds as they are very brittle. They will be showing up now like little parcels and the leaves will not be far behind.

Q What about staking?

A If your hydrangea has a corner to itself, it does not need staking; the large 'mopheads' will be beaten down by a heavy thunderstorm, but they will pick themselves up and the 'lacecaps', the flatter kind, can do without staking unless in a very confined space.

If you need to stake, put a stout one right in the middle and tie the branches to it as a support – you may need two or three round the edges as well. It is well worth doing this early on, nothing is worse than trying to rescue a plant which has collapsed from heavy rain or strong wind. Use stout bamboos or the modern green metal stakes which are strong and last well. Don't forget

when buying them to allow for summer growth and that part of
the stake will be in the ground, so you will need a foot extra.

SOWING SEEDS

Q If I leave the real planting until the autumn, there are going
to be quite a lot of empty spaces. Is it difficult to bring things on
from seed?
A Sowing seeds straight into the ground is not difficult, but it
can be a great source of disappointment to the first-timer. We
must realise, that to scatter seeds about and hope for the best is
no good unless the soil is very light and sandy. The small roots
of the seedlings must be given a chance, so there has to be
some preparation first, with the removal of stones, weeds and general lightening of the soil by forking and crumbling by hand, or
even sieving; here adding sand to a heavy, sticky soil is a help.

At the end of this month and in early May we can sow seeds
straight into the ground. They need to be hardy and it will
always say on the packets, which will be on sale by now in the
shops as well as garden centres. The letters to look for are HA,
Hardy Annual. HHA, Half-Hardy Annuals need a little heat to
bring them on and would not be planted out until the frosts are
over, around mid-May. Some of the latter, such as asters,
though fairly easily raised are not for the first-timer; in any case
we have missed the bus as they are sown earlier.

In choosing the seeds, we want to look out for seeds labelled
"not particular as to soil or situation", or something of the kind;
though sometimes a bit on the hopeful side, they are a guide to
the easier seeds. Here are some ideas which the reader may recognise from his own garden as a child.

Alyssum	'Little Dorrit'. We have already mentioned this for the rockery as it is a great 'self-seeder'. Does for edging too and spreads well. Needs sun.
Candytuft	*Iberis umbellata* fairy series is small and compact for the rockery or edging. 'Pink Queen' and 'Red Flash' are taller varieties at about 8ins. Very easy and do not mind a little shade.

Convolvulus Minor	This is not a climber but a smallish bushy plant for the front of the border. Mixed colours, or 'Blue Ensign' (blue with a yellow centre).
Convolvulus Major	This is a very pretty climber but not to be confused with the *ipomoea*, the blue morning glory which is half-hardy. These are different colours: purple, pale blue, pink, red. Its only drawback is that it needs a sunny summer to bring it on, or it will not flower until September. Unlike the white wild convolvulus (bindweed) it is an annual, so leaves no roots for the next year. Very easy to grow.
Clarkia	Slightly taller, 10–12ins. Pinks and reds, some white. Easy to grow, but it will straggle unless it has sun.
Digitalis (Foxglove)	Comes at a very useful time in the shady garden. It needs a little sun such as the dappled shade it gets in clearings in woods. Very easy to grow and will seed itself. Choose the one most like the wild foxglove.
Larkspur	These are tall and bushy, very colourful, pink and blue. Very useful for filling a space, not just for edging. They are rather tall about 12–18ins. Easy to grow.
Virginia Stock	The easiest of the lot – it sometimes seems as though every seed must have come up. Does not need thinning. A small 'edger' or a mass for the rockery.

Before seeds are sown the earth should be prepared by digging with a small fork, removing small stones at the same time, (we are assuming that the ground has been dug already). If the ground is fairly dry you can sieve it through an ordinary little sieve such as one uses in the kitchen. Add some sand and 'Growmore' to the soil as the seed will need something to feed on while they are growing.

Sowing seeds can be quite a fiddly business. Remember though, like the picture of 'The Sower' we used to see so much when I was young that you are scattering not planting. If you want them in a line, make a little dent as a trench for them, then cover over lightly with your sand, sieved earth, or seed compost.

Q Should one use a special compost?

A I never used one out of doors until quite recently, but if you do use a seed compost you will still have to remove any stones. Then put a thin layer of the compost, just enough for the small roots to get hold of, fork it in lightly, making sure no stones or lumps of earth have got mixed up with it and scatter the seeds as thinly as possible. Making a hole in one corner of the packet is the easiest way to sow evenly and is worthwhile because it saves thinning afterwards.

The sooner the seeds come up the less likely the birds are to get them. It is worth noting that the nylon threads we put out to discourage our feathered friends are not meant to make a kind of net; too many threads and they will see them when they are on the ground. Therefore the fewer the better, within reason, because the birds do not see them and catching their wings on something mysterious is what keeps them away. Do not plant seeds anywhere in deep shade and remember to water in a dry spell.

Q How long will they take to come up and how shall I know they aren't weeds?

A You will know more or less where you have planted them; they take at least a fortnight, or more if the ground is cold, to come up. Usually after warm spring rain, one comes out into the garden to find a mass of green has sprung up just as one meant it to, with all the leaves matching as it were and looking orderly. I am sure you will have no difficulty and all your troubles will seem worth it after all.

Q I think it is beyond me, though I might try just a small patch.

A You will only have to wait until next month when you can buy similar seedlings grown in 'strips'. Perhaps that is the best way if you are struggling with doing up a house at the same time and it is not very practical for the second home either. The seedlings will have grown into small plants but will probably not yet be in bud.

Q I seem to remember planting **Nasturtiums** as a child. They came up very well, but I'm sure I planted them in little holes seed by seed.

A Yes, there are one or two seeds of this kind, sweet-pea seeds are another. The trouble with nasturtiums is that one has only to plant them to see nice little plants come up, when suddenly they are attacked and ruined by blackfly. They are too small and tender to spray as one would a rose and most people give it up as a bad job. Whether the climate has changed, making it less dry and hot, or the pests have suddenly 'got the message', I don't know, but I would not try nasturtiums for the present.

THINNING OUT

This whole book is geared, as it were, towards the first-timer and much as I long to say there is nothing in thinning, I have got to admit that it is a very fiddly job and I haven't really mastered it in all this time. There are one or two things to remember; do not try to thin too soon and when the plant is small leave it alone as much as possible. If you find a mass of seedlings all in one place, lift them out gently without handling the frail stalks, dig a little hole with the dibber and drop the biggest ones in, but do not try to press down as ten to one it will break the stalk.

Otherwise, the great art is to remove the weedy ones without disturbing the others, which is easier said than done. Leave them until they are fairly well grown; the minute they show signs of getting leggy, take a little pair of pincers (like eyebrow pluckers) and just go as gently as you can. The firm of Sutton Seeds, which my Mother used and which are still going strong, recommend quite rightly not to discard the less well-grown ones automatically, it may only mean that they are the more uncommon colours.

Q What happens if you don't thin them?
A They will crowd each other out and stay leggy.

Before the first-timer gives up in despair, thinking seeds are not for him, let him try one of the very simplest, say **Virginia Stock** which doesn't need any thinning. See if I am not right in saying that there is nothing quite like the satisfaction of seeing the seeds come up and having a show all through the summer which owes nothing to any nursery or garden centre (if one forgets the seedsman).

There was a Victorian 'weepie' called "Misunderstood", about strong silent Humphrey, the misunderstood one, who contrasted with soppy little Miles, who was the favourite son. Humphrey goes out into the garden the day after his mother's death and sees the green of her initials which he has planted as a surprise for her and which have come up too late. I have never met anyone who has read the book who does not remember the green initials, which shows there is a gardener deep down in all of us.

SOWING HALF-HARDY SEEDS

This is probably not for the first-timer, but I must put in a short note because with our centrally heated houses nowadays, it is perfectly possible to grow half-hardy seeds in the ordinary warmth of the house. I had long admired the way our neighbours left their flower-beds planted out before they left for the South of France in May, exactly calculated so that they were coming into bloom on their return in July. I have only recently discovered that all the plants were raised on window-sills in the house. They are sown early in January, take a month or so to germinate and by the time May comes they are ready to be put out to 'harden off' on their veranda, before being planted out.

Like myself, our neighbour learned her gardening from her mother and though undoubtedly she has 'green fingers', she is an artist as well as a gardener. What particularly impresses me is the quality of the plants. She gets her seeds from Suttons of Suttons Seeds, Hele Road, Torquay TQ2 7QJ and grows them in seed compost in little plastic boxes saved from the supermarket, having first pierced holes in them for drainage.

This year it was African marigolds, large and small, with Busy Lizzies in the larger bed. Another year it might be pansies (once so difficult to raise from seed), sweet william, Canterbury bells or asters. Anyone who has been hesitating should certainly try, as I have, with varying success. I found the *Impatiens* very difficult to grow (they are said to be notorious), but asters and convolvulus were easy. It helps even the hardy ones to bring them on in the house, then they are more forward when one puts them out. There are many Qs I am sure who will soon be trying their hand at perhaps just one box. It is nice to be able to choose exactly what one wants and of course *much* cheaper.

For hardening off, as I have no veranda, I put my boxes on the compost heap, but of course do not add to the heap when they are

there. There is a certain amount of protection from the house, and
'bottom heat' from the rotting leaves and they stand the cold of
early May quite satisfactorily.

SOME MORE PLANTS

Before we turn into May, let us have a last walk round the garden
to see if anything is coming up of any note.

In a shady corner there might be a bigger hellebore with green
flowers, which would be a **Helleborus arqutifolius**. This, like
the *H. orientalis*, lasts well through the early part of the summer
and would be a good addition to our shady bit if not there already.

If there are **Lillies** coming up, I do not think anyone could
mistake them for anything but some kind of choice flower. They
keep a very regular timetable whatever the weather, with the
early ones often appearing in the second or third week of April,
about Easter time, as is appropriate. One of the first to show is
the regal or regale lily, the white trumpet with the beautiful scent.

Lily-of-the-valley

These sometimes disappear completely, or leave some very dreary
and bedraggled leaves behind and certainly there will be a tangle
of roots. If they are coming up now, the green shoots look like
rather badly furled umbrellas. Look carefully at one and you
may see the flower bud already coming up beside it ready for
flowering in May.

Q Mine seem to be all leaves.
A They are sometimes very difficult to get to flower really well –
try them with sulphate of potash in the autumn as they are beginning to die down, or after flowering. They may need dividing,
which is done in the autumn and one could work in a little bonemeal as well. They are always said to like leaf-mould, but stone
edges or between flagstones seem to be favourite spots, so try
them with a little lime as well if your are on an acid soil.

We noted the **Viburnum x burkwoodii** earlier on. Having
shed the dead-looking leaves it has hung on to through the
winter, new spring growth will be bursting forth together with
flat scented white flowers at the end of the stems. Cut the dead

heads off, when the time comes, as far down as is necessary to trim your plant. My own V.x *burkwoodii* is very accommodating and has flourished in spite of having been cut fairly hard each year – I had not expected it to grow quite as fast and as far!

In my opinion the two best months in the year are coming, so with this pleasant thought we will go on into May.

Lily-of-the-Valley

May is here and at last we can look forward to the summer. It often starts with a cold spell, which is rather useful to the gardener, for it prolongs the life – that is to say the flowering – of the late spring bulbs, meanwhile giving him the chance of getting the garden into order, before the summer plants are on sale in the garden centres and nurseries.

Q Would you call May summer? It seems very much between seasons.

A As the end of March is officially spring, I suppose we must say the end of May is officially summer. The fact is, suddenly a warm or even hot spell comes towards the end of the month and we may be passing a field where the buttercups have seemingly come out overnight, the trees are showing their fresh green leaves and the heart lifts making it impossible not to feel that summer has come.

In the garden lilac and laburnum are out and in the town our front gardens and window-boxes are suddenly full of colour; the poets who sing about this time of year have got it right.

THE CHELSEA FLOWER SHOW

We move from the real world of our gardens to the Chelsea Flower Show, which comes at the end of the month. It is almost literally out of this world. The plants have been brought on by experts regardless of season and there are daffodils, tulips, early and late, as well as the monster delphiniums and of course the roses.

The new gardener would not be the only one to come back rather despondent from all this perfection, particularly as the end of May can coincide with a gap in the garden; summer has come but not the summer plants for another week or two. We should think of it more as a showcase and remember that this is a marvellous opportunity to see plants actually in flower, which is far better than any picture or description of colour. You can see the names for yourself and order for the autumn if you wish, small orders are not despised.

Q Isn't the Show impossibly crowded? I went once and it nearly killed me.

A The RHS has introduced a new system for members which has helped to overcome this problem. As the benefits of membership are liable to alteration from time to time, these are sent to members annually.

SOME THINGS TO LOOK OUT FOR AT THE SHOW

Darwin tulips

These beautiful tall tulips are the last of the tulips to flower. May is their month, but if they have been held back by bad weather, they may still be flowering away happily in June when you will want to get them out and summer plants in. The firm of Walter Blom always has a marvellous display at Chelsea and I recommend them, though they are not cheap. The new gardener often has bright dreams – as do all gardeners – of what his garden is going to look like and it is most satisfactory to be able to recommend something which I know will make as good a show in a first-timer's garden as in anyone else's.

Q Are they the ones I have seen in the parks and can they be grown in an ordinary garden?

A Yes, in a small space, the open front garden is probably the best. Anyone who has seen a display in the park, such as the bed in Hyde Park near the gate which leads out into the Edgware Road, would naturally want something of the kind for his own garden. The park gardeners get over the late flowering difficulty by following them with dahlias; they cannot go in until the frosts are over and so the changeover is exactly right. On the grand scale of a park, when other things are happening in other parts and one has all the trees to look at, it is an ideal scheme, but in a smaller space the gardener would not be so content to look at stakes and leaves until the flowers come out in August.

We might do better by planting **Fuchsias**, they make a good show whatever the summer and if bad weather holds them back, they will go on doggedly flowering right into December as they did in 1988. Though some kinds are permanent and hardy, the tender ones can be treated as annuals and ordered in the autumn with your bulbs – they will arrive as little plants round about June.

Q Are there any earlier tulips and when do the lily flowering ones come?

A **Lily-flowered Tulips** are most attractive and a good deal earlier, not much after the early daffodils. There are also **Cottage tulips**, not so tall and slightly earlier but with the same cup-shaped flower as the Darwins. The last two would be best for tubs. Remember also that the Darwins must have space and light or the stems go 'bendy' and spoil the effect. Bulbs can be ordered at the Show or by post; you can take a catalogue and browse through it at home and having seen the real thing is a great help.

Q Should one leave tulips in the ground?

A For the sort of bed we have been planning, we will have to take them up anyway to make room for the summer display. The bulbs can be saved by digging them in temporarily as we did with the daffodils, then they can be laid out on newspaper in a garden shed to dry them out, as my Mother used to; her bulbs lasted year after year but the modern bulb does not take so kindly to this treatment. Some of the ones heeled in or left in the ground will flower for a second year, but one must not depend on them for a display. Do not plant more than two or three years in the same place for fear of disease. I heard the gardener for Buckingham Palace say on the radio, that the famous 'Grenadier' tulips grown outside the Palace are renewed each year.

Delphiniums

Q I bought some of the big delphiniums at the Show but the have gone much smaller, does this always happen?

A It is no wonder that people are tempted by the magnificent display of delphiniums, which is always a feature of the show. Delphiniums in general like a rich diet and I have no doubt that under a professional gardener or in a rich soil they would stay the way they are in the show, but the ordinary gardener will find that they will not last much beyond the first year as far as size goes. However, he will have a very satisfactory border plant and the smaller spikes are much better for picking. Remember too, that we are seeing everything at its peak, brought on specially for the Show.

The **Belladonna** strain of delphinium is a smaller fairly compact bush, which does not usually need staking. They can be cut down after flowering and will flower a second time, like the taller ones, given a reasonable late summer.

Roses

As the flowers will have been cut, the new gardener will not get much idea of how his roses will grow in the garden, but they are a most beautiful sight to enjoy. Of course he can take away lists of names from the grower to study. The Rose Society have a show at Vincent Square in the RHS Hall in September which is well worth a visit and is nearer planting time. We are going into more detail of the different kinds of roses in June, which is their month.

Rhododendrons

We must not forget the acid soil gardens where these grow so well and are in bloom now. The first-timer will know from looking round his neighbourhood whether or not he is on rhododendron and azalea soil and if so, perhaps has made up his mind to have a display in the new garden. Obviously these are not the kind of plants one can go into a garden centre and buy; a specialist firm is needed to advise and supply the plants. One of the best-known is Waterer's of Bagshot.

Q Can one grow them in tubs? I only want two.

A Yes, they do well in tubs because of their compact ball roots They should have a peaty leaf-mould mixture with a top-dressing of compost manure. I had two tubs in my front garden – actually it was a courtyard – where I planted two 'Pink Pearl'. I found they did not flower so well after the first year and needed some extra feeding to bring them on again. In the end, as there was no gate into the courtyard and the flowers used to disappear in the night, I replaced them with yuccas. This was in a town, I daresay in a country neighbourhood things would be different.

Clematis

One of the other famous displays is the clematis. Most of them would actually be out in the garden much later, but we are trying to plan our garden from the start so that we have a succession of flowering plants, whether climbing or in the borders and beds. The early clematis will be out in the gardens already, the later larger flowered ones come late June to the end of July. The ones to look for when ordering are the *Clematis jackmanii* and its hybrids, which are easy to grow and can be cut down in the autumn, so that one is not left with an ugly bunch of dead leaves all the winter.

Q I have had no luck with my clematis. I put their roots in the shade and they grew out towards the sun just as I was told they are meant to, but they never did well.

A The advice to grow their roots in the shade and their heads in the sun is about the only thing the experts seem to agree on, but the advice about pruning varies so much that it makes the head spin; likewise the number of hybrids (cross-breeds) nowadays makes it very difficult to sort them out. There used to be the two main kinds amongst the large-flowerers. The *Jackmanii* which is purple, its hybrids and the *Viticella*, the one pruned in the spring. The first-timer could not do better than to consult the expert on the stand. One or two which are often featured in catalogues are notoriously difficult to grow and 'Nellie Moser' the lovely pink and white one, must be the chief. Having failed in my own garden, it was irritating to say the least to go and stay with friends in Antwerp and to see the plant careering all over their garden! It was a sheltered town garden with high walls, but facing South and with a lot of sun in the summer; it had had no particular attention according to the owner.

Of the ones that succeeded, '**Ville de Lyon**' (red) and *Jackmanii* '**Superba**' (a later larger purple than the ordinary purple *Jackmanii*) were cut down in the late autumn; the '**Comtesse de Bouchaud**' a pretty pink was a spring pruner but very easy;

there is an elusive mauve clematis, '**Lady Cholmondeley**', which was much easier to grow than the mauve ones now offered and flowered all the summer. The reader might have some luck in tracking it down. There is a '**Mrs Cholmondeley**' however which is early and has light bluish-lavender flowers and perhaps this has taken over from Lady C.

THE OUTSIDE GARDENS AT CHELSEA

All the plants we have been thinking of will be found in the giant tent or marquee. Of course there are many many others which will give ideas and inspiration, but I have to confine myself to the ones I have had some experience with and ones which the new gardener can try. When we come to the outside gardens, we must remember the short time available to assemble them; in spite of the marvellous effect, it does account for a certain artificiality which can be a little disappointing if we are looking for the dream garden.

In all shows and exhibitions there are set pieces and although we might use the bedding *Impatiens* in its modern form in our scheme, we do not plan to build a little house and cover the roof with them as seen one year, that is strictly for the professionals to show and for us to enjoy but not to emulate.

In the same way, many of the gardens do look rather formal and too full of paving and bricks, but remember the idea is to show off the garden design and materials. You might well pick out a brick path which you would like to copy and the details will be there in a leaflet for you to carry home and study at leisure. If you want your garden designed from scratch by a professional, they will come with different designs, or if you particularly like the one you saw at Chelsea, it can be copied and modified to suit your particular site. You can obviously choose your own plants and they will advise as to how they would fit in to a formal design.

Q I hate those modern gardens. I wouldn't mind just the end bit paved, but I would like the rest to be grass.

A If your garden is a rectangle (the usual shape of the town back garden), provided there are no overhanging trees, a lawn edged with flower beds with paving and a tree at the end may not sound very original, but it is hard to think of a better and simpler plan for the town or half-country garden (I do not say 'suburban' on purpose, it sounds condescending). If you can make arrangements to get paving and edging at Chelsea, you will be saved a lot of worry later and a lot of hard work. If you go to Chelsea with something like this in mind, make a plan of your garden first with the measurements. It is essential to get some sort of rough estimate.

If the first-timer still has the energy there are masses of little booths, for want of a better name, which sell tools, books, garden machinery and anything else connected with gardening that one can think of. Luckily they are all in or near the main walk, where one can turn off to the refreshment tent when the feet give out, not to mention the brain in my own case.

It is worth a bit of planning in the early summer months to prepare for the autumn, meanwhile having a chance to enjoy the summer, always hoping it comes.

BEDDING PLANTS

Back in our own garden we must turn our attention to the empty flower-bed; the tulips or other bulbs have been lifted, or there was nothing planted at all and we want some sort of colour for the summer. The new gardener is more likely than not to go to the garden centre and buy himself some bedding plants.

Q What are bedding plants and are they the only thing to have?
A Bedding plants, or bedding out plants, are very largely sold for window-boxes, tubs and other formal designs. The plants themselves have been brought up in the cool greenhouse through the winter, ready to sell at the end of the month. They will be already in flower or anyhow in bud, for the growers know that people want an instant display. This means that they have been forced on a little so beware of buying them too early. Growing plants of this kind is big business nowadays and in towns at any rate, the general trend is for two or three main deliveries from the wholesale growers, the rest is a topping up with later more tender plants. We therefore have both to be careful not to buy too early and on the other hand to be ready to pounce when the first wave comes in early in June or late May, when one will get the best selection. They are not the only plants to look out for, in July the border plants will start

coming into their own as well as roses, early and late, not to mention trees and flowering shrubs, but for the present we are concentrating on the summer bedders.

HOW TO CHOOSE BEDDING PLANTS

If the weather is still cold when the plants first come into the shops, it is important to see that they have been 'hardened' off, as we know they will have been brought on with a certain amount of heat. Never buy any plant which is not standing outside and if it has been a cold night and there are signs of wilting do not buy. Wait until the weather warms up. Even with a sheltered garden or window-box the end of May is time enough and the choice will be greater.

Plants grown like this are expensive on the whole and the colder the winter the more expensive the early bedders. Most people will not worry too much if they only have a window-box or tub to fill, but a larger quantity for planting out in the garden can be quite costly.

Many garden centres and nurseries, particularly ones a little out of town, sell the young plants in strips which are much less expensive. The 'strip' is a small narrow plastic box, bound round with tape which is removed to get at the plants. They usually contain six plants not so far on as the ones sold in pots, but easily brought on in the garden. The only difference being that they will not make the instant show of the more expensive pot-grown ones.

When choosing plants, whether in pots or strips, look for bushy healthy plants and do not buy them if they have become drawn up and leggy. Touch the leaves gently, they should feel springy and the stem should not wobble. Look under the pot, where the drainage holes are and do not buy ones which have a lot of root coming through, as they have been too long in the pot.

If you buy at this time of year there will be plenty of buds on the plants, but when the season has gone on a little beware of anything which is all flowers and no buds. It has had most of its life already in the nursery. In fact in many ways bringing up from the strip-size is more satisfactory even if one doesn't get a show so quickly.

PLANTING THE 'BEDDERS'

The time has really come now and here you are with your first plants. If it is fine and sunny put them in the shade and wait until evening, or until it clouds over! Plants always do better if they go in on a cool day. If you have to leave them unplanted for any reason, leave them outside in a sheltered spot.

For the actual planting, the idea is for the plant not to realise that anything is happening, we want it to slide out of its pot easily and drop straight into the hole prepared for it.

The ground should be prepared beforehand. Dig in a little bonemeal and have some compost ready to put in the prepared hole, which you will have to make a little deeper than the pot. Bio, which is rotted seaweed, is good. When planting, the plant should go into the earth up to the same level as it was in the pot.

With our hole prepared, hold the pot slantwise on the palm of the left hand, give the bottom of the pot a sharp tap with the trowel and the root will come out nicely, all in one piece as it were. Do not disturb the roots, but if there are one or two sticking out through the drainage hole, they can be cut off cleanly without doing any harm. Water after planting and any day in the first fort-night when there has been no rain; sprinkle the leaves as well. Water in the cool of the morning or evening and your plants should not flag at all.

The cardboard or thick paper pots need not be removed before planting as they rot in the earth. Indeed the plants do surprisingly well if left in the plastic pots, but I do not recommend this if plant-ing out in a bed as they get in the way of the fork or hoe when one is weeding, but in a window-box they are quite all right. If you plant in pots, keep a little extra compost handy as the earth will settle and even though you have seemed to dig a deep enough hole, the pots have an annoying habit of appearing above the soil level and spoiling the effect. Press them down and add more soil or compost. Plastic pots can be saved and used for pot-ting up seedlings.

PLANTING OUT STRIPS

Here the little box must be broken up; take the tape off and pull the box away from the plants carefully. It is much easier to divide the plants from the roots, rather than by looking at the leaves, remembering to check where the stems go into the compost and when they have been planted water them. I have found that plants from a strip often need a little bringing on. Leave them for two or three weeks and if they do not seem to be on the move (not growing or showing buds, or if in bud not showing colour) give them a tonic in the shape of liquid manure. I have already recommended Liquinure which is excellent, but Phostrogen which is a powder you mix with water is recommended by all who have tried it. It is not expensive to buy and besides the powder one can also get 'phos-tabs', little tablets for individual plants. The latter are especially useful for indoor plants.

WATERING TUBS AND WINDOW-BOXES

May can be dry and cold so we might have to water for a day or two. Of course we are not likely to get the baking heat of the later months, but we can learn one or two hints straightaway.

If the tub or window-box has not been watered for a while and you are wanting to plant in it, you may find that a can of water will go straight out through the drainage holes at the bottom, showing that it is too dry to plant.

Q I thought it was a sign it had had enough.

A No, just the opposite. It is probably a peaty compost, very good if kept moist, but when it gets dry it will take a day or so with several more cans before the compost 'takes up' and will hold the moisture. This is why one reads so many warnings about not letting peat or peaty compost get dry, as it can act like a barrier to keep the rain from penetrating.

Water the window-box or tub once or twice more and then leave it. The next time you try you will probably find the water is lying on the top and taking a little time to work through. It is probably ready, but you will soon see when you dig your holes for the plants. Plants in tubs and window-boxes like being close together, so do not give them space around them as you would in a flower-bed.

Q I don't like seeing the roots coming out all in a lump and I am told one ought to tease them out.

A I know they do and I am never quite sure why; one does not see it in the books and I feel it must be the remains of some garden lore handed down from a long-forgotten expert. It is true that if a plant is badly 'pot-bound' and has outgrown its pot completely, it should be treated at the root, but this teasing out or pruning is much more tricky than one would think. It is an expert's job and if an amateur tries it always seems to end in disaster. Anyhow, we are not going to buy anything which has outgrown its pot. Modern compost is very different too, probably the seedling plant has been grown in a peat 'block' and is meant to stay as it is.

WHAT PLANTS TO CHOOSE

Of course the reader will make his own way to the garden centre and will buy what takes his fancy, it is therefore not my idea to write strings of names of plants which can be found in any good gardening book. We will go through a few of the favourite kinds which are also easy to grow.

Petunias

Everyone will know this bedding plant with its trumpet-shaped pink, blue and white flowers, which one sees so much in window-boxes. No wonder it is such a good doer.

Q I tried some my first year, in 1985 and they were a terrible failure. I was very disappointed and haven't tried them since.

A If I remember rightly 1985 was a dreadful summer, very wet and sunless. Petunias do need a certain amount of sun but they should not have been a complete failure.

A possibility is disease – these very popular plants and bulbs can be over-produced and it leads to virus diseases. There is no doubt that petunias went through a bad patch in the mid 80's, but they seem to have recovered now. One cannot blame the plantsman who is only supplying a demand when I suppose he should be giving his stocks a rest, but people *will* go on wanting the same things.

Another reason for not buying plants too soon or too far on, is that the partially heated greenhouse will encourage greenfly, which they may arrive with and once they really get a hold it is too late to do anything. Spraying is difficult with a half-hardy plant as the spray has to be weak and is therefore not so effective; I give a good puff with a Derris pack if I see the least sign and although it spoils the look for the moment it is worth it in the long run.

The large flowered, plain coloured petunias are the easiest to grow, stay in flower well and if they are not too far on when bought should last you through the summer. The ideal is for them to grow and flower at the same time, not to flower all in a burst at intervals, which is very annoying if one is depending on them for a good continuous show.

The smaller striped or double petunias appear a little later in the season, but although they make a change I have never found them as easy as the big single-flowered ones.

Geraniums

We can't get away from these if we are thinking of bedding out or window-boxes and in any sort of formal gardening it would be hard to do without them. There are so many different varieties that the first-timer may be quite bewildered as well as rather horrified by the price. Again, there are some nurseries which will sell geraniums before they come into flower. These will be cuttings from last year that will soon grow and flower 2–3 weeks later. For a window-box though, there is nothing like a fat red, white or pink geranium and in this case I should buy the best you can afford. We have already warned against the Regal pelargoniums which are very tempting with their showy large flowers, but they are really indoor and conservatory plants.

The buyer may be drawn towards the smaller geranium with the coloured leaves. They will never look dull, because of the attractive colouring in the leaves themselves, but on the whole they are not such reliable flowerers. A grower told me that they need to be starved and left alone or they go to leaf.

Ivy-leaved Geraniums

These are most useful for window-boxes and hanging baskets, since their habit (the way they grow) is creeping or trailing like ivy. The leaves are not round but more of a pointed ivy-leaf-

Geranium
As well as the fat red varieties there is also a hardy variety
ideal for the borders

shape, which makes them very easy to recognise. The colours are mauve and pink, which look very pretty together. The new gardener will soon find out that there are easy and difficult colours in all plants, as the flowers tend towards the wild plant from which they originally came. At one time the mauve was much easier than the pink but the modern varieties seem to have got over this. They also had a bad name for flowering early in the season and then going over to leaves until late August. This too seems to have been overcome, but it is always well to give some sort of tonic like Growmore or liquid manure mid-season. The fertilizer Phostrogen, which I have already mentioned, is much recommended by friends who use it for this purpose. Look out for new buds waiting to take over from the ones which are flowering and if there are none, or they seem to be hanging back, act with a booster.

A year or two back there was a new 'Mexican' variety which was bi-coloured red and white, but which I have not seen recently. It is always difficult when trying to recommend a variety by name as they vary from year to year and appear under different names. However, the reader can be sure of getting either mauve or pink.

The expense is the big snag – every year I am horrified at the price – however owing to their spready habit three or four would be enough to fill most window-boxes and one would make a centrepiece for a small tub or urn. With any luck and protection such as I had with the glass panel on my south-facing balcony, they will survive all but the coldest winter.

Geraniums of all kinds root very easily from cuttings, which we are going into in more detail in August.

Lobelias and White Alyssum

These are very popular plants for edging, particularly lobelias, of which there is also a trailing variety. One should be able to buy them as little plants in strips by the end of May or early June.

Q People keep talking about lobelias but I'm not sure which they are.

A They are the ones with the small blue flower, very often mixed with red geraniums and I am struck each time by the effectiveness of this simple arrangement. The tall, rather stiff form of the geranium, with its true scarlet flowers is a marvellous foil for the dainty lobelia covered in small blue flowers. They all trail a little, softening the hard edge of the box or container and the trailing ones will hang right down like ivy.

If you buy before they are showing colour, note that the light blue lobelias have pale green leaves and the dark blue, dark leaves, which is very convenient.

The alyssum is not so often seen in window-boxes as it spreads, but does not trail, making a little mound of honey-scented flowers which the bees love. It is very pretty mixed with lobelias on the rockery or along the edge of a flower-bed, but does need sun to bring it on or it can be rather a late flowerer. This is not necessarily a drawback, if one thinks of the second home which is a week-end and holiday house; it is often an advantage to have something planted which will come on over the summer holidays, when the earlier flowers are beginning to go over.

Q   Are Busy Lizzies any good for tubs?

A   Yes, I tried these marvellous little plants in a West facing tub in a very wet and sunless summer and they stayed in flower all the time, really saving the day, for the petunias which like more sun were very much 'on and off'.

Q   Will they hang over the edge or should I plant lobelias with them?

A   The modern *Impatiens* is much more compact than the earlier varieties but it spreads quite enough to soften the edge of a tub or container. I would not grow them with lobelias, the fleshy leaves and stalks of the *Impatiens* do not go well with the daintier lobelia. Lobelias do better in window-boxes which are always inclined to dry out; *Impatiens* is a water plant in the wild and still needs a deeper container to keep the moisture in.

Q   Is there anything else one could have for a change?

A   You may well ask, with the mass production of plants nowadays, we are bound to get a surfeit of certain plants. The ones I have mentioned are by no means the only 'bedders', but they are the ones which are most generally on sale in the early part of the summer. I have not mentioned **Pansies** or **Polyanthus**. These appear early in May, but unless your soil is rich and the position open, the pansies will soon go straggly; the polyanthus (the coloured primrose on a long stalk) look beautiful in a window-box, their extra height is an advantage when looking up and they make splendid early summer or late spring bedding plants, but when a hot spell comes as early as the end of May, they will be finished and we will have to move on to some other scheme. Say you have had an early spring display, then replaced it with a stop-gap like polyanthus or pansies (very good when first bought) you will find yourself replacing it again with later bedding plants, which is not impossible at all but rather more expensive and time-consuming. If we are thinking of a display in the wild garden, polyanthus can be left to die down under the shade of shrubs as they do at Sissinghurst, where of course one can simply move on to another display in another part of the garden.

There comes a time when new gardeners cannot stand the sight of their empty tubs or flower-beds a moment longer, out they go with the car to the garden centre and buy what takes their fancy. Sometimes this has very good results, most often the the things stop flowering and do not make the expected lovely display. Very few people buy the same display two years running as it seemed so expensive and the results were not what they had hoped for.

Here are things to keep in mind. Bedding plants *are* an expensive way of gardening so if you have a garden keep them to one bed, or to tubs or containers. Help out with sowing annual seeds if you have the time. If you buy a geranium say, for your centrepiece or window-box, it pays to buy the best you can afford so go for the healthy-looking ones with plenty of buds coming on. Later on in June, there will be a bigger choice, when the later bedding plants coming on. One does not see much written about **Calceolarias**, to name but one, until we come to June. This is a bright yellow and it will often 'lift' a mixed collection of plants in a container and also go on flowering without much difficulty. The flower is irregular, something like a slipper but is not a cushion and stands 6–8ins in height making a contrast with the flatter or trailing plants. If you have had a fatality with your early planting, the calceolaria makes a good replacement.

FLOWERING SHRUBS AND TREES

Flowering trees and shrubs are so much a part of the late spring and early summer display that for the moment we are considering them together.

Q What's the difference?

A A shrub is the gardener's name for a bush and it is as well to keep this in mind when returning from the garden centre with your neat little plant in its pot. Many people are very disconcerted at the speed at which their shrubs grow, overlapping their allotted space and hiding everything else.

Q How can I tell how big they are likely to be?

A Look out for them in other peoples gardens as this will give you a fair idea of whether they are inclined to grow upwards or outwards, most things do both. The 'maximum' height on its label or in the catalogue is not very accurate and is said to be about ten years growth. However, many of the fast growing ones will reach their 'maximum' in three or four years without any difficulty, but it does give a rough guide.

Q Do you advise against shrubs or trees in a small garden?

A Anyone who has lived in a town or suburb will know how much they would miss the marvellous display of the flowering trees in the early summer. Most people will know the **Flowering Cherry, Lilac** and **Laburnum**. Though they have flowers they are none the less trees; true the lilac is a shrub, but it is quite as tall as a cherry tree when full grown and with a spread to match. We can find room for them in all but the smallest garden, for one thing it is possible to have small and neater versions of the same tree, as we shall see later. The great thing is to be prepared and plan accordingly.

My first garden was by no means large, perhaps a little longer than some town gardens at 90ft and I planted two flowering cherries there. One a very pale pink, an unusual and attractive colour but not such a reliable flowerer as the other, a **Morello** which was always smothered in white blossom in the late spring. It was a neat grower too and by no means too big when I last saw it 25 years later when it must have been about 30 years old. The other had sadly been cut down, so perhaps it had overgrown in the end.

Q Is 'Morello' the one for jam making?

A Yes, that was the idea but the sparrows ate the lot before they were even swelling, let alone ripe. Nowadays one could put a nylon net over it which would be enough to get some of it covered and stop the birds landing for, as with the cotton, the idea is to frighten them away by fear of catching their wings or feet.

Q How should one choose a flowering cherry? I suppose one should go to a nursery.

A Yes, a small garden centre would have little choice. I went and saw my two growing. The best part of going to a specialist nursery is the expert advice one can get and the way one can see the shape of the tree, which is impossible to tell from a catalogue. Get the nurseryman to give you some idea of its real maximum height and how long it will take to get there. Choose a straight-growing tree with a nice sturdy trunk.

Q What names do you suggest?

A It is difficult enough recommending plants or trees by name, but with the Japanese cherry there is such an enormous choice, mostly with Japanese names, that the first-timer might give up in despair. If the nurseryman has suggested one or two trees and you have seen the colours and gone home to think about it, the catalogue will list them under the Latin name *Prunus*.

Some Shapes and Sizes

When these trees first became popular over here, particularly for planting along the roadside, we saw a great deal of shapes resembling umbrellas blown inside-out, presumably to keep them from overhanging paths and the roadway itself. They somehow never looked quite right and latterly much more compact versions of the spready kind – the umbrella the right way out – are planted. The two favourite colours are dark pink with dark leaves, which are also beautiful in Autumn and the pale but still quite intense pink with the lighter leaves. All these will have double flowers for they are purely ornamental and not grown for their fruit.

Any reader who was given prunes in the nursery diet will not need to be told that *Prunus domestica* is the wild plum, closely related to the cherry and so they say, the originator of the 'Blackheart' eating cherry. The native wild cherries are *Prunus avium* (the Gean), the dwarf *Prunus cerasus*, whose flowers the reader may have gathered in the spring wondering what they were and the third native cherry is the bird cherry *Prunus padus*. I include them amongst the garden trees because some people feel that there is something rather bogus about a 'fruit-tree' which only has flowers. Any would be appropriate for a wild garden. The gean is a really big tree and can hold its own with anything in the woods where it grows wild.

Q I would like a double-white cherry even if it is the only tree I have. I thought of putting it at the bottom of our back-garden where it could spread out on its own.

A It is my favourite and a lovely tree with a beautiful shape. There was one in the church garden near our first house and the whole neighbourhood looked forward to seeing it come out in the spring.

Q How big would it be at first?

A It depends a bit on how much you pay, but an affordable size would look like a little 'weeping' tree. You could fill in, for instance with roses, climbing up the back wall. Have your tree centred so that when it spreads backwards as it were, it will not overhang the neighbour's garden, then no one will be tempted to chop it about just as it is reaching its peak. It is a fairly slow grower so your children are more likely to be saved from this annoyance than you! Meanwhile, you will have a lovely little centrepiece for that part of the garden.

Q I would like something smaller, a real weeping cherry.

A I have seen the single wild cherry made into a real weeper, the stems touch the ground if not pruned. It would have to have been trained over a wooden frame which is quite an elaborate business.

The pink double cherry grown as a standard weeps in a rather more subdued way and looks very well in a small front garden, say one with a courtyard.

Another way of coping with limited space is to use a fastigiate tree, like the Lombardy poplar that one sees so much on the roads in France. Its great advantage is that it does not overhang or have to be trimmed. The cherry which goes by the name of *Prunus* 'Amanogawa', has large semi-double pale pink flowers and is ideal.

Laburnum

Q Do laburnum trees come out in May? I'm not even sure which of those yellow trees mine is but, it was out in March.

A If it came out in March it was almost certainly a forsythia. They are seen so much round towns and on the edges of roads these days that they are almost wild and give the appearance of trees. The early shrubs which are not evergreen come out with flowers before the leaves, but now we are coming to the summer the flowering shrubs have flowers and leaves together. The laburnum has one main trunk unlike a shrub, however big, which has probably four or five stems growing from the base. The laburnum flowers, which are shaped like a sweet-pea, hang down in clusters. They come as the weather warms up and the late spring bulbs are over, so they make a very useful bit of colour before the summer plants have come on.

If you find a well-grown laburnum in your garden as we did, it will be the old-fashioned variety which grow like a weed in towns, but are not to be despised on that account. They flower magnificently about every two or three years because, like apples, if they have had an especially good flowering they will take a rest the following year, when flowers will be scarce, but there is nothing wrong with the tree. I feel obliged to add that the seeds of the Laburnum are said to be poisonous and though I never heard of anyone actually being poisoned, it would be as well to be careful with small children. The seeds certainly do not poison the ground, for I grew Solomon's Seal and the small cyclamen under mine.

The modern laburnum is a far more certain flowerer and the first-timer would probably prefer this; they can be bought as well-grown little trees of about 6–8ft – make sure of its size when full-grown, but my guess would be not more than 15–20ft.

Lilac

Q   What about lilac? It smells so good.
A   If you find lilac bushes in your garden which may have grown very big, the chances are that the former owners planted them as a screen, so if you feel inclined to chop them down have a good look first at the scene around them. Again they will probably be the old-fashioned mauve ones, but in this case they are the best flowerers.

The two mauve and white lilacs I planted were a present from a friend. They never grew unduly large, nothing like the size of the cherry trees. The mauve one was deeper than the common lilac and was most probably '**Louis de Spaeth**', a variety I still see quite frequently in the catalogues. The white did not flower well and I eventually got rid of it.

If the new gardener is wanting something rather more choice

Lilac

there are double varieties, particularly the white which seem to flower quite well. The growers describe some plants as 'shy' if they are reluctant to flower and I am sure first-timers will agree with me that there is nothing more exasperating in one's first garden, than having a lot of green and flourishing-looking plants which produce no flowers, so different from the garden of our dreams. For this reason we are trying to stick to varieties which at any rate are sure to flower, even if they are of the common or "*vulgaris*" kind, as the botanist rather woundingly puts it. Who cares if they give us pleasure and make part of our scheme?

If you are going for scent, there is usually nothing to beat the old-fashioned variety of whatever you are choosing. Many people have remarked how the scent seems to have been bred out of the modern plant.

Q Can one get a standard lilac?

A Yes, the growers train one stem from the base so that it grows like the trunk of a tree. They can be kept really dwarf and are sold as "Mini-Lilacs", but should not be confused with the *Syringa macrophylla* which we have already come across on the rockery. You will have to keep a look-out for any shoots from the base or further up the stem and rub the bud gently away when you see it coming. Otherwise if it gets to the state when it has to be cut back, this will do no harm but of course will show a mark on the stem or trunk.

SUCKERS

Q We have two beautiful lilac bushes at the bottom of our new garden, but we are never going to be able to grow anything in the bed as it is a mass of suckers which of course don't flower. The bushes themselves flower beautifully.

A We have already come across suckers. The wild plant from which the cultivated one came, comes up from below the graft straight from the root, which is why they are such difficult things to get rid of. With a lilac, one of the worst, it is definitely a job for the male first-timer unless it should put him off gardening for life. One often sees advice to go right down (seemingly to Australia) and find out where the sucker starts, then wrench it off. I have never discovered anyone who has gone as far as this and we are trying to be as realistic as possible, so cut the suckers off at ground level to discourage them as far as possible. Then when they spring up again, wait till after it has rained when the soil is softer, dig down to the really tough root-like stem you will come to (about a foot down) and saw it off. As far as I am concerned this is the best I have achieved and it works reasonably well.

Though we are getting towards summer when the flowering cherries blossom, they can still be affected by the night frosts at that time of year and Shakespeare's rough winds will often finish them off if they have escaped a frost. The laburnum and lilac are both less vulnerable as they come out later.

Q I am quite happy for other people to have flowering cherries, but I would sooner have the lilac as it is better for picking than the laburnum, but does it do it any harm?

A No, it should do good if cut reasonably carefully; a flowering shrub is not harmed by cutting or pruning after flowering, so a little picking for the house is quite beneficial.

FLOWERING CLIMBERS

Q What is the difference between a climber and a creeper?

A Most climbers would creep if given the chance and vice versa. I am told that the ones one reads so much about in the tropical jungles creep along the ground, but will go up any convenient tree to lead them to the light. The ones we are concerned with now are the flowering shrubs, which are used as climbers on walls and fences and come out at this time of year, that is the late spring and early summer.

Wisteria

If we leave out roses, which in any case will not be out yet (their month is late June or early July), the two most planted climbers for this time of year are wisteria and the early *Clematis montana*. The wisteria is another member of the sweet-pea family with flowers that hang down in mauve clusters, the same shape as the laburnum.

Q I love wisteria and am very keen to try it on the house; I thought of planting it by the front door but would it grow too big?

A   In a town, where houses are built together in a terrace, people sometimes share their plant with a neighbour which gets over the difficulty. They are indeed very tall plants and if allowed would climb the height of most houses quite easily. Yours would not be difficult to train sideways or laterally; let it go over the door as far as the first floor (this will take up ten or twelve feet), then let it go on along the front of the house and to your neigh-bour's if this is practicable. Otherwise, a rather grand and expensive idea is the brick pergola which are now coming back into fashion with the formal garden and would be ideal. I saw such a one with 'white' wisteria (really a very pale mauve) blooming in the Blandy Gardens in Madeira, an unforgettable sight which made me long to copy it, but one needs the space.

Q   But surely Madeira is much warmer than Britain?

A   In general it is, but these gardens are high up in the hills and do not escape frost. In fact the camellia flowers had been ruined by unseasonable snow during another visit I made in March.

Wisteria likes a sheltered environment, it does well in towns and enjoys a sunny summer, but it likes plenty of rain too which we can provide more easily.

Q   What about pruning?

A   Needless to say a plant on such a grand scale needs expert pruning. The accepted time to prune is between July and August, when the lateral growths are cut back to within about 6ins of the main branches. These spurs are then shortened again to two to three buds in the winter (Dec/Jan). The flowers will be borne on these spurs. I know of one very successful plant which was always cut back in the spring, before the leaves had come. There is a three-house Wisteria just round the corner where they all prune at exactly the same time.

Q   What happens if you don't prune?

A   The plant will grow quite successfully, but all its effort will go into the leaves and you won't get so many flowers.

Clematis Montana

The reader may be more familiar with the large-flowered purple clematis which comes later on in July. The early small-flowered *montana* is a fast grower and often used to hide an ugly fence or make a nice background for other plants. Its habit is much more like the wild 'Old Man's Beard' and is equally difficult to control, for last year's growth has to be left for the flowers to come there the following May.

Q I have a lovely deep pink *Clematis montana* with rather bigger flowers than the ordinary one. The trouble is that it is growing all over a rose, but they both seem to flower very well which is rather strange.

A The *montana rubens* is pink but the best variety is '**Elizabeth**' which it seems you must have and it would be a great shame to lose both it and the rose. There is the danger that the rose and the clematis, but particularly the rose, are now holding up the fence or railing which originally held them and if you cut back too vigorously everything might collapse, fence and all. If it is not a boundary fence I would leave well alone and just trim it. Left to itself a white *montana*, the ordinary colour, climbed right up a silver birch tree, really in the tropical manner and must have been all of 40ft. The plant in question came from a neighbouring garden and had strayed up the tree. Rather sadly it has now been cut down from the rear, so has had to be pulled off the tree, but it had done no harm at all. Many years ago, I read a book which recommended a clematis climbing in this way for the small garden. However, it does give one an idea of what one is up against in trying to control it in a confined space.

A neighbour who declares that he knows nothing about gardening says that pruning is a design problem and there is a great deal in this. He has made a better job of cutting back his own *Clematis montana* than the professional did with ours.

We are coming now to two useful rather unsung shrubs, the flowering currant and the *Kerria japonica*.

The 'American' Currant

This is a real bush but does not grow too large and ungainly. The flowering time is rather uncertain as it depends very much on the weather, but it is late spring for certain and sometimes a great deal earlier. It is very easy to grow – a **Q** tells me it is growing up through the cracked asphalt of a tennis court in the jungle of her town garden. It has soft pink hanging flowers and very pretty fresh green leaves to go with it. Perhaps its easy habit made people despise it, or perhaps they made the mistake of bringing it into the house. It produces a very unpleasant smell, so much so your cat might be wrongfully accused. The latin name is *Ribes*, and the one most often grown *R. aureum* comes from N. America, hence 'American Currant'.

Kerria japonica

I was surprised to find it listed under flowering 'trees'. It looks exactly like a bush, deciduous (that is it loses its leaves in winter) and the pretty little balls of yellow flowers come out with the leaves. It too is easy to grow and does not get too large or ungainly. I have never owned one but I think it would be very easy to trim and keep tidy and I have seen them trained more or less into a hedge as can be done with forsythia. The kerria is said to be tender, but I first saw it growing in my sister's chalk garden 700ft. up on the Downs, in the shelter of the walled garden, but otherwise was unprotected. The *Kerria japonica* is the only variety I have come across but I find one listed in the catalogue, *K. pleniflora*, which sounds tempting, not that there seems any lack of flowers on the one most generally grown.

EVERGREEN SHRUBS FOR CONTAINERS

We are moving on now to the more compact evergreen shrub which is not usually grown for its flowers, but in order to have greenery all the year round.

Q I suppose one can buy plants in tubs at any time, I was thinking of a pair of **Bay Trees** by the front door.

A Of course if the plant is already in its tub or container one can buy it at any time but as bay trees, particularly the clipped ones, are very expensive, now is the best time when the winter is over. Bay trees are slow growing and can be killed by an unusually cold winter, when a nurseryman could lose a lot of his stock, so he takes the risk which is reflected in the price. A bad place for a bay tree and where one so often sees them, is outside a restaurant where they are subjected to draughts and pollution, not to mention litter. Even outside a front door one should be careful that they are reasonably sheltered and if the door were a little recessed with some sort of ledge above this would be best. The tubs would need watering in the dry weather and if partially sheltered from the rain.

Q   I wanted bay trees because of also being able to use them for cooking, at least if they are the kind they call the culinary bay.

A   This is the name they are usually sold under, perhaps to reassure people that the leaves are the same as the ones sold in little packets in the supermarket to flavour meat. It is a pity, for its Latin name of *Lauris nobilis* is so much more romantic and was the laurel which was used to crown heroes in classical times. It can be seen growing wild all over the Mediterranean shores with yellow flowers in the spring.

Q   They look quite different – much more bushy.

A   Clipping them is a great art and could be called real topiary. At home in the garden the idea is either to buy them ready-clipped, or as little bushes which is much cheaper of course. Then you can train them into either a triangular or circular shape.

I took the advice of an expert at a nursery and bought two bushes about 2ft tall and the same round, which grew to 5ft all round in ten years, as tall as most people would want. The time to clip and shape, on the same expert advice, is just as they are producing their new green shoots in about April/May. It seems hard to cut back the new growth, but one is only shaping and it does not all have to go. If you are trying to match the heights, you may be faced as I was with two which match in size, but are slightly different in shape. If one has already decided to be a standard with a round top, the other must follow as best it can as you will never be able to train your first one into a triangular shape. Put the clippings (leaves only) in a screw-top jar in the fridge and they will not dry as much as if they are hung up in a bunch.

Q   They sound rather difficult to grow. Somehow the Bible saying 'that the wicked flourish like the green bay tree' gives one the wrong idea.

A   As anyone can see on holiday in the lands of the Bible, they do flourish there, the climate being that much warmer than the British Isles. Here it is simply that they are a little tender, need a sheltered position and some attention. A good idea is to give them compost manure before the cold of winter and to keep them watered in dry weather. Water the leaves too as all evergreens suffer from pollution in towns and although our usual rainy summers are a great help, the last very hot and dry summers have spoiled some trees. If you don't want the bother of clipping, nearly all garden centres sell the ready-clipped bays and the favourite shape nowadays is a tall, narrow triangle.

Yucca

This is the spiky rather cactus-like evergreen, with long pointed leaves and a huge white flower on a long stalk. It only flowers after a sunny summer but is well worth waiting for.

Q I thought they only flowered every hundred years.

A Years ago in one of the hothouses at Kew Gardens I dimly remember some sort of plant with a white flower which was said to flower every century and one had to be content with a photograph. This must have been handed down as a sort of legend because so many people believe it applies to the yucca. Actually, in a sunny climate they flower every year and given a sheltered South-facing position one should see them bloom every three or four years. They can do surprising things as I saw after a hot summer and very warm autumn, when the two in my South-facing courtyard flowered on Christmas Day!

My variety was the well-named **Yucca gloriosa**, but there is a **Yucca filamentosa** with thinner spikier leaves which has three or four heads at one time, but I prefer the *gloriosa*. Many plants flower best if the roots are restricted and this is one of them; I planted an offshoot of one of the front garden yuccas at the sunny end of my back garden, in a tub. It grew very well, reaching well over six feet in height, but it never flowered. The offshoots which appear at the base of the parent plant, should be removed in spring by cutting them off cleanly where the stalk joins the main stem and repotted in leaf-mould with a little compost manure added. They will take five or six years at least before flowering.

If you buy your yucca already planted in a tub, they are quite expensive, so look into the centre of the main spike to see if you can see a bud and choose that one – you might as well get your money's worth. I was advised to protect the roots, which are shallow, for the first year or so and I used sacking pinned down with a staple at each corner. Any loose-woven material that lets the rain through would do and blows about less than something like bracken or straw.

WARNING ! Do not have these plants where young children are running about. A child has to be quite tall before its face comes above the level of the long spiky thorns at the end of the leaves, but everyone should take care. I got a thorn in my face when tending one of my yuccas and the end must have broken off for it didn't appear for months – it could have gone into an eye!

The Spotted Laurel

This is another Victorian plant making a comeback. It looks very well in a large tub with its spotted green and yellow foliage and red berries in the autumn. You will need two plants, male and female for the berries. The Latin name is *Aucuba japonica* 'Crotonifolia'. There is no end to the surprises with Latin names, for this one has changed its name from *Aucuba* to *Prunus lusitanica* and is to be found amongst the flowering cherries – ours not to reason why! They did well on my exposed roof-garden with a little protection.

Fatsia

The *Fatsia japonica* is the fig-like plant still firmly listed as a house or greenhouse plant, though to my certain knowledge there has been one growing at the entrance of the walkway to the Imperial College, South Kensington, for forty years or more. I first noticed this strange plant because it seemed to be a fig, but had greenish-white round umbels (umbrella-spoke shaped flowers) instead of figs and this in mid-winter. It will do well with a little protection – again it survived on my windy roof-garden. Planted outside in a sheltered spot it will grow very big, so be warned of this if by 'houseplant' you think of something small. You would be better to think of a smaller fig tree. It can be pruned quite easily and one very near my present garden, in a sheltered close, is cut back each year.

MAY IN THE GARDEN

We have finished with tubs and containers and into the garden again. If May is cold the early summer plants can hang back and we shall be glad to know of ones which flower earlier to fill the gaps.

Lily-of-the-Valley

We saw those starting last month and they should be out in May.
Q Mine haven't flowered, is there anything to be done or are they in the wrong place?
A Lily-of-the-valley are notoriously difficult and only beaten by the house plants African violets. They will sometimes move, that is they disappear for a year or two and appear where it suits them better and one hopes that this means they will flower. There are several things to try such as dividing them in the autumn and replanting in leaf-mould with the addition of lime and bonemeal. You will find I think this will produce marvellously healthy plants, but still not many flowers. If so after flowering, or after they should have flowered, give them a sprinkling of sulphate of potash, thus they will have the maximum time to form flower-buds for next year. They should also have a little sun.

Solomon's Seal

This has the rather formidable name of *Polygonatum multiflorum* in the catalogue, but it does have plenty of flowers and is like a bigger lily-of-the-valley, but arched over. It is very good for picking, standing up well in a bowl and lasting well in water. It flowers, given leaf-mould, much more reliably and will grow well in all but the deepest shade. Its natural home is in clearings in woods, or in a lightly wooded place such as a hazel plantation.

London Pride

This is a saxifrage, *Saxifraga x urbium*, a great stand-by in towns at this time of year and growing to about 12ins. The leaves are spoon-shaped in a neat rosette and they have feathery pink flowers. It is very useful for the front of the border or the shady rockery. It will not grow well if it is too enclosed by high walls, otherwise it grows like mad and has to be thinned fairly often (in autumn). They are ignored by garden centres and catalogues so beg some from a friend. Another plant, **Heuchera**, can be bought in garden centres. Its flowers are deep pink and red, and it is equally useful for the edge of the border but it does not increase in quite such an uninhibited way as the London Pride.

The Bearded Iris

For a long time the mainstay of my first garden at this time of year was the bearded iris. Bearded irises are similar to the flag iris but are available in more interesting and varied colours and flower that much later. They will be coming into bud when the late tulips are out and will come into flower when they are over. The main colours, as in the wild, are mauve and yellow, but an amazing range has been developed and if the first-timer has a chance he should go to see them at the Chelsea Show. They can be ordered now and will be delivered some time after August when they are usually lifted and divided. Prepare the soil with a little lime and bonemeal, otherwise they are not partic-ular, but like sun and an open position.

FOR THE ROCKERY OR EDGING

Two kinds of **Primula** come on a bit later, *P. auricula* and *P. denticulata*. They look uncommon and will carry on after the early rock plants.

If we think over our imaginary garden we have not done so badly already with some flowering shrubs for the dead of winter, early spring bulbs, followed by early and late tulips and the early and late daffodils. May has produced some flowering shrubs to take over later and with the help of bedding plants we can go on to June without even having to mention the mainstay of the English garden, the rose. But we are coming to them!

There is no doubt that June is the summer and we are coming to one of the loveliest times of the year. Soon the trees will be in full leaf and in this respect the towns will be ahead of the country; driving down to the coast we would leave the green trees in the parks and then pass bluebells in leafless woods in the country. Sometimes it was foxglove time before the big trees had their summer leaves; then the country would catch up gradually and leave the towns behind.

Autumn flowers are for the country as town gardens get exhausted and are past their best by the end of August, particularly in a hot dry summer.

ROSES IN THE NEW GARDEN

Roses will be coming out in the beds from mid-June onwards with the climbers coming at the same time as the bush roses. Some ramblers are early but one or two of the old-time ramblers come much later, in July, where they are a great help in bringing colour at a difficult time of year.

Q   Would that be why my roses aren't flowering? I thought my new garden was full of roses, but as they are so thorny and tangled up I haven't looked at them properly and now wonder if they could possibly be brambles after all. Would one get them in a town?

A   It astonished me when I had my first London garden to find a path nearby, behind some little cottages (worth a mint of money now of course), which had become overgrown with brambles just as it would have done in the country. The path was an old right of way as similarly would be the case if one's new garden was part of an old estate, or near a park as my present garden is and all sorts of unexpected wild things can appear, even the wild briar rose. The thing to do is to look for buds, if they seem fairly plentiful and in clusters, you just have a rambler gone wild. A wild blackberry lies much flatter, does not have woody stems and its flowers do not come until the end of the summer.

Just for fun, before you have a friend or expert to make sure, have a look at the leaves and compare them with the ones on the bush roses, or in a picture. It is not a bad idea for the first-timer to take a good look at the different leaves on whatever plants he may find and get into the habit of recognising them by their leaves and not only by the flowers. Most first-timers are worried by not being able to name their plants – they may know the names when they see them in bunches in the flower shop or market, but will have no idea what sort of a plant they grow on.

To go back to our tangled web of roses, one of the loveliest gardens I ever saw was a country garden where the roses just went their own way. The owners having become elderly and not able to do the heavy work of pruning and tidying. This house and garden stood alone, with a view over the fields of the Kentish Weald, a lovely sight in itself and the kind of view which goes with this sort of wild garden.

In towns one is always up against dirt which is the only bane, for the 'soil' which blows about in the air and settles on old plants and bushes makes them look depressing instead of wild and beautiful. One cannot blame the first-timer who cuts the lot down and hopes for the best and indeed if it should turn out to be brambles and roses mixed, that would be the only way.

Wild gardens are all the rage now and it is notable that when things grow themselves they never seem to flop or get diseased; I suppose the ones which have survived are growing where and how it suits them, as a wild flower does.

Q It might not be a bad idea to prune the roses eventually. When should I start?

A The rambler should be pruned in the late autumn, about October or November. The idea is to cut out all the wood which has flowered the previous season and tie the new shoots in their place. Of course cut any dead wood right out. You may remember your father or grandfather struggling with the pruning while the air turned steadily bluer. If you are leaving the roses to grow more or less as they please, I should modify the pruning. After getting rid of any dead wood, if the rose is settling down again and has plenty of room, I can't see why you should do anything more. The great thing is to allow plenty of space for it to have its head.

Q My roses are quite different. It is more or less a town garden and they are bush roses in a bed by themselves. Some of them have got very out of shape and some are much bigger than others. Is it too late to prune them?

A It is too late for the sort of pruning one does in spring or autumn, but they can be trimmed and tidied. The flowers will be coming out soon and as you cut them for the house, cut so that the balance is better and with a longer stalk that you might have otherwise. If any are looking very small and stunted and showing no signs of new growth it would be better to get rid of them now. If you see no signs of disease, in the way of black spots or rust on the older leaves, it may just be that the rose has not done well and should be replaced.

Q I think several have suckers coming up from the root, but how can I be sure?

A As with all suckers, they will be coming up from below the graft and in this case it will be a briar, from which the rose was cultivated. The sucker will be all green, have no reddish tips to the new shoots and there will be seven leaflets instead of five. Get rid of the suckers by digging down as far as you can, then saw or cut it through.

Q What about replacing the roses? I suppose it isn't the time.

A November is the month for planting bare root roses but if the gap is very conspicuous, we live in an age of instant gardening and your garden centre will have many already growing in pots. I came across one, 'Papa Meilland', a lovely dark red, quite by chance and put it in a tub on my roof-garden where it did very well.

SOME SUGGESTIONS FOR ROSES – THE DIFFERENT KINDS

Though this is not the time to plant bare root, you will have a chance to see the roses in bloom in gardens and in the nurseries and be able to order them ready for delivery in November.

Q Are roses difficult as I would like to grow some up my wall.
A Roses are not difficult and they are not expensive which is
cheering. They need moisture round their roots, which like it
cool, so that the clay of so many town gardens suits them. However, they need good light and air circulating round them. If they
are grown up a wall, the front of a house is a good place if it faces
South or West. A sunny wall or fence in the garden would be suitable, provided the rose is not hemmed in by other things, such as
overhanging trees or plants grown by neighbours.
Prepare the ground beforehand, all roses like a bit of nourishment
and some material to keep the moisture in, such as peat or leaf-
mould, with bonemeal added.

CLIMBING ROSES AND RAMBLERS

Q What is the difference between climbing roses and ramblers?
A The old-fashioned rambler was more like the wild rose in its
habit, not only in the way it rambled (a word which explains itself)
but also because it only flowered once in the season. The hybrid
tea (HT) bush roses, which flower twice at least, were often very
successfully turned into climbers. They grew more or less as if
one had trained a large bush against the wall (and indeed it can
be done) and the flowers were like those on the bush rose; thus
Etoile d'Hollande, a fragrant dark red rose which I had in
my first garden, made a very successful climber. The growers
have now developed a climber-rambler which is said to have
superseded the older varieties. They are not quite so wild in
their growth and flower "perpetually" – that is more or less
through the season.

   If the reader should find himself with an old-fashioned climber,
it will have thicker stems and less of them and will flower twice,
with flowers the size and shape of the bush rose. The thing to remember is that they are pruned like a bush rose, mostly in the
autumn.

SOME OLD FAVOURITES

Rose growers have long memories and if the first-timer has a
favourite rose remembered from childhood or has been recommen-

The hybrid tea Rose
The HT varieties are available as a bush or climbing rose

ded a certain kind, they are very seldom stumped and can supply many of the old varieties or recommended a modern version of old favourites. I have been surprised at the number of older varieties still appearing in catalogues, so it is worth giving the names.

We were thinking of a climbing rose for the front of the house and it would be difficult to beat **Gloire de Dijon**, (a French name is often the sign of a tried and trusted rose of the old gardens). This rose though not modern to say the least – it dates from my childhood and before – could have been called a climber-rambler. Its warm creamy-buff flowers are scented, unlike so many modern roses and they have a much longer flowering time than the ramblers. They are not too difficult to keep in order for there is plenty of room up a house and along the windows, where the scent is so welcome.

Two other old favourites, '**Albertine**' and '**Alberic Barbier**' are still much grown and both are ramblers, no doubt of that. They only flower once, fairly early in the season, round about the middle of June. 'Alberic Barbier' has cream buds followed by masses of creamy-white flowers. 'Albertine' is salmon-pink, has slightly larger flowers and perhaps an even better show of blooms. Both these look well together.

Q I was told 'Alberic Barbier' was going to be evergreen, but mine lost all its leaves last winter and they only came back in May. **A** Some people call ramblers which hold onto their summer leaves for a long time in the winter, semi-evergreen. The same is said about the rambler 'Mermaid'. I think this is misleading for the first-timer as they can be disappointed just as you were. In a milder winter your rose would have held its leaves right up to January and very occasionally until the new ones come in the spring, but they are not a proper evergreen like a camellia.

'**Mermaid**' is seen a great deal in towns. They do need a lot of sun and like shelter if they are not actually enclosed and a front garden, or on a wall in a sheltered square or close, would be ideal. They have large single primrose-yellow flowers, not produced in clusters like the other two, but flowering through the summer and often into the autumn. Mermaid cannot be cut back easily and should be given plenty of room so that all one needs to do is to cut out the dead wood. Train the new shoots as much as you can so that they grow sideways, for it is impossible to cope once they get out of hand, as the woody stems are really more like branches and tend to die back if cut.

Q I think 'Mermaid' sounds a bit tricky, are the other two easier to grow?

A Yes they are both easy to grow, the only drawback is that nothing is left except some quite pretty leaves once they have flowered. 'Albertine' in particular is so spectacular when in flower that many people are willing to settle for the one glorious burst. A lot depends on the size of the garden or pergola, but you could have another one to take over later, growing with it or near it. In my first garden I had two later ones on the opposite side from 'Alberic' and 'Albertine', the rambler 'Dorothy Perkins', a late flowerer and 'climbing Etoile d'Hollande'.

The '**Dorothy Perkins**' was something of a mystery; the beautiful healthy rambler, with huge trusses of double-pink flowers, that my parents grew over the tunnel pergola, seemed to have degenerated into a miserable little weedy affair with small flowers rather sparsely produced. At the time I put it down to poor stock after the war, but this is still the plant sold under that name and no wonder it went out of fashion. I can only think that the one grown at that time, in the '20s and '30s, was an improved variety now sadly lost. Perhaps some grower will find the secret and we shall see it again.

'**American Pillar**' has huge clusters of single deep-pink flowers and is very good while it lasts.

The '**Crimson Rambler**', also much grown before the war, seems to have disappeared from the catalogues. It was a pleasant contrast in colour to the other ramblers and flowered in July with the old 'Dorothy Perkins', bridging the gap of the first and second flowering of the bush roses.

'**Paul's Scarlet Climber**', a bright scarlet crimson, is another good choice, easier to control than the ones we have previously mentioned and it will grow and flower well in semi-shade. This is an early flowerer coming with the bush roses and only flowers once.

THE NEW RAMBLERS

Here we come to the modern varieties, though I note some of the old favourites included amongst them in the catalogue.

The '**New Dawn**' is probably the best known, I believe partly on account of its attractive name and also because of its easy habit. Though not quite so rampant as the old rambler it certainly puts out plenty of new shoots, but they seem fairly flexible and manageable. I had a surprise when I saw the growth it had made in a new garden. It has pretty, pale pink, fragrant flowers and shiny leaves which grow neatly.

Q I thought the flowers looked rather washed out.

A These delicate shades do literally fade in the sun which is rather surprising somehow, but also when they fade in the poetic sense and start to die the colour goes. Certain soils encourage pink and in my old gravel and clay garden the 'Iceberg' was noticeably pinker in the bud than the one in my present clay garden. There must be traces of iron in the soil, for the hydrangeas turn blue in mine and neighbouring gardens, when they remained obstinately pink in my old garden.

If you like a stronger colour, my own choice would be **'Breath of Life'**. It has large double apricot-pink flowers and started to flower in our neighbour's garden in mid-June, going on steadily right through July into August and from August only slightly diminished until the frosts. Tie it in sideways, don't let it shoot upwards which spoils the look and discourages growth lower down.

'Golden Showers' must be one of the best ramblers ever grown. Yellow roses are often difficult, but this is a very strong grower and flowers in great profusion all through the summer. It is said to be a medium grower, but I have seen it go halfway up a neighbour's house and cover all one side of another, so give it plenty of room. The neighbour's plant had to be cut down for want of space and has never really recovered.

Before leaving the rambler rose we should not forget its usefulness in growing quickly to hide an ugly wall or shed, or to soften the bare new pergola or trellis. One or two of the old ramblers combined with the newer 'repeat-flowering', a much more accurate description than perpetual, would be a good combination and make your new garden come to life in no time.

THE HYBRID TEA (HT) ROSE

This is now often described simply as a bush rose and is indeed what most first-timers would think of as a rose-bush.

Q Did they really come from China?

A Yes, all the books agree that they came from China when the bulk of tea was imported from there, so there was felt to be some connection. A hybrid is just a mixture, bred into the plant for some such purpose as to make it more hardy, keep a special colour, improve the shape of the flower and generally turn the plant more into a garden plant and less of a wild one.

There is a vast choice in this kind of rose, so the first-timer should keep his head and think calmly. Roses like moisture provided the garden soil is not water-logged; so clay is good, sand with manure added is good and ditto chalk. If the chosen site seems rather shady, but not actually overhung with trees, he would do better with the polyantha or floribunda bush rose, now sometimes called a cluster rose.

If the soil is poor, we will look for strong growing varieties such as **'Peace'** and its relations. A bed of these would be hard to beat, they do not mind a little shade and are resistant to disease. If you want a mixture of colours, choose one of the same kind; 'Pink Peace' is a warm cream tinged with pink, 'Grandpa Dickson' has huge yellow flowers and 'Papa Meilland' is a dark red. They are all taller than most HT's and the vigorous growth is inclined to overshadow other roses in the bed so keep them together. The flowers are large, not as many at a time as in some other kinds, but beautifully shaped so that they show up well. They have two flowering times, from about mid-June to mid-July, then again from early or late August according to the weather. The second flowering of all roses can be delayed by a bad sunless summer. These marvellous roses are listed as "show blooms" in the catalogue and they deserve it. My only reservation in recommending them to the first-timer is that he should realise that they are such strong growers that they can look out of scale in a small space. However, if your front garden has a straight path with a bed either side, provided it is wide enough so that the plants do not encroach on the pathway, 'Peace' bushes planted either side make a very impressive entrance.

New roses are developed every year and it is impossible to keep up with them. If the new gardener is thinking of having a rose garden, not just one or two for the sake of having a rose, he should take the opportunity to visit a rose nursery in July when he will get the best display. Meanwhile, here are some old favourites in the HT's set out by colour.

RED

Most people will be interested in colour, so if we start off with red roses, I have already mentioned '**Etoile d'Hollande**' as a climber, though as a HT it is not seen much nowadays but is a lovely dark red and very fragrant. '**Ena Harkness**' is another favourite. It is a lighter red, rather more scarlet, which is as good when in full flower as in bud and does not fade to an ugly colour when full blown, as so many red roses do. '**Fragrant Cloud**' is another good red rose, rather more coral coloured. '**Super Star**', from the famous firm of Wheatcroft, is a lighter red but good for its long season of flowering and is disease resistant.

PINK

Pink roses are often to be found amongst the old fashioned 'cabbage' roses, now back in fashion. '**Pink Favorite**' is a nice deep pink and '**Lady Helen**' a paler pink with a beautifully shaped flower. The firm of Cants from Colchester produced '**Beauty Queen**', which looks a real beauty and now can be bought from Warley Rose Garden Ltd in Essex.

YELLOW

If one wants a good yellow, '**Spek's Yellow**' used to be the favourite, but if not obtainable, the nearest (from the famous firm of Wheatcroft) would be '**Miss Harp**', but I am only judging from the coloured photograph. One should be wary of colour printing so look out at a show or at the nursery itself. For an outstanding colour '**Harry Wheatcroft**' stands out even from the other Wheatcroft roses. The colour, orange with yellow edging, is so unusual and striking that it is obviously best on its own.

CREAM – PINK – MAUVE

Q   I don't like those garish colours much in a rose. I prefer something softer.

A It is no good recommending '**Silver Jubilee**' then, because it is a deep rather hard pink. There are some very lovely creamy-pink roses. One of the old favourites, '**Ophelia**', has been brought up to date with its faults (it was very prone to black-spot) all bred out of it, or so we are to understand. '**Madame Butterfly**', like the up-dated 'Ophelia', of my youth still goes too. I hesitate to recommend two new 'blue' roses, '**Blue Parfum**' and '**Godfrey Winn**', because so many people dislike them. They are a shade of mauve like a sweet-pea which appeals to me, with 'Godfrey Winn' being the deeper in colour of the two. A rose like '**Lady Helen**' or 'Ophelia' with their soft colours would combine beautifully with the 'blue' roses.

Q They aren't a proper blue though.

A No, if one accepts that all 'blue' roses are a shade of mauve, perhaps they would be better liked. The first varieties were rather grey and drab, particularly when they began to fade, but the new ones are greatly improved.

FLORIBUNDA OR CLUSTER ROSES

Q Are there any kinds of roses which go on flowering all the summer, more like a bedding plant?

A If you take a look at an outside display, say in a public garden or park, you are bound to see the modern floribunda. It is usually planted in one colour and treated as a bedding plant in the sense that they are intended to give colour all through the summer, though as we have seen they are strictly speaking perennial shrubs.

They are fairly tall bushes and rather less branched than the HT bush roses. Several stalks come up from the ground and the flowers, usually single, are clustered together and rather smaller individually than the HT. They are good for shadier conditions and will do well in the North of Britain – for instance there is a very good display in Princes Street Gardens, at the foot of Edinburgh Castle. They originated in Scandinavia and have retained their hardiness, which caused them to flower late in the season, but the modern ones are very good for a display all through the summer. One of the best is '**Frensham**', a dark red variety.

Q They tell me that '**Queen Elizabeth**' is foolproof and I need something which grows itself.

A This is indeed a wonderful 'doer' and many beginners are attracted to it for that reason. It is totally different in its size from anything one could call a bedding rose and is really more the size of any other shrub. The pale pink flowers are lovely, as long as they are not all clustered at the top of an overgrown monster, such as one sees so often if they have not been kept in hand. Like all strong growers, they can be cut down to three or four inches from the base and will grow up again quite happily. I would prefer '**Elizabeth of Glamis**', the same idea but more compact. Another rose which grows in difficult conditions is '**Iceberg**', the white floribunda, which is growing at this moment under the shade of the forsythia in my front garden.

I would certainly never mix floribunda with the hybrid tea, their habit is so different and I am not sure that I would mix different kinds of floribunda with each other either, as they do not show up at their best.

Q What about those mixed collections they offer in the catalogues?

A I imagine every new gardener has been tempted by these, I certainly was. They will all be worth growing if you go to a reputable firm, but the grower will have hedged his bets a bit. That is, of six roses, he will have tried to cover six different possibilities in the way of aspect and conditions generally, not knowing what sort of garden his collection is going to. While some will succeed, some will probably fail because the conditions were not right for them.

It is easy to preach after years of trial and error, but I ought not to forget how the new gardener longs to experiment and try everything that takes his fancy. If you prefer a collection of different roses you will have the fun of seeing how they turn out. By the way, keep the names, as you will forget as I did and not know which ones have done well and which haven't. If there are some failures, get rid of them as you do not want to spoil the look of the others which have succeeded. If there is any gardener in the land who tells you that he has never had to do this, I fear he is not speaking the truth.

As usual, we have tried to get some idea of the roses most likely to succeed and where they would be most suitable. The bush roses, floribunda and ramblers or climbers suggested are some of the most seen and grown, but the new gardener has plenty of choice if he would prefer more unusual ones and new varieties.

Meanwhile, in the mind's eye, we can keep a place for the roses of June and July ready for planting in November.

SOME PLANTS & QUERIES

Q My garden is no good for roses as they never flower well and to tell the truth I don't want to be bothered with all that spraying and pruning. About the only other thing I can recognise is a tree in the front garden, which has pink flowers and is very thorny and I assume to be a May tree. Is it late in flowering?

A The **May**, which is a hawthorn, doesn't come out until June and this is what makes people say that it is the May tree which one should follow before casting that clout and not the month of May. As soon as the weather warms up in early June it will start blossoming and is a very welcome 'gapfiller', for the roses will still be in bud and the spring bulbs over. It was and in some cases still is, considered unlucky for the flowers, which have a very heavy scent, to be brought into the house and certainly they are a little overpowering indoors. It is not a very large tree, about the size of the 'medium' flowering cherry and the clusters of pink flowers with fresh green leaves are a sign that summer has begun at last. It makes an effective screen even in winter because the branches are very dense and there is no need to prune which is lucky as it is so thorny. I was surprised to see it listed as "quickthorn", which I had always called the hedges which farmers used so much in my youth and into which the riders came a cropper in the old hunting stories. This is the white hawthorn that with the little celandine, I remembered as a child from cold country walks, as signalling the beginning of the end of winter.

Perhaps the May is a bit untidy-looking for a formal town garden, but makes a lovely part of a wild garden and is not seen so much nowadays. If the reader should want to order one, it appears in the catalogue under **Crataegus monogyna**.

Q I would be very happy to keep the May tree as I don't like being looked in on. What about the back though? If I get rid of the roses there won't be much else, except for some summer jasmine which is doing very well growing near the house. I don't mind shrubs except that I find evergreens dreary, but I would like some sort of screen, particularly at the end of the garden.

A The summer jasmine is rather a find, for although it is *Jasmi-*

num officinale, a politer way of saying the common jasmine, this summer cousin of the winter yellow-flowered *J. nudiflorum* is very easy to grow, provided it gets enough sun and a bit of shelter, which it has in your case from the house. It has lovely scented flowers and will grow as much as you will let it, I know one contented owner of a small patio garden who has nothing else – it started at the back of her house and was on its third wall when I first saw it.

There are some very easy shrubs which we could think of for the end of the garden, which will flower between late June and early July, though sometimes earlier sometimes later, because June can vary from cold and wet (the Derby was once run in a snowstorm) to very hot and dry. The sun is at its highest at this time of the year, though one would not think it some years. This explains why so many catalogues are reluctant to name dates of flowering, as it is so uncertain. However, one can say which are amongst the early ones; philadelphus, buddleia and the lilac, which we have already been considering.

Philadelphus

It would be just the thing for a screen at the bottom of the garden, as it grows very rapidly and even in winter is so branched and twiggy that it is almost as good as an evergreen. The one I grew in my first garden was the common or *vulgaris* type which is very free-flowering and a bit untidy if one has the sort of garden where it is competing with other things. Left to itself, it will be smothered in the white scented flowers which give it the name of mock orange.

Q Should I have to prune it?

A From what you say, it will be up to you. As it will have plenty of room to expand, it is rather a fruitless task making a shrub of this kind into a tidy bush. For others who would wish to keep it in hand, the thing is to cut it back after flowering which will shape it automatically.

Q Mine never does flower, but I thought a bit of pruning might help it.

A It either doesn't get enough sun or perhaps it is a rather superior kind, which are always more difficult to get to flower. The double **'Sybille'** I have seen in several gardens, is much

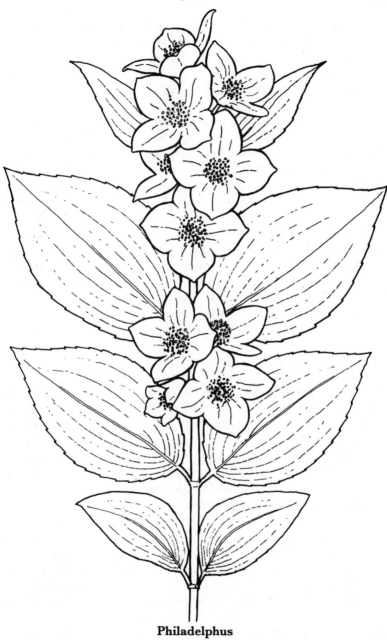

Philadelphus
Popularly known as the 'Mock Orange'

more manageable and flowers quite well, but by no means with the glorious burst of the *vulgaris*. As for pruning, cut it back after it should have flowered (late July) and give it something like composted manure or 'Growmore' and add a sprinkling of sulphate of potash for good measure. If it still won't flower, get rid of it. In the old translations of the Bible, the gardener asked if he could "dig about and dung it" before consigning the plant to the bonfire and the advice is as good as ever. Sometimes plants will grow quite vigorously after such treatment and often this is a prelude to flowering, but if they stay leafy they do not like the situation and their fate is sealed.

Q Didn't you find the philadelphus terribly difficult to get at once it had grown? I had to leave mine as there was nothing substantial to lean the ladder against.

A Yes, this is indeed a problem unless you can get it done when you have professional tree pruners in, when the experts will have long pruners and special ladders. I used to use a long rake and hook the rake onto a branch and pull it down (the stems are flexible luckily) and get at them standing at ground level.

Buddleia

This plant is often seen in deserted gardens and was one of the bomb-site plants in London after the war. One or two bits have survived to this day at St Katherine's Dock near Tower Bridge. The common one has sprays of mauve flowers, is attractive to butterflies and grows rapidly to a good height of 8–10ft. It can be cut right down in the autumn and will grow up again the next season quite happily. There is a variety **globosa** which has flowers like little oranges. I have never grown it myself but have seen it too in a deserted garden, so it would not be difficult.

The one I planted either side of my philadelphus was **B. alternifolia**, recommended for its quick-growing habit and ideal for when I had had to cut down a mass of dead creeper, which had half killed the philadelphus I found beneath it. Removing the creeper and replacing the fence which had rotted during the war must have been rather the same situation as we are thinking of now. The *B. alternifolia* has long sprays of mauve flowers which spread out laterally and therefore are so very good for hiding a fence quickly. If one thought of these it would be better to have two the same, one each side, rather than one of one kind and one of the other as they grow so differently.

Q I should only be sitting out in the summer, that's partly why it seems unnecessary to have evergreens which never flower, so something like the buddleia would do me very well. I would probably pave the rest so as to have somewhere for a table and chairs.

Weigela

Another good grower which flowers well, with a mass of pink or red trumpet shaped flowers, but is not quite so tall as the lilac, philadelphus or buddleia. It might do for a side fence or wall.

Q I hate it as it is so ugly when the flowers are over.

A It flowers early in the summer and is amongst the shrubs which grow very rapidly after flowering. The have to be caught and the stems which have flowered cut back just as the flowers are over, before they have a chance to overgrow, but at best it is an untidy grower. If one has a formal garden there is nothing much one can do about this kind of plant. It would have been quite in keeping with the summer jasmine and the three bigger shrubs though. There is however a variety, *W. florida aureovariegata*, which has leaves with broad creamy-white margins and is a vast improvement on the common one.

Rhododendrons

Anyone who has soil which suits rhododendrons and azaleas can forget about anything else at this time of year, unless he should be particularly fond of any other plant. Grown more or less wild in a large garden or park, they will start to flower in May, or earlier, and go on right through the summer. They are probably at their best and most colourful in late June and early July. Driving through the heathlands of Hampshire and Dorset in the early summer we are treated to the lovely sight of huge bushes of the wild *Rhododendron ponticum*, with its masses of mauve flowers. Then there are yearly planted 'treats' at Exbury, or in the houses of friends or strangers, who have considerately planted their bushes so that they go right down to the river and can be seen by all. Don't go to Kew only in lilac time, go from now onwards when the rhododendrons are out in the Dell.

Q I'm afraid my garden isn't up to that sort of thing. Can one get any smaller varieties?

A Yes, the last years at Chelsea they have been showing 'mini' rhododendrons and I now find them in the catalogues, not just from the specialists, but from bulb growers who sell some plants and shrubs as well. This is always a good sign that a plant has 'caught on'. They are small bushes but have full-sized flowers, not like azaleas.

Azaleas

Q Are they really all called rhododendrons now?

A Yes, they are so closely related that I suppose the botanists gave up the ghost having got in such a muddle trying to sort them out and have now lumped them all together as rhododendrons.

It makes it very difficult though for the first-timer. If he is ordering from a catalogue, he might be better off with the Bulb/Plant catalogue sent by firms like Walter Blom and J. Parker. These have coloured illustrations and are not so technical and tend to keep more to old names. If the new gardener is after the small evergreen bushes, mostly with pink or red flowers, he should ask for evergreen azaleas, sometimes called Japanese evergreen azaleas. The grower is used to these naming difficulties as we were saying earlier on.

Q Are they the ones that one grows indoors? I hear that they can be grown outside.

A The indoor azaleas are brought on specially in hothouses, are mostly from Belgium and have bigger flowers than the real outdoor ones, but will succeed sometimes in a mild situation.

Q We have an azalea in the garden but it is not evergreen and is quite tall, with yellow flowers. It has an annoying habit of dropping its buds just as it is coming into flower. It's frightfully muddling if these are called rhododendrons too.

A The way to track down these azaleas is amongst the rhododendrons, but they usually have a little section to themselves – the Knaphill hybrids (azalea) are mostly yellow or orange. They are very useful for the wild garden as their taller habit competes better with other shrubs and trees. Even the experts are not always able to stop the buds from dropping, which is sometimes the result of an unseasonable frost. My Mother was a great believer in dried blood to bring things on and give them a boost just as they were going from bud to flower.

Q   Do you mean dried blood? I should feel rather odd asking for it.

A   It is a well-known fertilizer and as far as I know dried blood is exactly what it is and it seems to act as a kind of blood transfusion. Sprinkle a trowel-full round the plant about two or three inches from the centre. Water it well in as roots take in nourishment in liquid form, but do not try to mix it in the can as it is very difficult. Roses benefit too from dried blood.

All azaleas, indoors and out, hate lime in any form and should be watered with rain water or softened water. If the soil is not naturally peaty add plenty of leaf-mould and peat when planting. In the towns, or in any new garden, beware of builders' rubbish which is always limey.

At the beginning of June it is possible to buy an instant plant from the garden centre, first checking that it is the hardy kind. They are very useful at this time of year to fill in before the roses are fully in bloom.

Q   Our house is in Dorset where azaleas like the soil. Even so they can die in a hot summer and they don't much like a cold winter either, particularly when first planted. I think they are tricky things myself though very beautiful.

A   Perhaps first-timers should leave them alone for the first year or two unless the soil is really suitable. I planted them rather against my better judgement to please the Q who shares my life; married Q's may have similar requests from their partners, so why not try? I smother mine with leafy compost each year and they haven't done too badly. They are the kind of plant which passers-by admire which is always gratifying.

Perhaps the botanists are not all that wrong after all, for the little pink flower which is the third of the wild Swiss trio – we have come across the gentian and edelweiss already – has always been classed as an alpine rhododendron, though in its native land rather confusingly called an alpine rose. It is a smallish shrub much in evidence near the Reichenbach Falls, where Sherlock Holmes nearly met his death. The nearest to it in the garden is the *rhododendron praecox*, which comes out very early in April or even March in a mild winter.

Q I thought the early azalea was mauve. I tried one in my garden but it died.

A The one I tried in my first garden was 'Blue Bees', but like the blue rose, this was really mauve. Mine failed too. I think now almost certainly because my garden was only just reclaimed from a bomb-site and must have been full of rubble. As a grower said, however careful one is to put down plenty of peat and leaf-mould, the roots may come across something deeper in the soil which they dislike.

This azalea was not evergreen, so it would be found in the Knaphill section, so look for an early rhododendron which has (azalea) in the list. If you are buying to bridge the gap between the bulbs, roses and early border plants, ask for the later ones (May to early June) which will be among the evergreens.

EARLY SUMMER PLANTS

If there is a long border in your new garden, the plants which looked so unpromising in the winter months should all be anyhow in leaf and some will be budding and nearly in flower.

Chrysanthemum x superbum

It is always referred to as the 'Shasta Daisy' in catalogues though I have never heard it called any name but 'Esther Read', the name of the most-grown variety. The correct name for this is now *Leucanthemum x superbum* 'Esther Read'. It looks like a garden version of the wild marguerite which grows by the road-side. With border perennials the thing to realise when planning is that they will not go on producing flower after flower like the bedding plants, but have one main flowering period and only rarely a second one. This 'daisy' is a good mixer, middlesized and about 3ft. so it is not so tall that it would overwhelm things planted at the back while still making a show on its own. It is good for picking and will flower well into July, sometimes longer. If you should want to divide it, it is one of the few border plants which should be divided in spring and not the autumn.

Coreopsis

This is another 'daisy' plant, yellow this time, with a much lighter and more graceful look than 'Esther Read'. It is a favourite of mine but it does need replacing, as having done well for two or three years, it will suddenly disappear after a winter for no apparent reason.

Q I don't want to be difficult, but I don't like daisy flowers.

A Many people feel the same way as we were saying earlier on. I suppose nowadays, when we are so keen to label everything, they could be called "daisyphobes"! It is a bit difficult to get away from daisies in the border, but we are coming on to lupins now.

Lupins

The really good news about lupins is that the **Russell Lupin** has made a great comeback. It suffered from over-production just because it was so outstanding; easy to grow and perennial, lasting over many years, yet very easily raised from seed. If you find them growing in your new garden, just leave them alone except for keeping them weeded. They too are for the middle of the border and make nice compact plants. If you want to plant them, there might be nurseries still selling plants which you could put in straightaway, but if the season has already started to show signs of being a hot dry summer, June is too late.

Earlier on we were thinking of the soil in the new garden and I recommended a sprinkling of lime to sweeten neglected earth, but never let lime near your lupins.

Delphiniums

When we were visiting Chelsea, with its monster delphiniums, I mentioned the feeling of disappointment one has if the flowers became smaller in one's own garden. Delphiniums need sun, a fairly rich soil and manure should be added when they are planted. Like lupin plants they might still be available from nurseries, but do not plant in a dry spell. If you find delphiniums already growing, this means the soil is right or they would not have survived. They should be out in a week or two and expect the spikes to be medium-sized, dark or light blue. If cut down after flowering they will have a second flowering in the late summer.

It is difficult with a poor soil to struggle with things which really like a richer one, but an early blue flower (and not a daisy) is so useful in the border, that I recommend the **Belladonna delphinium**. They make no pretence of having huge spikes, but grow very prettily and as a rule do not need staking. They can be middle-border plants as they are not so tall as the large-flowered delphiniums. As they succeeded in my gravelly first garden, I feel safe in saying that they will do well in a poor soil with a bit of feeding. They look rather more like the annual lark-spur than the big set-piece delphinium.

Paeony

Q Is that how you spell it?
A Yes, it trips me up every time. The diphthong, the two vowels squashed together, has gone out of print now but one can still hear the double vowel in the sound, making everyone unsure whether to look up 'pe' or 'pa' – such is simplified spelling! So many Q's give up looking for plants in the lists for reasons of spelling, or not being sure what category they come under, that I make no apology for digressing.

To get back to our paeony; *Paeonia Officinalis* is the red paeony so often seen in cottage gardens. If it likes the situation which should be open and sunny with a fairly rich soil, it will look after itself, and need no top dressing or extra attention. *P. lactiflora* is said to be the origin of many of the other garden kinds, with huge double flowers in red, pink or white. The 'Chinese' paeony with single flowers, three or four inches across with a prominent centre in a contrasting colour, is easily recognised from the ones painted on Chinese bowls.

The time to plant is in the autumn but because their tough roots "resent disturbance", as the catalogue says, they may take a year or two to settle. Once growing well and given a sunny spot they will flower very reliably towards the end of June. Though they only bloom once they have very pretty leaves and given a corner to themselves they will look spectacular when out and can then subside as a background to the later plants.

Like roses when established, they often survive in a deserted garden. I have seen the old-fashioned pale pink double paeony, which smelled of equally old-fashioned cold-cream, almost filling the border against the wall of an empty house.

In my first garden the red cottage paeony settled quite well but never really flowered satisfactorily, as I fancy the garden was not open enough. The deep double pink '**Sarah Bernhardt**' did magnificently, a real star turn, but perhaps my favourite of all is *Paeonia lactiflora* '**Bowl of Beauty**', which is rather an expensive purchase but worth it. It has huge pink single flowers with a creamy centre and was one of the few plants which had survived when I visited my first garden some ten years later. 'Sarah Bernhardt' was already past her best when I left and one was tempted to be fanciful and think she had thrown a tantrum after the arrival of the 'Bowl of Beauty'; probably I had disturbed the roots and she resented it. In any case, the plant must have been all of twenty years old.

Make as rich a mixture as you can when planting for they will not be moved again and growers recommend a top-dressing of manure after flowering.

The **Tree Paeony** is a shrub. They are beautiful plants but need a rich loamy soil and are therefore not for the town or first-timer. If one turns up in the new garden though, it should be made welcome and fed as much as possible. They can grow as high as six feet depending on the variety, so of course belong more to the shrubbery than to the border, but I have known the smaller ones of 3–4ft settle down quite happily with border plants.

Aquilegia or Columbine

The *Aquilegia vulgaris* is the old garden columbine. The first-timer is more likely to find it already growing in his 'new' garden than on sale in a garden centre or nursery, as they will be selling the modern hybrids with larger and more colourful flowers with longer spurs.

Aquilegias can go near the front of the border. The old columbine will make a bushier more compact plant, but both will seed themselves. The leaves are very pretty and easy to recognise when they reappear in the spring and look something like a Maidenhair fern. The flowering time is late May or early June.

BORDER PLANTS FOR THE SHADE

Hostas

Q I have a plant with huge leaves in a shady corner. A tree must have been cut down there and it has settled in well so I don't like to move it. It has quite pretty flowers, but it doesn't fit in with anything else.

A The succession of wet summers in the British Isles (said to be the 'greenhouse effect'), has led to great popularity amongst flowers which like shade and moisture and don't mind a lack of sun generally. The big hosta and the easiest to grow is the *H. sieboldiiana* 'Elegans' for all the world like a huge plantain such as one digs out of the lawn and whose cousin it is. They have shallow roots so that if they get too big they are possible to move. I had to do it when mine showed signs of wanting a stately home in which to spread and accommodated it in one short border at the shady end of my first garden. The smaller variegated ones which I tried did not do at all.

In your case, one well-established in a difficult corner comes into the "better than nothing" category. I appreciate that if one is looking out at a garden, the eye will look down its length and focus on the end or on corners and we all have the feeling that something more dramatic than a hosta and if possible with flowers would be more suitable. If there is a tree-stump it is an expensive business to have it removed and if the hosta is growing well, an idea might be to have rather a showy border plant or flowering shrub such as a hardy fuchsia, to hide it as one looks down the border. Then when walking round and looking at the border close to the hosta would come into its own.

Astilbe

If by 'shady' we mean facing North and if there is moisture in the soil, the astilbe is a very good choice. They are pretty feathery plants and cousins of the wild meadowsweet, the white flowered plant which grows in water-meadows. Beware of calling it spiraea as I ordered one under that name and what came was a cultivated Meadowsweet, intended for a water garden. The astilbes are hybrids and leaf-mould in the soil will usually keep them moist enough. They are coloured pink, deep pink and red and there is a white which is really a very pale pink. They come at a good time, near the beginning of June.

BEDDING PLANTS

We promised some more bedding plants for June and now is the time for the best selection. We have already mentioned petunias, *Impatiens* and geraniums which are probably the best known. A very useful little plant which will flower better in the shade than any of these is the little bedding begonia.

Begonia

Begonia semperflorens which lives up to its name and once started, a little later than the first bedding plants, goes on well into the autumn. It does not do so well in an exposed position and got rather 'nipped' on my roof-garden, which must have been too sunny and windy for it.

The bigger begonias are first seen in July and make a marvellous later show, which is very good if one wants an instant effect for whatever reason. They are rather expensive though.

If the first-timer should become more expert, they are not at all difficult to raise from bulbs grown in leaf-mould – I used stuff straight from the compost heap. They will even come up outdoors if planted the previous autumn, but it is preferable to have a little protection from a verandah or greenhouse.

Q Mine seemed to deteriorate and the flowers fell off.
A I would not go for the huge ones as big as cabbages, such as one sees at shows, but settle for the smaller ones about an inch across. The male and female flowers are separate but borne on the same plant and one must say that the showy ones are male and the smaller ones female, NOT degenerate!

Salvia

These are greatly used as a bedding plant in parks and public gardens, (they replace the 'Grenadier tulips' outside Buckingham

Palace for example). Most first-timers will know their scarlet flowers when they see them in the garden centre. They are nice neat growers and make a bright show, but they need an open position and sun. My attempt at planting them the sunny end of my North-facing garden was a failure, after their first flowering in June they went in and did not flower again until September. In a small garden this is not acceptable, especially as the eye tends to focus on the end of a garden as we have been saying.

Q Those sort of plants are all very well for parks, but I would like something which reminds me more of the country for my own garden. Are there any less formal?

A You will probably know **Canterbury Bells**, **Stocks** (single and double), **Sweet William** and the **Heliotrope**, or perhaps under its old name of 'Cherry Pie'. There is no difficulty over names here and they do give a nice countrified feeling to the town garden and are rather more like border plants in their flowering. You will buy them now as plants just coming into bud, probably from a nursery rather than a garden centre. They all flower well, but once over that is that for the summer. The sweet william will come on a bit after the first blooming but not quite in the same way. The exception is the heliotrope, which can be bought at garden centres and should flower all the summer – its scent is what gives it its old-fashioned name. My feeling is that it is rather too dark for a bedding plant, it can look a little dreary, but mixed in a group in a border it is unusual and less formal than other bedders.

Q I was looking at some stocks and thought they were hollyhocks.

How can you tell the difference?

A I must admit I was baffled at first for I couldn't see the connection, as hollyhocks are very tall plants for the back of the border and the stock is about 12ins. If you were looking at the double stock, the flowers themselves do look very like the flower of a double hollyhock and they grow up the stalk in the same way, but one has to see them both growing to appreciate the difference.

Q What about **Hollyhocks**? I like those old-fashioned plants.

A If you can't find any plants, they are very easy to grow from seed. Buy the double ones and they will seed themselves. However, they are inclined to revert to the single ones or change colour and if they seem to be doing this just buy more seeds.

They need sun, or they will be rather weak-stalked and fall down untidily.

BEDDING PLANTS FOR CONTAINERS HANGING BASKETS

Q Don't you hate them? I do.
A That is a little hard I think, as so much depends on where they are placed. If they are seen hanging from a door which looks perfectly all right on its own, they can look quite ugly; or if one has to crane ones neck to see them, they lose half their point. I have seen them hanging from the underside of a terrace-balcony and as one approached the front door, the passage way under the terrace would have looked rather dismal but for the four hanging baskets, which looked very attractive in that setting.

If the first-timer should fancy a hanging basket, especially if he should find a hook where one has been (which would look rather sinister on its own and probably be difficult to remove), he is lucky. It goes without saying that such baskets are heavy and preparing their hook is no DIY but a builder's job – a misplaced hook could be very dangerous for all concerned. Baskets have special compost and they can be bought, compost and all, ready planted which is ideal for a beginner; one can choose the plants first of course.

BASKET FUCHSIAS

Apart from geraniums and the lobelia which are obvious choices, there is a big choice in fuchsias. These are not the hardy garden kind, but specially grown for containers and the like and look very well as the centre-piece of a basket. The kind to buy are the 'spreaders' grown for the purpose and many firms specialise in them. Of the basket fuchsias, I have only grown **'Swingtime'** which is a very pretty red and white; the red sepals (top layer of petals) and the double white 'underskirt' of petals are very effective. If you prefer something upright, **'Winston Churchill'** is a robust grower as one would expect, with red sepals and bright purple petals which is the 'easy' colour combination in a fuchsia.

The ones you buy at the garden centre will be in flower having been brought on for you, so simply buy the colours you prefer. The growers tell me that none of these kinds sold for baskets and containers are really hardy, but they will last until well into September and usually until the first frosts. As they are late starters, this is an advantage at the end of the summer when other things are going over.

Q Should one protect them in winter?

A They are not as expensive as they were, coming out no dearer and sometimes less than geraniums, so it seems rather a waste of time and energy worrying about protection. If they do survive in a mild winter it is a bonus, if not replace them. They will lose their leaves in all but the mildest winters, so your show will be over in any case.

The exception is the variety *Fuchsia magellanica*, which is generally hardy and survived the very cold February of 1987. It is easy to grow and has a mass of flowers. It will lose its leaves in the winter, but soon comes on when the weather warms up.

The hardy fuchsia for the garden is a bigger thing altogether and we will come to it in July.

Watering hanging baskets is the big snag and though I have never had one myself, have seen neighbours struggling with cans and drowning themselves with the hose. I understand there is now a pulley available by which they can be lowered and the extra expense would be well worth it. There is also all the tidying and perhaps replacement if a plant dies to consider and they MUST look tidy and cared for.

TENDING THE GARDEN

We have had some pleasant dreams and I hope real experiences in the new garden in June, but now we must become real gardeners and cope with pests and diseases. Mildew, black spot and rust are mainly leaf diseases on roses.

MILDEW

This is the white powdery substance which may well be on the roses already. It attacks the young shoots in bud and can spoil the look of the rose, as well as pre-disposing it to disease.

Q My 'Iceberg' rose is covered in it but I am told it does no harm.

A If it attacks the new buds badly it can harm them, for they don't flower properly. I would never leave a plant, particularly in a town, with anything which can weaken it. Mildew should be dealt with straightaway with a copper-based fungicide spray, such as we were laying in at the beginning of the year. I find Murphys very effective. Spray again in a fortnight's time, but not sooner and that should get rid of it.

BLACK SPOT

This is not seen on the new growth but usually comes later in the season on the old leaves. The huge black spots need no further explanation. Early signs are older leaves turning red and yellow for no good reason, but the young growth should look a darkish red as it is a sign of flowers coming.

The spores which cause this disease and can kill your plants lie about in the ground, therefore pick up any infected leaves which have dropped and burn them if possible. Do not mulch the rose by giving it solid feeding like compost manure or even peat, as the spores can breed in it particularly during the winter. A badly infected rose which has made no new growth as it should have at this time of year, should be got rid of; then the ground should be left clear of roses for a year. Otherwise, cut back the infected stems and spray with Murphys' fungicide as before.

Q I suppose the spores can't be seen.

A No, I should have explained that they are no more to be seen than our own germs or viruses. The sooty air which used to attack them has gone in our towns and as I write there is quite a plague in my own and neighbouring gardens. As I was saying in April, this is what causes me to prune in the autumn instead of the spring.

RUST

It would be hard to say which is the least welcome on a rose leaf, rust or black spot. Like black spot, the name explains itself and if the older leaves are turning rust-coloured for no good reason they must be sprayed at once. As for something specifically against rust, there used to be a very good powder, Tulisan, which one mixed as a spray, but most are sold in liquid form now.

It is many years now since any of my roses were badly affected by rust and I used to find that ramblers and climbers were more affected by it than bush roses. It chiefly comes from growing roses without sufficient air circulating. Our neighbour on the old bomb-site side put up a trellis, thus enclosing the roses which had been free before the site was built on. As this was obviously the cause and after struggling with not much success to cure them, I cut down the roses and grew something else in the end.

Q I don't think I have ever seen it.

A Let's hope it is less common now. The treatment, with a different spray, is just the same as with black spot.

Speaking in general, if plants of any kind get leaf-disease do not be fooled if it produces a lot of buds, as in these circumstances it is a bad sign.

Q Surely buds are always a good sign?

A I used to think they were and a sign that the plant was recovering. Actually a plant with all buds and no leaves (when they should be there) is a cry for help; I discovered this from an expert on the radio some forty years after having worked it out for myself, though had never been quite sure. He said the plant was trying to compensate for the loss of leaves by producing more flowers.

It is hard to have to say to a new gardener, but do not keep roses badly affected by either black spot or rust, as they will only give it to the others.

To be more cheerful, many roses are labelled "disease-resistant" in the catalogue, so go for these if you have no particular preference and you will not go wrong – many of them have the best flowers as well.

LIVE PESTS

The leaf diseases are caused by a fungus or virus, but the pests we are after now are the live ones.

THRIPS

We have not met these little pests before. They go for the new growth which will have the buds, particularly roses and the hardy fuchsia which will be coming into leaf now. Look for little pinholes at the top of the stem, where the new growth is coming and spray at once; this time with something like Sybol, which I have used for years. Derris powder, sold in a puffer, is very effective but disfiguring and is rather like mildew to look at. This would not matter in the second home where you can go away and leave it, to come back and find it washed off and hopefully the thrips with it.

Once is usually enough, but if not, leave a fortnight as before between spraying. The thrip in the singular is unknown, which is a measure of the numbers of these horrid little pests, but a good spray will do them in.

We have already met greenfly and blackfly. In a warm winter they can linger on for most of the year, but this is the time when they really get under way.

BLACKFLY

They usually settle in a solid mass along the stalk of their chosen plant – syringa for instance. Mine always got infested at this time of year and I used to cut off the little stem, blackfly and all, before it got a chance to increase. Earlier on, we were advising the use of the little modern plastic sprayers (so much handier than the old brass syringes), but with a large bush, if one of the old kind should be around still in the shed, they are best for shooting the spray (Sybol as before) a long distance. Don't forget though to soak the washer first and let it take up the water, or you will spray yourself more than the bush.

GREENFLY

Greenfly is not always bad and sometimes a spray early on will clear the bush for the whole season. Sometimes though, one has only to go away for a week to come back and find the roses thick with the wretched things. I have heard many good reports of 'Roseclear' which is easily obtainable.

Q Do they really do much harm?

A They suck the sap of the stems which can't be good and though I have never heard they are actual killers, are certainly very unsightly.

If you have to water the garden anyhow there is a lot to be said for using the hose against greenfly. Go up close and using a fine spray simply drown as many as possible and chase them when they go under the leaves, which is what they do when dislodged from the stems. Some people prefer using a really strong spray which is a bit messy but effective.

CUCKOO SPIT

The name is only too appropriate as the 'spit, houses the pest.

Deal with it by using Sybol or a derris product as before.

SLUGS AND SNAILS

They are not much seen in the daytime and must be trapped at night. Put out the slug-bait, I use Slugdeath, where you see the slimy trail or if the petals of your pansies, which slugs are fond of, suddenly develop holes. They are worst in wet summers and heavy soil, like clay. There are a couple of new products on the market I have not tried, but which sound good as they work both above and below ground. One is a liquid called Murphys' Slugit and the other is crystals containing aluminium sulphate. A great bonus is that the latter is described as being safe for pets.

Q Which are the best, the pellets or the powder?

A I have tried both and can't see any difference in the results, so I confess I buy whichever comes to hand. Either kind needs renewing after rain, or in any case after three or four days. Then put it down if and when they come back again.

Q How depressing all these different pests sound. Are the remedies any good?

A They will all succeed if things have not gone too far. With thrips particularly, the plant recovers almost overnight and the new growth rushes out again, as if the plant was as pleased to see the thrips go as we are – just keep an eye that they don't come back again.

For **EARWIGS** see Dahlias)

STAKING

1) Staking as a Protection

Not all our live pests are small, there are pigeons, squirrels and cats to be considered. Pigeons are at their worst in the spring as they go after new growth of all kinds but are not usually troublesome once summer has come. However, there are places where they like to sunbathe and my rockery is one of them, where of course if they see anything which they like the look of they will polish it off and have to be discouraged.

In a town garden the neighbouring cats are always a problem. The best hint I ever read pointed out that cats will never jump if they do not see their way clear; if they want to drop from a wall they will be deterred by spiky shrubs, or on the ground itself by stakes. I have found nothing which deters squirrels who have a fondness for bulbs, except actual netting, which I am forced to use in the spring. Then they usually disappear from the garden until the autumn. (For netting use Netlon garden net).
Staking 'Dragon's Teeth' fashion:

The little sticks which are sold to support pot plants are not expensive and can be used in quantity. Place them sticking up out of the ground in a criss-cross pattern in the manner of the wartime 'Dragon's Teeth' tank-trap. These will stop birds landing as they like a clear patch and I have often seen cats sizing up the situation with a view to jumping down and finally deciding the landing is not safe enough. Anything may walk along the wall, it is jumping down onto the bed which does the harm!
Q Do you use cat-pepper?
A Yes, I find it quite effective, particularly in the spring. It should be sprinkled over what seems to be a favourite patch or piece of wall. Use plentifully as it does not keep well.

2) Staking for Support

We touched on this, to say how important it is to stake early. June is only just in time with the border plants in your new garden, which have no support of their own. Even if they are little bushy plants at the moment, do not fail to stake them. The difficulty with herbaceous non-wood plants is that they haven't the firmness of the woody shrub and often grow out towards the light and therefore need staking. The expensive metal supports are much more effective if they are placed round the plant really early, so that they grow through them. It is enough if you are busy to get a stout stake at the back of the plant and enclose the whole with some string (the green garden kind) – if you fasten with a bow it can be adjusted if necessary.

There are not many things I really dislike about gardening. I rather like weeding and have thought out many bits of this book when wielding my little fork, but I absolutely detest trying to tidy up a flattened border when the plants are more or less fully grown. They never seem to go back naturally when placed upright again; the plants have, almost unnoticed, developed a bias and when one tries to get them straight even the leaves look inside out and the last state is worse than the first. However tidy they look when they first grow in June, let the reader be warned by me and stake things in good time.

TIDYING UP

Gardeners vary over this; some cannot see a leaf out of place and some feel a sweet disorder in the garden, even in a town one, makes it more home-like. Of course the first-timer must please himself. There is no point in saying obvious things like, 'the lawn will probably need cutting', as he may be quite happy with a rougher effect. So much depends on the design, which we will go into more fully in July.

As for cutting and pruning, as we said at the beginning of the month it is too early for real pruning, so tidying is at the new gardener's discretion.

Q   Even now, I am a bit worried about pruning things. What I am never sure about is how easily one can kill things by cutting the wrong bits.

A   There will be a lot of new growth about and some of it is surprisingly brittle, so unless your plants are diseased I should leave well alone. If there is new growth coming amongst dead, or what looks like dead growth, I should leave it until July at any rate, when the new growth will be less tender.

If you can pick out any border plants which still have dead stuff from last year, feel right down by the root, the stem may have rotted off and can be easily pulled up. If it resists, it is not dead and may be about to sprout again. You may be handling something like a hardy fuchsia, which will be making new growth and sprouting from the old.

In six months we have seen enough plants to make it worth our while, next month, to think out some simple plan and to decide what space we have left for the later things and how they will affect our design. Are we going to keep the design we have, have one thought out for us, or put some cherished scheme into practise? With some more plants in July we shall have a difficult choice, but an enjoyable one. Anyone with a garden will agree that planning is half the fun and what is more we shall make our dreams come true if at all possible.

July can be a difficult month; the weather is often sultry and thundery with heavy rain and not many really sunny days, which the plants need to bring them on. A heavy storm can put paid to the roses and other flowers hanging on from June and suddenly the garden has gone over, but we are going to plan ahead and not be disappointed.

LATER BEDDING PLANTS

Q I must say I was a bit disappointed, as when we first saw the house there were quite a lot of roses in flower and it looked very colourful. Now there doesn't seem to be much coming on. Is there anything I could put in?
A If the garden is free of the worst weeds (nettles, ground ivy, docks and coarse grass) you can still plant some annual flowers. They will need a sunny aspect to bring them on, otherwise they are easy to grow for they have been started for you by the professional grower.

Try some 'strips' or small plants of **Asters, African Marigolds** (tall or short) and **Snapdragons** (*Antirrhinums*). All are colourful, but will not flower until later in the season, so will not provide instant colour. You might be able to find some bedding begonias, which will be in flower and even geraniums and fuchsia going more cheaply as the grower will not want them left on his hands.

It is getting near the end of the season for selling these kinds of plants, so do not buy anything straggly, weak-looking or already in full flower. Remember that the earlier bedding plants have been brought on to sell in late May or early June – they are mostly

182

annuals and the earlier they can be planted out into beds or containers the better. In July we are looking mainly for plants which have been brought on to flower later.

Q Isn't it a good thing to buy a bigger plant then?

A It is not so much the size, look to see whether the plant is still coming on. Are there plenty of buds and has it got 'drawn up' by being left too long in the pot? Never buy anything which is long and thin as the plant should look bushy whatever the size.

Coleus

This is the time when the coleus will be appearing. It is the ornamental nettle plant which is very good for a more shady bed, where the sun-loving bedding plants would not flower well and be disappointing. The coleus is grown for its leaves, which are in very pretty patterns of green and pink. Choose ones with plenty of pink if possible, or dark red, because they can revert to mostly green when fully grown – 6–8ins approximately. When we become more ambitious, they are not difficult to raise from seed in the ordinary warmth of the house. Though the coleus has quite a pretty blue nettle flower, do not let it flower as the general effect is too leggy and it looks like a lettuce which has 'bolted'. When the flower buds form remove them gently with finger and thumb to keep the plant bushy. The young coleus stems are very easily broken so be careful when transporting them.

Ageratum

We have mentioned the ageratum briefly, because it appears to have no 'pop' name. It is a neat little mauve bedding plant with a flower which looks like the middle of a daisy, but without the outside ray of petals. This gives it rather a special look and makes a change from the more usual edging plants. There might be some still about, for they are less well-known and therefore less in demand.

African marigolds

The little orange or yellow African marigold is good for backing the mauve ageratum, otherwise they are plants which look best on their own. The taller African marigold is good for standing out in a window-box. Slugs eat their roots, so put out slug-bait when planting. If one wilts, dig it up straightaway bringing up plenty of earth with it and if done in time, one can sometimes catch the slug at it. Look for it near where the stem meets the root underground and it can then be disposed of underfoot. Put the plant back at once, watering it in if at all dry and put out more slug-bait.

Snapdragons – (Antirrhinums)

As snapdragons flower in August this is a great bonus for the second home which is used for the long summer holidays. The large varieties are about the size of wallflowers and could go in when the latter come out, though there would be a long gap between the flowering times. There is a smaller bedding variety of snapdragon called **'Magic Carpet'** or sometimes 'Persian Carpet', which looks like an oriental rug in its colours and is easy to grow and will sometimes survive a mild winter. Older readers may remember the pink and yellow snapdragons which grew more or less wild in country gardens, especially wall-gardens. The really wild flower, the little toadflax, is yellow.

We were talking of planning ahead, so we must not forget that if we had been able to buy our bedding plants in June, they would have been coming into their own. Things like lobelias, salvias, Busy Lizzies (*Impatiens*) and many more will be at their best in July.

Q They are all right in tubs, but I want more of a garden.

A What about the **Asters**? They don't come on until September, but most people would think of them in the garden and not in tubs or window-boxes. There is the single, or the more artificial double one **'Ostrich Plume'** which if planted needs plenty of light or their mop-heads will flop about. 'Daisyphobes' will not like the single ones.

LATER BORDER PLANTS

Arriving at a garden in July is too late, or too early, whichever way you want to look at it, to plant anything perennial unless you use container grown plants and ensure they are kept well watered.

The best time is in the autumn. We have already been planning some early border plants in June. Now the lupins, delphiniums and paeonies may be over and the later border plants only in bud and giving no colour. Apart from the work involved, it is not possible for the small garden to have sufficient space for a succession of colour throughout the summer using perennial border plants only, but we can mix in shrubs in the modern fashion.

Q   I don't particularly want shrubs with all that boring green.

A   I don't mean the rather dreary evergreen bush, which is conjured up by the word 'shrub' or still more by the word 'shrubbery'. The sort of house which would have been called "The Laurels" and probably been planted with the poor brave things, for they tolerated the sooty air of olden days, is now the height of fashion and the garden can be as good as any country one in the cleaner air.

We are thinking of flowering shrubs such as roses or hydrangeas. Roses are all shrubs and a climbing rose is listed as a climbing shrub. We could have a modern climber-rambler at the back of our border, climbing over a post or up a wall. **Hydrangeas** are just starting at this time of year and they will go on all through the summer, turning to lovely autumn colours when the early frosts come. They look very well at the corners of a bed where they have plenty of room.

Q   Would the **Queen Elizabeth** Rose do as a shrub?

A   It can certainly compete with other shrubs as to size, but remember that like all roses it needs air circulating round it and should not be hemmed in by other shrubs. For the mixed border, it could go at the back instead of a climber; the long flower-bed which is called a border is not always backed by a wall and a row of 'Queen Elizabeth' roses would be attractive. They can actually be cut into a hedge, but I feel the first-timer does not want to burden himself unnecessarily. Although all roses need pruning to a certain extent, the 'Queen Elizabeth' needs more than most, but it would only be once a year.

At the present time in our border we are considering the transition from June to July, when the rose would not be at its best. The point of hydrangeas is that they would be in bud early in July and will then last, showing colour until the autumn without a break.

Another useful climber would be the large-flowered clematis, which is coming on now and will flower all through July. Earlier in the year we were thinking of sowing the easy hardy annuals (HA) straight into the ground, as part of the display in the front of the border. **Clarkia, Virginia stock** (the small annual, not the bigger biennial stock) and **Candytuft** are all easy and will be at their best, making a colourful show and getting away from the formality of the bedding plants.

For the moment we will consider border perennials, which fill the gap between early and late summer and should come out amongst the other perennials which have flowered in June.

Pyrethrum Daisy

This is the cultivated feverfew, about 3ft tall and with pretty feathery leaves. It is 'out' for country gardeners because rabbits, who should not be encouraged, like them. Otherwise, they come when the late tulips have finished and will flower when there is nothing else coming on. My mother planted them at the front of a large flower-bed behind the tennis-court (grass in those days) and they left behind a pretty feathery hedge when the flowers were finished. In this bed, when the tulips came out dahlias went in, which is a very good idea if one has sufficient space. The flowers are pink and red and there seems no point in having white ones if the Shasta daisy 'Esther Read' is grown as well in the border. They make good cut flowers.

Lychnis Coronaria

Lychnis, which used to be known as agrostemma, is a smallish plant for the front of the border. It grows to about 18ins, with silvery rather woolly-looking leaves and purple-red or white flowers. In spite of its impressive name it is not as showy as some border plants, but its time of flowering in early July is useful and it does well in a sandy soil near heathland, which is often difficult ground for the gardener.

It is a plant often seen growing in friends' gardens who do not know its name, though most of us know the look of it. Some people may call the red one rose campion, it is very useful if a friend gives you a bit.

all. On looking them up I find they need a rich soil and plenty of sun, neither of which they were getting. I have tried them in a tub on my new patio with no better luck, so I must say that unless your garden is famed for growing lilies, do not try this one as a first-timer.

PLANTING LILIES

Though this is rather out of season we will go on to planting lilies, because for the first-timer it is all a part of the decision whether or not to have lilies in his first garden. Though he won't be planting until much later, the lily catalogues will be arriving with their tempting pictures in August and he must be prepared. First of all, although everyone talks of lily bulbs strictly speaking they are corms, where the nourishment for the new plant is stored up in buds. The 'bulb' looks rather like a huge head of garlic and should look fresh and juicy – good enough to eat as it were.

If ordered from a catalogue, they should be planted directly they arrive and this is the snag, for it can be the coldest part of January. The only solution is to have pots ready. Put the corms in and protect them on a verandah or balcony, or in the open against a wall under leaves as I do. They can be put into the ground when the milder weather comes. One is sometimes lucky and has a mild January, 1989 for instance, when the weather is 'open', not too wet or frosty and they can go straight into the ground, provided it has been prepared beforehand. The corms are lifted when the plant dies down, which may not be until late in the season, but they cannot be stored like bulbs.

Q I should never feel sure. January can be very cold and supposing there was a terrible frost that night.

A Yes, the weather can change very suddenly, but one would only get a really hard frost after several days of cold weather. Once in the ground I have found that the lilies in both my town gardens survived very cold winters. They are better protected than in a pot, where the frost can get at the roots through the sides of the containers.

Q How long do the flowers last?

A Each individual flower would not be fully out for more than a week, but if one thinks of the buds coming out all up the stalk, the total flowering time would be more like three weeks. If the lily gets

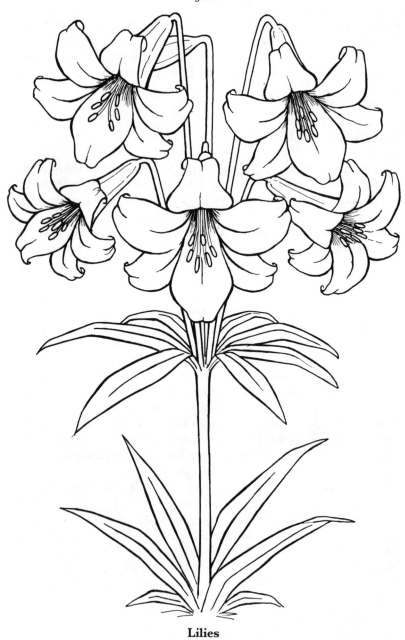

Lilies
These plants are suitable for growing in the garden or in pots

established in a clump in the border, different plants will be out slightly later or earlier and you could get a month of lilies.

If the regal lilies seem to be doing well, you could try '**Pink Perfection**' or *L. regale album*, both a little more difficult but a little later than *L. regale*.

PREPARING THE GROUND

Though loam, the rich crumbly clay we were discussing in 'Soils', is recommended for growing lilies, we are not all so lucky as to have such a soil. Therefore material from the compost heap with well-rotted manure or Levington compost will have to do instead. Mix plenty into a good big hole if your soil is poor and put a little sand (ordinary builders' sand will do) under the corms which should be four to six inches down. Excellent instructions will arrive with the lily corms.

PLANTING IN POTS

For a single lily use a pot 6ins across and put extra drainage 'crocks' (broken clay pots and similar) over the drainage holes. Make a compost of leaf-mould or peat mixed with compost manure, or simply use Levington and put a little sand on top. Place the corm on the sand and cover with about 2ins of the same compost. In both the garden and if using pots, remember that your corm is alive and be careful of its roots; spread them out gently when planting.

Lilies once established increase by seedlings. You will see tiny leaves by the main plant, so include them in the top dressing of compost and don't 'weed' them by mistake.

Q My lilies decrease. They tend to disappear in the winter and if they do come up the second year the flowers aren't as good.

A If even the easy lilies do this, my feeling is that the soil is not suitable and one should grow them in pots rather than in the ground. In general though, if there seems no particular reason why the plant should not be doing well in its second season, when other lilies are doing well with you or your neighbours, my own explanation is that the corms have been fed and brought on to sell. They will often rest in their second season while they are getting accustomed to their new home. Feed them with something slow-acting like bonemeal, then bring them on again in the spring with something like composted manure or Growmore.

When they disappear one sometimes finds sad remains of corms, half eaten or rotted and it's hard to say which. One of my lilies disappeared one winter from the balcony pot and I was able to search right through the compost but found nothing; not a withered corm, not a single scale, only a very fat healthy earwig. I suppose the poor corm had been its winter food and that can happen in the open as well. One could dust round with Derris powder when planting and put Derris at the bottom of the pot, where the earwigs can get in.

Q It sounds altogether beyond me.

A Why not buy a lily in June or thereabouts already growing in a pot? Lilies are not particularly cheap, but to be able to buy *L. speciosum rubrum* (the pinky-red incurved one) already growing for round about £2 seems to me a bargain. This was what I paid a lily grower at an RHS show in Vincent Square, but they have them at garden centres too and you can plant them pot and all in the border if you wish. It is an easy lily and if you bring it indoors as we suggested it should do well. A small packet of Levington would see it through the next year. The lily pots must be kept damp in winter, so water occasionally if there is no rain.

Arum Lilies

Q I would love an arum lily as I remember them from years ago.

A It is very pleasant to see them coming back into fashion. They were a great feature on the altar at Easter when I was a child, having been brought on in the greenhouse and returned there in their pots when Easter was over. Of course these had been gently 'forced' (brought on in a little heat) as their natural flowering time is not till late June or early July.

All the lilies we have mentioned so far and even garlic, come from the big lily family, but arum lilies are quite different. They are bought as plants and are called *Zantedeschia* not *Lilium* and are related to the wild 'lords and ladies', which grow by the sides of paths and ditches in the spring. Even though these lilies do like a wetter environment I was a little startled to find the wild arum, *Arum maculatum*, sharing a page in the wildflower book with the bulrushes and burweeds. However, if you look at the centrepiece in the huge 'petal' or spathe, you will see a mini bulrush.

Arums are bought in pots, already growing and the variety **Zantedeschia Aethiopica** was also on sale for £2 at the RHS show. They can be ordered by post, as I have seen them in the bulb/plant catalogue. They are even listed now as house plants, but I have doubts about this.

Q Could you leave them outside in the winter?

A I should bring them in, giving them the sort of shelter we advised for the other lilies. I have not tried one myself but they were never considered hardy in the old days, so it would be safer.

The variety which is said to be the hardiest is **Z.** *aethiopica* **'Crowborough'**. Certainly arum lilies grow almost wild in Ireland where there is plenty of rain for them and mild winters. If arums are put out in the summer they should be given shade and not be exposed to the full sun.

Agapanthus

Before we leave the lilies, we must not leave out the agapanthus. Many readers will have seen the blue South African lily in tubs, coming out when the frosts are over as a sign that summer is here.

Our neighbour's front courtyard faced due South and his agapanthus used to go back to the nursery which had supplied them, in the winter – possibly rather a costly business. However, they can be planted outdoors as I am told that hardier varieties have been developed. One would not think of Lincolnshire as a county with the ideal climate for tender plants, but I have just heard of an agapanthus which has survived and flourished there in a sheltered corner. It could be another sign that plants are more protected in the ground than in pots.

Pinks and Carnations

We cannot let June and July go by without saying something about these. The carnations and pinks don't usually flower when the Lilac is in bloom, but two or three weeks later. The poet is right in his imagery though, because of the lovely scent of all three plants, which is sadly so rare nowadays.

Q What is the difference? Those spray carnations look like pinks to me.

A The spray carnations we buy from the florist are all very well for a vase, but we want the larger-flowered border carnation if possible. The kind sold by the florist for buttonholes (the dark red clove carnation with the heavy scent) is less and less grown, because they start going black at the edges when only a day or two old. For cut flowers though, the other colours are unrivalled and although a greenhouse is outside our scope as first-timers, it is worth knowing that they can be brought on in a greenhouse without too much heat in a normal winter, though an unexpectedly heavy frost can lead to tragedy, even amongst commercial growers.

Q Are they the ones they sell in the flower markets in the South of France?

A Yes indeed, at all times of the year it seems. I have asked several French friends what they call pinks as opposed to carnations, but they never know – to them they are the same thing. Mind you I don't remember seeing pinks growing in France, so perhaps they concentrate on carnations.

If we want to grow either border carnations or pinks, both like an open position with sun and good drainage. They are not very happy in a town garden, unless it is a little way out or unusually large and open. Carnations need staking and here the metal supports sold in garden centres and often advertised in gardening 'ads' in the newspaper, come into their own and save time for the busy gardener.

Pinks are for edging and the firm of Allwood have produced a range of plants so successfully, that the Allwood pink or carnation is as well-known as the Russell lupin. The first-timer should try for an easy colour such as pink or white. The white is a modern version of the 'Mrs Sinkins', that older readers will remember from their childhood and rather puzzlingly known as a 'pink'. The calyx (the cup which holds the bud) used to split and spoil the shape of the opened flower, but nowadays things are different and both white and pink 'pinks' are beautiful compact little plants. Both pinks and carnations are sold from the nursery or garden centre by colour rather than by name, but the named ones can be bought from the specialist Allwood themselves, or a similar nursery. Of the collection I grew in my first garden,

when it was still unenclosed the one which did best was appropria-
tely 'Winston Churchill'.

LAYERING

I mention this because so many garden books and books about
carnations have good descriptions and pictures of this way of pro-
pagating or increasing plants. It is worth knowing because of the
cheapness and satisfaction of increasing one's own plants.

Briefly, the cutting is not cut right off and planted (as for a pink),
but severed at a joint, opened up and fixed to the ground with a
kind of staple, so that the opened stalk roots at this point. For
the first-timer with a good diagram, the difficulty is not doing
the layering, but looking after the plant thereafter. Once the
plant has rooted it should be kept an eye on to see if it is
making new growth. If it is, then cut it away from the parent,
plant into a sandy potting compost and keep watered before planting out. Many people would prefer to keep the little plants in a cool
greenhouse for the first winter. Few first-timers would feel like
doing this in the first year or two, particularly as it would coincide
with a busy time in the new garden, but it can be stored away in
the memory for a more leisured time, if that should ever come!

Phlox

Here is good news, a perennial border plant which is not a daisy.
They have colourful heads of flowers smelling pleasantly of honey
and can be back or mid-border, according to the height of the
other plants. They did well in my parents' garden in the
Thames valley, but the light soil meant a great deal of watering;
one whole border was given over to them and they were an unforgettable sight.

Not many readers will be able to grow phlox on this scale and if
one or two are added to the mixed border be careful which colours
are chosen. The common colour is rather an unattractive red, neither crimson nor scarlet but the colour of faded red roses. I suggest
white with a pink 'eye' and deep or pale mauve; the deep mauve is
pretty because it is not a sombre purple and mixes well. There is a
good scarlet and deep pink but these are not so easy to grow.

Phlox was a plant which disappeared from the growers' catalogues and is now making a welcome return. Their height is
about 3ft which is just right and they like an open position, but
will grow in towns now the air is cleaner. They flower soon
after the early border plants which is useful when planning.

The annual phlox is **Phlox drummondii** and the only reason
I did not recommend it is because it needs a sunny position and
does not flower well in a sunless summer. Otherwise, it is one of
the prettiest and least formal of annuals and a great favourite of
mine. Its height is about 8ins.

Poppies

Another poet got into trouble with gardeners when he made his
poppies hang in sleep amongst the cool mosses and ivy. The
latter do very well in my North facing rockery, but the poppies
are in the front garden where they get more sun and are facing
as near South as I can manage. We are all for lotus-eating
though and should not disturb this image of sleep. Provided we
plant things rightly, we should not be always fidgeting to get at
the garden, but should be sitting peacefully thinking of sweet
music when we see the petals from blown roses on the grass, without wanting to rush and sweep them up.

The poppies in my front garden are the pale mauve '**Shirley**'
poppies and it has just come to me that the mauve 'Shirley' tulips
must be named after them. I found one in the rockery which
seeded itself all over the place and when the weather is favourable
I tidy up the seedlings a bit, so that they make a nice pattern.
They are considered very uncommon; yet another instance of a
change of fashion, for they were weeds when I was young and
much despised. When they have finished flowering they do look
a bit tatty but they can be pulled up, leaving the one or two
which are least noticeable to seed themselves for the following
year.

Border Poppies or Papaver

These are the bright red colour of the wild cornfield poppy. The
leaves are an attractive light green making a good contrast with

the flower and are easy to grow in sun, but no good for picking as the flowers fade so soon.

Q Can't one dip the stems into boiling water?

A Of course you can try; the idea is that it stops them sealing themselves up and they will drink up the water but even so they will not last any longer than they do outdoors which is never more than a day or two. They have a quick succession of buds which keeps them showing colour for the early part of the border display. Any really bright colour is useful to 'lift' the effect.

Hydrangeas

We have mentioned hydrangeas in passing, but they are so easily grown in towns and sheltered spots without too much trouble for the first-timer, that they are in danger of going out of fashion, as the easily-grown plants did when I was young.

Q People do seem to despise them, though I think they are very colourful.

A It is your garden and if you like them why should you not grow what you please? I was very glad to see a nice bush when we arrived in our new house. At this time of year they are a great standby and to arrive in a new house and see plenty of colour in the garden is very cheering.

Q Can one grow them in tubs?

A The flower-shops will be selling them as house plants, which is rather an expensive way of buying them, but they can be planted in tubs or out into the garden and will survive. They need plenty of water so should have humus, such as leaf-mould or peat, to retain the moisture.

The ones usually sold as pot-plants are **Hortensias**, *Hydrangea macrophylla*, the **Mopheads**, with great mops of flowers which grow outdoors on a bush often fully 4ft high and the same round.

Q Do you mean they grow to that size from a pot-plant?

A Yes they do and this is one of their advantages. Look out for the ones with the uneven or serrated leaves. Give them plenty of room, leaf-mould, peat and a dressing of compost manure in the autumn, to help keep them warm in winter and you will have no trouble. The site should be reasonably sheltered and not in full sun; a corner is good because they can spread themselves.

Q I ordered some hydrangea plants from a nursery, but they were so small I thought they had sent the wrong thing. My memory is of really big bushes.

A The nurseryman would have grown the hydrangeas from cuttings, which are small at first, the equivalent of a seedling plant. The bigger the plant, that is to say the longer the nurseryman has been growing it, the more expensive. Your plants should soon grow and given the treatment we have suggested, it will be not more than a year or two before they are fair-sized bushes.

Obviously the grower is not going to make much money if he sells only full-grown plants and they are not suitable for moving anyhow. However, there is a difference between receiving a small bush, of say one or two stems and about 1ft high, which though different perhaps from the bush of one's imagination, will grow quite satisfactorily and receiving as I have, a small cutting about 3ins long, just rooted and badly packed; carriage and packing are quite heavily charged nowadays. No reputable nursery should send out any plant below a certain size. If the buyer is paying for a rooted cutting he should be told so and not charged for a plant.

The other type of bush hydrangea is the **Lacecap**. It has much flatter flowers, which really consist of outer sepals with a large flat centre of the true flowers.

Q How can you tell sepals from petals?

A To put it at its simplest, if there are coloured sepals and petals, the sepals will come on the outside, enclosing the bud. When the fuchsia is in bud it may look red, but when the bud opens the red sepals will curve back to show the 'petticoat' of the purple petals. The sepals which enclose the bud are usually green; the rose for instance needs no help from coloured sepals. With something like a clematis, or the exotic bougainvillea though, it is interesting to see the leaf-shape of the flowers. No grower is going to confuse the first-timer by saying anything more than that the flowers are purple, pink or mauve as the case may be.

With hydrangeas, they will also be said to have blue or pink flowers. What they have in fact is masses of tiny real flowers surrounded by round coloured sterile flowers with large petal-like sepals to make up the large head. The lacecaps have much larger centres which show up well, so nature has arranged fewer and smaller sterile petals round the edge. The daisies, with their ray flowers surrounding the centre of florets, work on the same principle; there is no end to the tricks which nature will play to lure the bees and ensure the plant survives.

Q Nature really *is* wonderful.

A Yes, this is half the fascination of gardening and why so many gardeners are believers, but of course we must stay firmly with the first-timer and not worry him with too much detail, which is just as well as I am no botanist. As for the unbelievers, I can think of no better retort than one of my uncle's sayings, "well, make it yourself then" − he was referring to the universe, not just to plants.

Q Can you turn the lacecaps blue? I tried, but a pale mauve was about as far as I got and they are going pink again.

A There are some alkaline soils, my first garden had one of them, where hydrangeas stay obstinately pink. I was given a beautiful blue pot-plant, which I planted outside when it had finished flowering indoors and though it flourished it went pink, having gone through such lovely graduations of pink, mauve, blue and blue-mauve in the process, finishing up such an attractive deep pink that I was not really upset.

Q All the same, people are always trying to turn them blue.

A Yes, there is a great deal of one-upmanship in gardening as you have already discovered. You can try a blueing powder, iron sequestrene and the instructions are on the packet, but in my experience it is more successful for pot-plants.

Rusty nails were said to be a help. Where there is iron in the soil, as for instance at Studland Bay in Dorset, the hydrangeas are so blue as to be rather hard and ugly. An Australian friend tells me that 'down under' they are considered very ordinary if they are blue and pink is the colour everyone strives for.

The prettiest of all happens by accident. Mine which were pink when we arrived have been slowly turning themselves blue. Possibly owing to having been staked with a bit of copper piping left over from the central heating, or possibly because there are traces of iron in the soil as people nearby have bluish ones. The best part of it is the number of different colours all on the same plant. It is a strange fact and I have double-checked this, but acid soil produces blue flowers and alkali, pink, which is just the opposite of litmus paper.

Q Is there such a thing as a climbing hydrangea? There seems to be one climbing up the wall of the house.

A Yes, the **Hydrangea Petiolaris** which flowers earlier in the season, but the huge white flowers hang on even when they are technically 'over'. They are a flat plate-like shape, more like the lacecap than the mophead, with few outer sepals and a large centre of the real flowers.

Q I tried to buy a climbing hydrangea but it has turned into something quite different with long heads of white flowers, more like a lilac than the ordinary hydrangea.

A This is the trap we were talking about earlier in 'Names of Plants'. What you have is a **Hydrangea Paniculata** and the panicles are trusses as you say. They are differently arranged from the mophead, but the 'flowers' are the same idea – small flowers of sterile petals with the real flower in the centre, arranged together in a whole, which does look more like a lilac.

Q I nearly threw it away when it wouldn't climb.

A I'm glad you didn't, as it is a really splendid sight with its big white flowers which turn pinkish before they fade. Once again we are left with having to say "be careful of the right name".

Q I just picked it up in the garden centre and they said it would climb.

A One has to be a bit careful in garden centres. There is a great deal of heavy lifting and students and young people are often given jobs on a temporary basis, more or less as 'humpers', so if in doubt find the gardener and ask him. *H. paniculata* is not suitable for a border as the heavy flowers make it inclined to flop, but it looks very well in an ornamental urn with a stout stake to hold it up.

Q My hydrangea is the mophead kind and a recent thunderstorm knocked it right over. It would be fearfully difficult to stake it.

A Hydrangeas are pretty tough, they pick themselves up amazingly well once the water has dried out of the heavy heads. If some are still lying about when the others are straight again you will do no harm if you pick them as cut flowers, in the same way as summer-pruning the roses. Later on when they have turned a handsome autumn red they can be picked and dried. Keep them in water until they stop drinking, then leave them to dry on their own.

Q Is it really that easy to dry them?

A The only tricky bit is knowing when to pick them. The flowers will start turning red but wait until they start feeling a little papery before cutting them. If you wait too long they will die on the bush, if too soon, they will just die and not dry.

The time to prune is in the late autumn when the leaves are off. If you decide to cut back in a big way cut right out from the base, for if you just shorten, you will only get a lot of small stalks in a bunch and the flowers will flop worse than ever.

Q Are lacecaps easier?

A Yes, the flowers are not so heavy and do not get beaten down by the rain in the same way. They are a big bush though, every bit as big as the mopheads and slightly more spready. They can be cut right down to the ground in the autumn and will flower again after only missing a year. It can be contained a bit if there is not much space by buying it in a pot and leaving it there when planting in the garden.

Q Do you leave the heads on in the winter to protect the new flower buds? People never seem to agree over this.

A I always leave them on and have never lost my flowers after a severe winter, though it seems tempting providence to say so. I can't see the point in taking them off for though they do look a bit untidy, that is only for the coldest part of the winter, when the garden is laid up and one is not walking round admiring it. As soon as the worst frosts are over they can be cut off; indeed for the most part the new leaves will push them off.

Q None of this is my problem, for the fact is I get very few flowers.

A I think you will find they flower one year and have a rest the next. The older variety of hydrangeas were not nearly such reliable flowerers as the modern hortensia ones and it would be well to change to one of this kind.

Roses – (continued)

We left roses unfinished in June with a promise to continue in July. This is the month of the later climber-rambler and according to the growers the month to visit the nursery. Seeing the 'maiden roses' in their first year of bloom would give the new gardener a much better idea of colour and habit (the way roses grow) than any catalogue, however colourful. You will be able to ask for advice on the spot, as well as looking at full-grown ones in other gardens. Just as we did at the garden centre when buying bedding plants, look out for the strong and healthy ones, as you do not want to land yourself with unnecessary problems.

Be sure to ask whether anything you like the look of is a hybrid tea (HT) bush rose, a floribunda or a cluster rose, or even a poly-antha, the kind with several flowers on the stalk and a different shaped bush. They do not mix unless with a purpose; for instance using an 'Iceberg' at the back of a bed to make a strong-growing background to the smaller bush roses. If you see a climbing rose ask whether it is a climber or rambler; a climber is best for a wall and a rambler or pillar rose for an archway or pergola.

The roses will not be sent until the autumn, probably in November, so you have plenty of time to plant.

Q The trouble about floribunda roses is they have no smell.

A Certainly none of the ones I have grown have had any scent, unless one counts a general sort of fresh flower smell. However, scented ones are being developed and are appearing in the cata-logues, some even marked as "v. fragrant" and are worth looking out for. The great merit of the floribunda is, on the whole, their strong growth and their long flowering period.

Q We have built an archway for the new garden. Would I want two roses for it?

A Some roses are such strong growers that I suppose you could say that they would go up one side and come down the other, but somehow it would look rather forced and unnatural. One would have to tie the rose down as it arrived at the far side! One could have a pillar rose, say 'American Pillar', but it only flowers once, or two rambler-climbers kept well in order so that there was not too much chaos when they met at the top of the archway. A grower advised me never to try and shorten a strong-growing ram-bler, it was better to cut the long 'streamer' of a new shoot right out.

Q It sounds rather drastic. What if there aren't many new shoots?

A Growers always say that the amateur gardener will never prune hard enough and that is in general and not only for roses. If a professional had a weak-growing rose he would simply replace it with something else. To go back to our rose, if it had only two or three rather long shoots, we need not worry that it will not mix in with the other rose, it is usually where they join that the problem starts. These same thin-looking new shoots which the rambler produces are going to branch out tremendously in the next season and produce flowers for the arch-way.

Q What about shrub roses and what are they exactly?

A What used to be known as shrub roses, particularly the kind which have ornamental fruit or 'hips' in the autumn, are for large gardens, partly on account of their size (they are real bushes or shrubs) and partly because in former times they only flowered once. Many firms specialise in them today and the reader may have seen a fine display at Sissinghurst. Nowadays you will find the modern hybrid shrub rose listed along with some of the old favourites. They have a much longer flowering period and some of the old French Bourbon roses have an old-fashioned scent too.

Q I was thinking of just one shrub rose. I haven't got a very big space, but I wanted something old-fashioned and unusual.

A **'Charles de Mills'** is a rose with very fragrant crimson-purple flowers of the old cabbage rose shape, but more elegantly called a 'dress rose'; it looks exactly as if it has been made of red velvet and is most unusual and beautiful. The catalogue says it is a vigorous grower 4–5ft which is not too tall as shrub roses go. The **'Rosa Mundi'** is my favourite amongst the striped roses, or bi-colours as they are called sometimes. It is red and white and often seen in old flower prints. It is small for a shrub rose, not more than 4ft and a very neat grower with pretty leaves. The catalogue warns against mildew but I can give it a clean bill of health as far as my own garden went, though it is just as well to spray in case.

There is a big choice amongst the repeat-flowering shrubs, which need very little pruning and will flower through the season. **'Ballerina'** is a very pretty little rose, with pale pink single flowers in large clusters. It belongs to a category, unknown to the catalogues, of 'leaners' (the kind of shrub which is half inclined to be a climber) and is happiest falling over a fence or half climbing up some other bush.

'Prima Ballerina' (not to be confused) is a hybrid tea rose happiest grown up or along a wall. The flowers are a perfect shape, like that of the HT, with long buds and flowers which when open keep in trim until they fade. They are also good as cut flowers with a lovely scent. The colour is difficult to describe – a lightish red, not crimson or scarlet, but a pretty effect unlike the phlox we disliked earlier. It is very nearly perpetual flowering, i.e. from early June to early Autumn.

The Bourbon rose hybrids are the old-fashioned flat shape,

crossed with 'perpetual' shrub roses, which will flower more or less through the summer. The old 'Malmaison', its title is now '**Souvenir de la Malmaison**', has come back in this new form and has pale pink flowers with a lovely scent which I remember when it was 'in' before. Perhaps we should prefer '**Boule de Neige**', which has very fragrant camellia-shaped white flowers, is a neat shape and of medium height. I envy the first-timer able to try one or two of these.

Q   Are there any more bi-colours?

A   If we go away from shrub roses, a fairly tall floribunda is '**Masquerade**'. It is about 3ft tall and has single flowers which are yellow in the bud and gradually turn to red. Though very spectacular, it is subject to disease and mildew as anyone who has grown one will tell you. A neighbour near my first garden had a lovely bed of them which were pruned right down every November or thereabouts and emerged in the spring as good as new. As the mildew or disease didn't appear until the flowers were nearly over, it didn't matter that much. I fear nowadays, when the town is not so sooty, that one would have to be more careful and spray in the spring with the new growth.

A smaller floribunda and more the patio size, is '**Regensburg**'. I found it very striking, with a beautifully shaped semi-double pink flower with a white centre. Its only fault is that it is so unusual that it looks a little artificial and would be best grown on its own. It would make a marvellous display for someone who wanted to use it instead of bedding out in the summer, as it really is almost perpetual.

Standard Roses

Q   I suppose a standard rose is meant to stand all by itself?

A   Yes, the old standards would be about 4–5ft tall, but there are also half-standards now if one should want something less 'stalky' and formal. They are great space-savers in a small garden as the bush is at the top as it were and there is room at ground level to plant something else if you should wish it.

Q   My new garden has a small round flower-bed in the middle of the lawn and I thought of planting one there.

A   Yes, it would leave room for some early bulbs or bedding plants round the edge and give colour for the summer. The alternative to a standard, is a weeping rose. A rambler like '**Dorothy Perkins**' or '**Excelsa**' weeps naturally and would not have to have a frame. They would cover the whole bed though and would not leave much room for anything else.

Q What about patio roses, or are they just for a patio?

A The growers are careful to point out that patio refers to size only, as they are shorter floribundas. We were thinking of 'Regensburg' amongst the bi-colours and three or four of them would make a very good show in a round formal bed. Grown in a patio, they would still need sun and air like any other rose.

Fuchsias

We have just mentioned fuchsias as bedding plants, now we come to the really hardy border shrubs which will survive a really cold winter in a sheltered town garden or similar situation. The **Fuchsia magellanica** is the hardy strain. This is the large bush seen growing almost wild in hedges in the West Country. The flowers are small but very plentiful and although it does not flower much before late July, it is a useful source of colour whether in the border or on its own. It grows to a height of 3–4ft with about the same spread. Look out for thrips in the early summer, as it will have died down in the winter and these pests attack the new growth.

If your flower-bed is bordered by grass, the fuchsia dropping its petals will make the grass go yellow which means they must be somewhat poisonous, so must be swept up to keep the grass looking well.

We have already come across the hanging *F. magellanica* suitable for containers. There is another *F. magellanica* which has larger flowers and would be better planted in a border as it is not so tall and spready.

'**Tom Thumb**', sold for rockeries, after rather a shaky start has proved hardy in my small rockery in the front garden. Starting off a real 'mini' at 4ins or so, it is now about 8ins and quite a bushy little plant, but has grown no further. All have the 'easy' colours of red sepals and purple petals. For the most part they disappear in the winter, leaving dead stick-like stalks behind. The winter of 1988–89 saw leaves all through and even some flowers, but this was quite exceptional. We should have to leave the plants alone

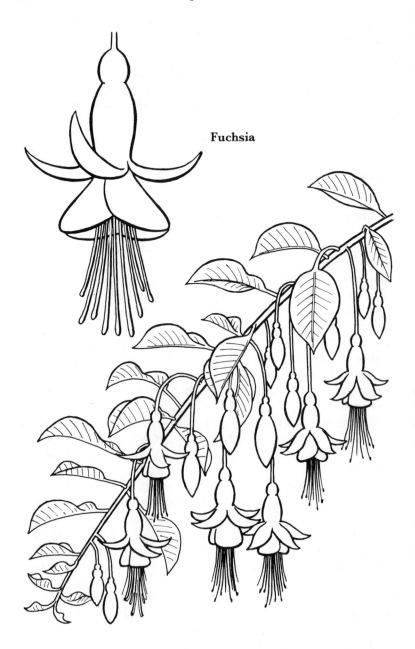

Fuchsia

in such a winter and cut down the old stems directly the new start
to sprout from the base in the spring.

Q What if the old stems have already sprouted?

A If the plant wants tidying up you can still cut them down without harming the plant. After a very cold winter though I should
leave them alone, for the stems sprouting from the base will probably be rather sparse and weak. Later cut off any dead bits which
haven't re-grown.

ANNUAL CLIMBERS

Morning Glory

At this time of year you may find the garden centre selling the
half-hardy morning glory – this is the bright blue *Ipomoea
hederacea*. They depend on a hot summer and plenty of sun to
show at their best and I recommend them. They are grown in
a very loose sandy compost by the experts and I should leave
them in their little pots when planting. Look for the sunniest
wall or fence in your garden and you will be rewarded by one
of the truest blue flowers which exists.

Q Do they only come out in the morning?

A If we were to have a really hot summer they will be in by
about midday, but in one of our normal summers they will last
until after lunch.

Cobaea scandens

A very easy climber which grows quickly and has quite pretty
flowers of a greenish purple, which are bell-shaped and look a
little like leaves gone wrong. It is not so spectacular as the morning glory, but not so dependant on a good summer. Neither plant
is expensive so worth buying in any case to try.

Passion Flower

This is also on sale in garden centres and with some luck will be
permanent. Formerly considered a greenhouse plant, it has

emerged into the garden with so many others of the same kind. They are strange and beautiful flowers; the arrangement of the stamens at the centre is thought to resemble the nails and crown of thorns of the Passion. They are not difficult to grow.

CONTAINERS

We have been out in the garden a great deal in July, but of course most bedding plants are suitable for containers as well. Now the frosts are well over, if you have a gap in your tubs, what about house-plants? Most of them can go outside in the summer and the fresh air and rain does them good, also nearly all house-plants like being close to other plants. What about the Christmas poinsettia for instance? Even if it is nearly all green by now, it can look surprisingly colourful among other plants and I put mine in my small border. The maranta tricolor, a very easy house-plant, flourished in a tub. Do not leave out too long, mid-September is the time to come indoors again, before there is any chance of an early frost.

We have not done so badly in the way of plants for our imaginary garden; some later or longer flowering roses; some later bedders; useful flowering shrubs and annual climbers and gap-filling border plants to keep the show going.

SUMMER BULBS

Q You haven't said anything about gladioli which are very colourful. Do you think them too stiff?
A It is not so much that they are stiff as the unpredictability of their flowering time and the fact that they can fail to flower at all. I do not like to recommend anything uncertain for the first-timer.

I am not being fanciful when I say that the ones I planted in my first garden were almost psychic, they waited until we went on holiday, whether in July or August and then came out and it was the neighbours who told us how well they had flowered. I gave them up in the end. The smaller daintier ones have often failed to flower at all, which is very annoying if one is counting on them for a display.

GROUND COVER ROSES

Q You haven't said anything about ground cover roses either.
A They are a new idea intended for difficult banks or something of that kind, but I have not heard good reports of them. They are a nuisance as they will grow up instead of along and are difficult to keep in hand. 'Snow Carpet' is so small, with a 'mini' flower, that I am trying it on my rockery. I have seen it doing very well in an urn, hanging down in a very attractive spray.

We are already at the end of July and coming on to August, when we have to consider holidays and the fact that the garden could be left for a fortnight or more. In August we will look at the problem of the second home and of leaving one's town garden at weekends or for holidays.

August

August is *the* holiday month for many people; the month for family and school holidays. We have to consider straightaway if the first-time garden is the second 'holiday' house, or whether it is the only one and will be left each year for at least part of July and August.

This will of course affect our planning. There is not much point in having later flowering bedding plants or border perennials if one is away for their flowering month or months. However, we have already noted in July that the later-flowering things are somewhat erratic in their habits, a wet summer can hold them back and a sunny summer bring them on, so it is better to plan for a succession of colour as best we can in a small garden. We might go away for a fortnight and find some favourite plant has flowered with no one to look at it, or we might return to find the garden the proverbial blaze of colour after a sunny fortnight. As far as established things are concerned, a fortnight is not long and the first-timer need not worry too much about leaving them.

Bedding plants on the whole do not mind dry weather. I have already described in April how a gardening neighbour brings up her seedlings in the house all the winter, puts them out to harden off after the worst frosts are over and then plants them out when she leaves for the South of France in May. On her return at the end of July, an absence of six to eight weeks, they are in flower and she is then abroad again in September and October by which time the plants are established. The first-timer will have to buy his bedding plants, but the principle is the same. My neighbour's permanent shrubs are the roses, hydrangeas and camellias which we have been planning for the mixed border.

Shrubs, trees and climbers can be left to look after themselves.

212

Roses need spraying but are not going to notice being left for a short time. Our garden was a town one and we were away for a great deal of the summer, on the boat at weekends and for longer holidays. Readers who have this kind of garden and are away a lot in the summer should give more attention to drying out.

A town garden like my first one with flower beds, trees and shrubs, but not many tubs, will survive as well as a country one provided it has plenty of moisture-retaining material. Compost, peat or spent hops can be used as a mulch to keep the ground damp whilst one is away. In any case, town gardens are at their best in the early part of the year and a dry hot summer will see most things looking as used up and exhausted as one feels oneself. This is another reason for planning the town garden mainly with spring and early summer in view.

Of course if you have the time before going away, it pays to get things as tidy as possible before leaving. The sort of things one can do are; weed, spray if necessary, look at stakes to see if they are firmly in the ground and that string is not rotting or getting loose, particularly on wall climbers; broken string can bring the whole lot down and that is the last thing one wants to see on return from holiday.

For the patio, roof-garden, or containers in general, if you are to be away a lot in the summer, avoid things which mind being dried out; hydrangeas and camellias in particular. Bay trees could stand being left for a fortnight, any longer and it would be a help to get someone to water them in a dry spell – they are so often seen outside the front door that this should be fairly simple to arrange. A roof-garden will be all containers, but as it gets the natural rain it can be planted up more or less as you please, provided you get back regularly to water it if it is a hot dry summer.

PLANTS IN THE AUGUST GARDEN

Q   There seem to be quite a lot of plants in the garden but not many flowers, though there are some in bud. It's been a terribly wet summer, would that be the reason?
A   Yes, they could be later flowerers waiting for some sun. I felt obliged to advise on drying out in a hot summer, because we have

had some unusually hot and dry summers lately, but the rainy apologies for summer we had at the end of the 1980's did nothing but hold things back. Plants need a certain amount of rain to bring them well into flower, but excessive rain and lack of sun can defeat any gardener. Perhaps it is not a bad thing to have some idea of just how late your plants can be in a bad year and whether it is worth keeping them for the future.

Certain types of **Chrysanthemum**, the hardy non-greenhouse kind, do very well in towns and make a lovely splash of colour, but even the so-called 'early-flowering' ones can hold right back until October and some later ones will be flowering in November when one wants to get things cleared. I had to let mine go in the end, together with some very attractive edging **Michaelmas Daisies**, as they flowered too late. The latter too are prone to mildew in towns, particularly the taller kinds.

Q   There are roses coming on, but one or two have gone rotten in the bud. Is this some disease?

A   No, if there are no other signs on the leaves and the plant is growing well, it is just the heavy rain and wet weather generally. One often gets a fine spell in September following a bad rainy summer and the roses will be flowering well then, probably right up to the frosts.

Q   What about pruning?

A   It is too early to prune roses. Wait until about November when they are dropping their leaves and stopping flowering.

Q   There are some shrubs I shall keep, but they are rather over-grown.

A   Earlier in the year we were speaking of the winter-flowering shrubs and these will be forming their buds now, so when you are trimming back shrubs such as forsythia or winter jasmine, look out for buds. The spring-flowering ones may be starting too, early camellias for instance. Once they have made the summer leaf growth they usually get down to forming buds for the next year.

At this time of year at any rate, it will be much easier to see dead wood which should be cut right out. One can always trim any awkward-growing branches which spoil the shape and branches which are growing crossways inside the bush – these will not flower and it gives the bush more light and air, which it specially needs in an enclosed garden.

Q   The trouble is with some of the older shrubs, cutting out the dead wood would mean cutting right into the bush. I should like to keep as many as possible, or would it be better in the long run to replace them?

A If one sees the experts talking on the television, over and over again one hears the same advice, not to hang on to older shrubs and trees which are past their prime but to replace them. To me, this advice is very hard to follow. In my own small garden I found two lovely camellias and an ornamental maple tree, which I suppose are really out of scale in a patio garden, but I would not dream of sacrificing them. In my case though there was no sign of dying back – dead wood as part of the tree or bush is probably a sign of this, unless a branch should have been damaged in a gale.

If the tree or shrub *is* dying back it should be replaced. Otherwise, if the tree is quite healthy and almost growing too well as in my case, give it a year or two and see how things go. It is extraordinary how cutting down mature trees and shrubs can alter a garden, taking away all its mystery and individuality and leaving an ordinary strip or back yard exposed.

Q We made a bit of money when we sold our old house and I have put a sum by for the garden. I would like to get it done and then leave it to a gardener to come in every now and then.

A There is nothing the professional gardener likes better than being given a free hand; readers of P.G. Wodehouse will remember Lord Emsworth's struggles with his gardener and they were most definitely founded on fact!

If you decide to make a clean sweep, or just to have a firm along to clear and trim where necessary, then you can plant any new things needed with their advice and they will bring them along when the time comes. The planting season is very near now and the end of September and beginning of October will see the spring bulbs and border perennials going in. Trees and shrubs follow in November so August is a good month to book a firm before everything gets busy. BUT FIND OUT FIRST IF THE FIRM KNOWS ITS JOB.

PROBLEMS ABOUT PROBLEMS

Q How do you find a good firm? I did go along to our local garden centre, but I wasn't very impressed with the advice I got.

A It is a little difficult just turning up at a garden centre or nursery. If you intend to give a big order such as we have been discussing, do not hesitate to ask for the owner and make an appointment with him if necessary. The nurseries to look out for are the ones which grow their own plants.

Q Supposing they don't do the kind of thing one wants though?

A If you have some definite plan in mind, for instance the sort of design we were thinking of at Chelsea, this is where the RHS comes in handy and I am sure they would be able to recommend a firm. If you just want the whole thing taken off your hands as far as planting goes and are content to let the nursery choose your plants for you, within reason, the boss will always advise and send his own people along to plant when the time comes. They will probably be able to come along at intervals and keep things tidy and replant if necessary. A reputable firm should replace anything which does not survive its first winter.

Anyone in the London area could write to the Royal Botanic Gardens at Kew; they have retired gardeners who will come and advise and possibly tend the garden when it is needed. For first-timers living further from London, the RHS Affiliated Societies welcome new members or there may be a garden club which you could join to make new friends and find out about the best landscape firms and nurseries in your area. There is nothing like a gardening friend's recommendation.

Q Anyone could take me for a ride as I know so little, hardly what to ask or suggest even.

A We have tried to deal with this problem in 'Clearing and Planning' earlier on in the year. As for being cheated, to speak plainly, it will be a sad day for all of us gardeners if growers become so commercialised as to rival the proverbial card-dealer (greatly maligned for all I know). For the real gardener-nurseryman it would go against the grain not to put his heart into a new garden, particularly if given a free hand. Don't forget though that everyone has different tastes and if you hate evergreens (the kind planted as windbreaks), or if rhododendrons remind you of school, you may feel that these are not horticultural reasons, but that should not stop you from saying you don't want them. Even the most dedicated plantsmen have their favourite plants which they may press on you, so don't be afraid to say so.

I have often noted how well plants do if supplied by and put in by professionals. They do know their stuff. The ideal is the sort of family firm which came out top in a recent survey, of a father and daughter who worked their own nursery and loved their plants.

Q I want to do as much as I can in my summer holiday.

A The amateur gardener is up against the sad fact that he has to work the garden in his time and not in its time. Wind and weather pay no attention to office hours or weekends and we have all been frustrated by a hopelessly wet Saturday and Sunday followed by a gloriously fine Monday. This must be another thing to understand and make allowance for from the start.

There are plenty of things one can get on with in the established garden in August, but for the new garden, if it is to be planted up more or less from scratch, August must be the month for planning and patience. "Time spent in reconnaissance is seldom if ever wasted" and August is when the catalogues come and we will have more to say about them later in the month. If you find your firm and book it, that is a tremendous step in the right direction and they may find jobs they can get on with right away.

SOME MORE BORDER PLANTS

We can continue to plant our imaginary mixed border which we started in June and July. The rest of the border plants can now be considered, for the majority of border perennials flower from the end of July until September and the frosts. Remembering that your border should have an open sunny aspect at least on one side, (backing onto a wall doesn't matter if not overhung by trees or large bushes), one can choose according to taste and the size of the border.

Aaron's Rod or Golden Rod – (Solidago)

The old-fashioned Aaron's rod is very easy to grow and may well be one of the plants surviving in an established but neglected garden. I was given 'bits' for my first garden and they remained until I left nearly thirty years later and were only just beginning to show signs of wearing out. Even the toughest plant grows tired in the end of being divided and the new 'bits' cease to form strong new plants, as they did when the parent was younger. Aaron's rod thrives on being left alone and does not need staking. Though not as tall as some things which grow at the back of the border, they do best if left there as they are rather late flowerers, but are very reliable and will go on for a month or so when they do come out. The modern varieties are much superior to the older kind, which were almost considered weeds as they were so easy and there is also a dwarf variety which might be useful for a narrower border, which would not want tall things at the back.

Q It doesn't look much like a rod to me.

A The flower is a yellow plume, not a straight rod, but I suppose one has to think of the rod when it has flowered.

Rudbeckia

This is the very tall coneflower, which also seems to survive anywhere and certainly needs no pampering. I am not sure if its yellow daisy flower, with the very prominent middle and not particularly exciting leaves, would appeal to everyone, but if you find it growing in the garden you can be sure that at least you will have something which always flowers, if rather late in the year.

Helenium

Another old-fashioned border standby is the daisy-flowered helenium. The colours are mainly pale yellow, dark yellow and bronze. If the latter is the older variety it will be taller and later than the other two. I do not name the variety as they keep on changing according to which firm is selling them, or perhaps as improved varieties come along. Garden centres will sell them by colour for the most part. They reach a height of about 3ft which is just right, as plants of this size are at their best grown in front of wall climbers. Taller border plants will get in their way and cause them to become 'leggy' as they reach for the light with all their flowers growing at the top.

Q Are there any unusual ones that are not difficult to grow?

A There are two I can think of which look unusual but are still easy to grow: achillea and acanthus.

Rudbeckia
A plant which does not need pampering

Achillea

This is the tall plant with the spectacular flat yellow heads and feathery leaves and is a cousin of the yarrow we dig out of the lawn. In the catalogue there is one given as only 2ft so that might be useful, but I feel it is partly the height which makes this plant such an ornament in the later border.

Acanthus

Acanthus have beautiful classical-looking leaves, (you can see them decorating gilt mirrors of the Chippendale period) and tall spikes of purple and white flowers. *A. mollis* is known as bear's breeches. *A. spinosus* has longer spinier leaves.

Heliopsis

It is very easy to confuse the two names heliopsis and helenium. Most people, particularly the 'daisyphobes', would prefer the heliopsis as it has a double yellow flower and hardly looks like a daisy, but it is tall and therefore less easy to fit into the general scheme unless there are other tall plants to go with it. It has always been one of my favourites and worth fitting in if possible.

Here are three more confusing names in the border: echinops, eryngium and erigeron.

The Globe Thistle – Echinops

As the name implies, the border echinops has a round not a thistle-shaped flower and is rather an unusual shade of blue-grey, which holds its colour well when dried. It is very easy to grow and is a tall plant for the back of the border. Even the English name is a bit confusing, for the globe artichoke is the one where the edible part is at the base of the spiky 'leaves' of the bud, which will turn into a large thistle flower if left alone.

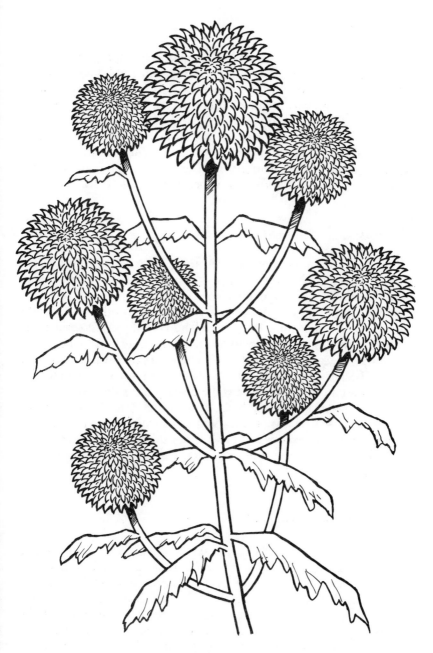

The Globe Thistle – Echinops

Eryngium

The eryngium is the sea holly. I bought this for my first garden thinking it was the globe thistle. It was not until I saw the sea holly growing wild on the beaches of Brittany that I realised why my plant was so much more exotic than I had remembered. It did not do so well when the house was built beside us, as it needs air and sun such as it gets nearer the seaside, but it is not all that difficult to grow. This is the cultivated border one of course and from memory mine was fairly tall at about 3½ft and was probably *E. giganteum*, which is listed as 3–4ft.

Erigeron

It is the most unexpected of the three and looks like an early Michaelmas daisy with its mauve flowers and so completely unlike the other two. I only include it to clarify the name, as it seems to me that one has had enough of daisies in the border particularly as the real Michaelmas daisies will be coming in September. If however the first-timer should feel differently, they like a light soil.

Simply because of its name I include **Erythronium**, which is not a border plant at all, but liable to get mixed up with the other three in one's mind. It is the dog's tooth violet, *E. dens-canis* and is a very pretty spring bulb. It needs the special conditions of moist peat and plenty of sun, neither of which I have ever gardened with, but growers tell me it is not difficult in the right soil.

Before we leave the August border, here are two plants for the front: geranium and nepeta.

Geranium – (Cranesbill)

After saying more than once that the bedding geranium is a zonal pelargonium, here is the true geranium, the hardy cranesbill. They flower in the summer over a long period, making bushy plants which might be as much as 2ft high, but they are for the front of the border because of their shape. More or less unstakable, they are leaners and like an edge to rest on; the variety *G. endressi* 'Wargrave Pink' is the most floppy. I should choose the blue *G. ibericum*.

Catmint – (Nepeta)

The most usual garden one is *N. mussini* and is another leaner which likes to sprawl over a sunny edging stone. Given sun it is not difficult to grow and has a pleasant aromatic smell, not exactly mint but fairly strong. Cats do like it as they enjoy the springy feel of the layers of mauve flowering sprays and of course the sun, but the plant (usually) comes to no harm. If the drainage is not perfect, catmint tends to disappear after a wet winter.

Q I have two fairly small plants at the edge of my border, but they are just leaves at the moment. One looks rather uncommon with heart-shaped leaves, the other has very fleshy leaves and is beginning to have buds.

A Doronicum and sedum; you could have added a third, the dwarf edging Michaelmas daisy and they would all have been in my first garden.

Doronicum plantagineum

This is the one with the heart-shaped leaves and is a very useful little plant which fills in the gap between the early and later spring bulbs. Even when the flowers are over it leaves neat attractive bright green leaves behind, as you have discovered. It has what I think of as very pretty yellow daisy-like flowers, but the 'daisyphobe' in my home disagrees and thinks them boring. The English name is leopard's bane, another which I have never come across outside a book.

Sedum

The sedums are the water-storing family with the juicy-looking leaves. The one often seen in gardens is the variety 'Autumn Joy'. Though listed as flowering from August to September, it is much more likely to be September or even later in a bad summer, especially in a town garden, so don't rely on it for the summer display.

Otherwise, it is a pretty neat-growing plant with pale green leaves which gives it its common name of the ice plant. When the flowers do come, they are a feathery pinky-mauve and make a good show much loved by butterflies.

Q My garden is nothing like big enough to take all those plants, particularly as the little borders are so narrow.

A I do think any kind of an herbaceous border should be wide enough to take three rows; either tall plants or something growing up a wall or fence, with middle-sized plants in front and then the edging plants. From memory my first borders must have been all of 4ft wide.

There are plenty of other ways with narrow beds, as we have seen and I have spent time with the border plants these last two months, principally because they are the 'herbaceous' months along with September, when most of the border perennials are flowering. Although these plants are coming back into fashion, they still make a lot of work and the first-timer must experiment for himself, which is half the fun, and not feel like a murderer if he has to get rid of some of them to save time and energy. Gardening is nothing if it is not a pleasure.

The 'rhizome' Iris

These are the flag and bearded irises. The rhizome is the swollen stem on the surface which looks like a root and the sun needs to get at it for the plant to produce flowers. These irises are perennials and can be divided to increase them and keep them in good heart and now is the time to do it. Flowering time is late spring and early summer, but the buds will have already formed and it is important to know how to look out for them.

Q I thought the spring ones were bulbs.

A The Spanish and Dutch irises are bulbs and very pretty, but unfortunately they do not always flower and I would not recommend them to the first-timer. The same applies to the little rock iris, *I. reticulata*, which can be a lovely sight in the early spring coming almost with the snowdrops, but it can fail to come up at all let alone flower.

The other kind of rockery iris (to make a distinction) is just a mini-rhizome, but is not too easy to grow as it needs more sun and a better soil than the two bigger ones. The reader might have seen the wild version growing amongst the ruins at Sunion, near Athens.

Q My bearded irises never flowered after the first year, then after a year or two they suddenly flowered again, but they had gone back to being purple. They aren't much to look at once they have flowered, so I am thinking of getting rid of them.

A Yes, they do tend to revert in this way and depending on the soil and situation they either, go back to purple (town soil on the shady side), or to yellow (country on chalk). The ones which seem to stay best are, the shortish pale blue varieties, the tall brown-yellow and the rare white, 'Gudrun'. The latter never backslid in my garden, but went a little mauve when it moved to a garden in Earls Court. In the same way, my yellow which refused to flower at all, flourished with bright yellow flowers in a sunny Fulham garden.

A sunless summer can stop them flowering the next year and they can flower badly if they need dividing, as the older rhizomes rot and the whole clump deteriorates, particularly in the middle. Giving a sprinkling of lime and bonemeal after flowering or after they should have flowered, is a good tip which I was given.

Q What about reverting? Though they are still very handsome even when all purple, I would like them to stay as they were at first.

A They have been brought on by the skills of the professional grower to produce a certain colour or combination of colours, but it is their nature to backslide in this way and one can only experiment and see which ones stay the course the best and increase them. They are very long-lived and can be divided more or less indefinitely.

The thing in a small garden is not to have too many, keep the ones that do well and when they are over hide the 'iris garden' with a later bush or plant. A slanting tree such as I found growing made a natural break. Unlike daffodils they can have their leaves neatly cut back and besides looking tidy it does no harm.

Q How can I tell which kind of iris I have? The leaves all look the same.

A I don't think there is any way of telling at this time of year. The flag irises in my present garden don't look any different from my old bearded ones, as far as I can see.

Q What is the difference?

A The flag iris is earlier than the bearded iris. They are not difficult to grow if they like the situation and need no attention unless to divide them occasionally. I think of them as the same kind of plant as the Madonna lily and the cottage paeony; where they do grow, they grow like weeds with minimum attention, but they will fail if there is something they dislike and that is usually lack of sun.

The bearded iris is the 'posh' one with the bright colours and usually taller than the flag iris. When the petals open the 'beard' can be seen as a fluffy bit down the middle of the petal, often in a contrasting colour. They flower at the end of May, a very good time as there is often very little else to be seen.

Q It therefore makes it all the more annoying when they don't flower.

A Certainly, if a variety hasn't flowered after two years, I should discard it and divide the others, which are hopefully flowering. A sunny summer is a help for the next year, but of course it can't be ordered! Add a little Sulphate of Potash to their lime and bone-meal.

DIVIDING THE RHIZOMES

Q How do I know if they need dividing?

A The rhizomes will go underground when the plant is growing – only the older ones will be on the surface – then suddenly iris leaves appear right outside the clump where they were planted, perhaps getting in the way of other things. The original clump may be all right on the outside but a mass of roots, that is rhizomes, in the middle, some of which may have rotted. The idea is either, to dig up the ones which have strayed and plant them elsewhere, or to dig up the whole clump if it seems to be going off and divide it, discarding the old rhizomes and keeping the new.

Q How should I separate them? I am not sure I should know which ones to keep.

A If we are digging up the whole clump, pull the outside plants gently from the old plant. Sometimes they come right away almost without trying and sometimes they will break away, but that does no harm. The ones to keep are the ones with a white swelling at the join of the leaves with the rhizome and these will flower next year. Do not start dividing until the swellings can be seen.

PLANTING

You will already have found that the ground can't be got at when the clump has a mass of rhizomes in the centre, so before planting, the ground should be dug well and the opportunity taken to add a sprinkling of lime and bonemeal. Leave enough time to do this when planting, as the less the plants are kept hanging about the better.

Once the soil is prepared, raise it slightly above the level of the bed where you mean to plant. Then plant the new pieces as you would any other plant. You will see the true roots hanging from the rhizome, cover them rhizome and all, with an inch or so of soil. Get them in firmly and a day or two later brush the soil away from the rhizomes, so that the sun can get to them. If you try to bury them only as deep as the true roots it is very difficult to get the plant in firmly, it tends to fall over and be very awkward. Shortening the leaves first is a help.

Q Should I water them?

A Not a bad idea for the first day or two. In a hot summer wait for a shower before dividing and avoid the heat of the day. If it should be a really hot summer one can wait right up to October.

WATERING

Q I never know when to water and when not. I don't have much time actually.

A For the most part, a large garden has to look after itself in a really hot dry summer, it is impossible to water enough to take the place of rain. Though the plants will look very sad and droopy, they should recover in the winter and may be all the better for the sun the previous year.

Town gardens benefit most from watering both on the soil and on the leaves, because the pollution will be much greater in dry weather.

A lawn needs a fixed hose with the kind of sprinkler that can be left on and moved about. It naturally means an increased water rate, but I would say it was worth it. If any Q should be reading this during a hot and dry summer, perhaps having been forbidden to use the hose, do not despair at the brown lawn, which is possibly bare in places, as it will recover in the most amazing way. In fact a hot summer is like a cold winter in that way. One says goodbye mentally to nearly all the plants which are looking so miserable and it is an added pleasure to find that ten to one they have been reprieved.

After the exceptionally hot and dry summer of 1976 we had one or two thunderstorms in London in September and the grass in the park went green literally overnight – I would not have believed it had I not seen it.

Occasionally one gets a dry winter, perhaps without even snow to bring the moisture and the grass won't grow until the spring. Sow grass seed to cover the bare patches and protect well with netting, as there is nothing that sparrows and birds in general like more than grass seed. You can now get treated seeds which are 'bird-proof' and seem to work. The time for turfing, strangely enough, is right in the middle of winter (January or February).

EXCEPTIONS

We have been speaking of the exceptionally hot and dry summer, but what about a dry spell that comes just as you have put some young plants in? As we said at the time of planting, if there has been no rain in the 24 hours, water for a fortnight. Always use a can and not a hose which is rather too strong. A border will benefit from a hosing in the evening if the rain has not fallen for about a fortnight. There is no need to begin watering too soon in the year, as you will bring the roots up to the surface where they can be burned in the hot sun and this can do real damage. Constant light watering which only wets the surface, encourages a sort of webbing of fibrous roots and the plants can never seem to have enough water for the mass soaks it up like a sponge – containers are the worst for this. So the rule is, ALWAYS either give a good soaking or leave well alone.

Many firms now print warnings on bags of peat to say that it is essential to soak the peat really well before adding it to the soil or container, otherwise it acts like a mat taking the water up and the poor plant gets nothing.

There are one or two shrubs which suffer in the dry weather, though most can look after themselves. Camellias which can start dropping leaves in a drought like a bucket or two of water after dry windy weather. Once you start though you must go on, as the roots want to be encouraged to stay down deep looking for water and it mustn't be just a surface trickle.

Evergreen azaleas can be lost in a very dry summer, but there is a snag here as they loathe the lime in the hard town water, so without a water-butt or softened water, it would really be the lesser of two evils to leave them unwatered.

Needless to say, it is rather hard work humping cans about and a hose in a garden of any size is a must in spite of the increased rate. A good guide is to see the water lying on the bed after you have finished watering. One has no need to do all the garden all the time; most shady or half-shaded bits will only need water in a hot summer and will survive the occasional dry spell. If the water pressure is high and plants seem to be getting battered by the hose, you will probably find the nozzle can be adjusted, by turning it to produce a finer and more gentle spray.

Gardeners of the old school like my father rather disapproved of watering in general. Gardens were much bigger in those days and he was convinced that most people did more harm than good by watering too early in the season and thereby having to go on all through the summer – summers seemed to be hotter then. The exception was his lawn part of which was a grass tennis court and which he watered religiously, so keeping it green was not just for looks.

CONTAINERS

With the best will in the world, it is impossible not to let containers get dry sometimes. For instance, you may have been on holiday with no one to look after them. When you first water, give them a whole can and pay no attention if the water runs out at the bottom, as it will take a little while before the earth is damp enough to take up the water. Leave for a short time and then give another can, the container will leak less and should be better still the next day. The disastrous thing is to think that the water running out means that the tub has had enough. In hotter drier climates, the rain when it comes runs away in the same way, often sadly to waste.

Q I know that it is like that with peat, you have to go on and on watering, but I did think when it ran out at the bottom it had had enough.

A If your container has not got too dry, you can scrape a bit of soil away and see what it is like underneath. You will not find the water runs through so quickly and the compost is absorbing the moisture. It is the time it takes and the amount which runs through which counts. Water lying on the surface and only seeping through very slowly is the best sign.

Q I have some hydrangeas and I do hate to see them wilt, but I have noticed that they pick up again in the cool of the evening.

A I have noticed the same thing, it seems that the flowers will always wilt if a hot sun is directly on them. They do pick up, but if the leaves droop too, they can do with a bucket or two of water when the sun goes down.

In our climate there is a certain element of gambling. Will it rain in time to pick the things up or not? Probably it will, but your time has not been wasted, as the softened earth will let the rain penetrate better. Later on in the year we have a section on weather, with the idea of being able to forecast rain as far as that can ever be done.

SOME RANDOM THOUGHTS ON A HOT SUMMER

Apart from watering, I have been caught out in other ways. In my first garden, the Japanese anemones at the shady end of our North facing garden, together with a mass of michaelmas daisies gone wild at the other end, were about the only plants to have survived the war. The anemones like real shade and in the very hot summer of 1947 they put out huge leaves to shade their roots, which are shallow, though so tough. I thought they looked untidy and in cutting them off very nearly succeeded where Hitler had failed. They did survive, but only just and I learned a lesson. They are strange plants, very difficult to start off, but once there nothing will dislodge them.

My next mistake was in 'pricking out' little seedlings. I had seen my mother handle tiny plants in the sandy soil of her Thames Valley garden and when I attempted to do the same thing in the gravel and grit of my own garden, they failed dismally. In general plants need to be well on before planting out in town gardens and in a hot summer it is very difficult to grow anything from small beginnings. I would always go for pot-grown plants which can stand sun.

Of course another side to hot summers is that one is persuaded that the climate has suddenly changed. In my case, having always heard people grumbling about the heat of the city when it was too hot to sit outside in July and August, I thought it would always be so, only to find that in the next year it was too cold and windy. That summer I planted chrysanthemums and fuchsias which were out fully by early September, only to see them hang back until November the next year!

Q What a lot there is to know.

A Yes, and I wish I knew the half of it. Luckily Q's will have access to plenty of books giving them much more detailed and expert knowledge. I am just trying to fill in a few gaps on the way through the year.

Another thought that comes to mind and which didn't help the young plants either, was giving them unrotted stable manure (courtesy of the milkman's pony in those days), which of course was much too strong and everything was scorched. Looking back I can't think how I ever got going at all, but I lived to see people admiring my garden and thinking I knew something about it.

Q Is farmyard manure dangerous then?

A Only when it is too fresh – real farmyard manure needs to rot down. It needs a bit of experience, as does liquid manure made of the real stuff, to make sure it is not too strong. The composted manure is already rotted down and is quite safe. What one doesn't realise in one's first garden is that it is a source of warmth as well as nourishment and probably in a cooler drying summer my manuring would not have been so disastrous.

One can put it round tender plants for warmth in the winter, but if it is used for roses, it should be dug in and not left to lie on the surface. For as I have already mentioned leaf disease, particularly Black Spot, leaves spores in the ground which can be encouraged by mulching or leaving the compost on the surface.

SOME RANDOM THOUGHTS ON A WET SUMMER

Just about the only consolation is that one doesn't have to water. Look out for mildew on roses which wet conditions encourage and oddly enough so do dry conditions. The maddening part of a wet summer when time is limited, is trying to find a dry spell, when it is not sunny or windy, for the spray not to be washed off by a heavy shower. An hour is enough to let the spray dry and it is worth doing because mildew weakens the plant and leads to leaf disease.

Q The roses are just coming into their second flowering but some have rotted in the bud. Just as they should be coming out they go brown and the petals fall off, have they got some disease?
A No, it is most probably the wet weather and disappointing though it is, we may have a fine September and the roses will re- cover and may flower until the frosts. A very fine autumn can quite often follow a bad summer.

Then there are the plants we take for granted which flourish in towns. Flowering shrubs and trees in the spring and early summer; real forest trees in the parks and streets; all these depend on the plentiful supply of rain which they get in the average year. Most of all perhaps we take the green grass as a matter of course. A hot dry summer will turn it brown in no time.

THE BULB CATALOGUE – PLANNING FOR THE SPRING

Anyone arriving in a house in August which has been lived in before, may well find bulb catalogues arriving for the previous owner. Hang on to these, even if you don't necessarily mean to order anything at once. Catalogues are a tremendous help as a reference for the different kinds of bulbs and with their marvel- lous colour photographs will help you to choose for the spring dis- play.

Allow a bit for wishful thinking (it is the grower's business though our hobby) and stick to easy bulbs at first, remembering what we said about aspect; nearly everything likes some sun in the day and an open situation. 'Open' does not mean draughty though and in towns one has to beware of wind funnelling down passageways. Remember if there is a draughty corner in the garden where you would not care to sit, your plants will not like it either.

Of course colour photography is not exact as we all know from holiday photographs, so allow particularly for differences in 'blues'. Some really blue flowers can come out quite wishy- washy or nearly mauve and you may easily find different tones of the same flower in different catalogues, according to the colour process. Other colours are pretty reliable, although red is a bit chancy but not as bad as blue.
Q Can I buy from the shops in August?

A Unfortunately the bulbs are not ready until late August or early September as a rule; like other things it depends on the weather, then they have to be packed and sent out to the different firms. Some are English, from the fields in Lincolnshire, but the majority are still imported from Holland. Start looking in the shops about mid-September or order now by post and they will probably come by the end of that month.

Gardening friends will undoubtedly recommend their favourite firms. The two firms I go to at present are Walter Blom & Son Limited of Milton Ernest, Bedford and J. Parker Dutch Bulbs Limited of Old Trafford, Manchester. Blom's specialise in tulips and are fairly expensive, but they are reliable for all bulbs and their giant daffodils are all exhibition size. They are costly if ordered in large quantities, but in a small garden like mine, ten of Blom's daffodils make a marvellous show if planted in a group near the house. There is an enormous choice. While on the subject of expense, it is encouraging for the first-timer to know that a daffodil like '**King Alfred**' which has been going some time, is cheaper than other varieties, simply because it has proved successful and easy to propagate; the easier to grow the less expensive the bulb will be.

Q I bought some special ones in the bulb fields which were terribly expensive and none of them even came up.

A Many amateur gardeners have had the same experience. We have to wait until the bulbs have been proven and the new exclusive ones are for the expert.

Though not 'cheap and nasty', J. Parker are much cheaper and operate more on a wholesale basis and as they say themselves, they save money by not having such an elaborate catalogue. Of course the choice is limited and one has to buy in larger quantities.

Beginning a garden with no plants in it at all is bound to be an expense and even with presents from friends, the reader may well be daunted at the high cost of postage and packing. Carriage etc is usually free for an order round about £30. However, if funds will run, I should not consider an order of £30 excessive in a garden of any size. Small bulbs like crocuses go nowhere and if planted in grass or round a tree a hundred is just a handful if seen from any distance.

Q What about planting daffodils in grass?

A The collections sold for 'naturalising' are very good value from both firms and though they choose the varieties, they can usually be trusted in what they send. If the first-timer wants a show for his front garden, where every bloom shows up, I should always go for the named collections and get say five each of five different varieties. You can see pictures of them in the catalogue and therefore will know exactly what you are getting. The more expensive the collection, the bigger the bloom, otherwise there is little to choose between the two firms. Both are recommended by the RHS by the way.

Q When should I order Christmas bulbs?

A As soon as possible. They should *arrive* by the end of September, but be prepared with bowls and bulb fibre for them if they arrive earlier, for they should be planted at once. If "specially prepared", this is even more important, because the bulbs have been refrigerated in order to persuade them that they have been through the winter and to think that Christmas is their normal spring-flowering time. Get them in the bowls and into the dark before they find out their mistake, as making roots is the important bit.

We will be going more fully into planting indoor bulbs in September.

Q To tell the truth, I meant the Christmas bulbs you plant outside.

A The ones labelled "for Christmas" or something of the kind, are meant for indoors. In a very mild winter, such as 1988–89, the early-flowering ones might be out by Christmas but it is very rare.

If you want your outdoor bulbs specially early, choose a sheltered sunny spot if you can. The early ones I plant at the sunny end of my North-facing rockery, are still firmly in bud when the identical kind is flowering away in my neighbour's sunny South-facing front garden. For planting outdoors I should try '**Paper White**', a bunch-flowered narcissus, which might be flowering by Christmas if planted by the end of September but a cold spell in November or December will hold it back.

'**Soleil d'Or**', a deep yellow and again bunch-flowered and '**Cragford**', which is white with an orange centre, are the other two narcissi most often recommended for pot-growing and though early are not certain for Christmas. 'Soleil d'Or' if planted outside is out in late February or early March, whilst 'Cragford' is later and more in line with *N. poeticus*, which is the sweet-scented single narcissi. The drawback of the bunch-flowered narcissi outdoors is that they tend to look leggy and are really best in bowls, particularly as all three are sweet-scented. ·

Q I am never lucky with 'Cragford' indoors.

A They are extremely reliable, but not for Christmas. I am sure much of the trouble comes from trying to hurry them on, as outside they flower quite a bit later as we have seen.

Some of the smaller trumpet daffodils are early; **'February Gold'** is a great general favourite and **'Peeping Tom'** has an attractive shape something like a cyclamen.

Do not be carried away by the coloured photographs of more difficult flowers such as freesias or lily-of-the-valley, which are forced (brought on early in pots). I am reminded of my early failures with both of these, when bulbs weren't nearly so expensive. Narcissi are not difficult but it is absolutely essential not to bring them into the warmth of the house, let alone a warm living-room, until they are nearly out and this takes a bit of practise – tulips are the same. For the first-timer I recommend hyacinths for growing indoors.

HYACINTHS FOR BOWLS

When ordering from a catalogue, the first-timer may be a little puzzled when trying to sort out the hyacinths. He may find the same varieties on later pages in the catalogue, offered more cheaply. The ones which have been specially prepared to flower at Christmas will be the more expensive, though the ones shown later are exactly the same quality, but have not been prepared to flower specially early. Even so, if the hyacinths are planted in bowls, they will be out in January/February and therefore much earlier than those outside. Choose the hyacinths recommended for "bowl culture" as not all are suitable for bowls.

A good indoor choice for flowering at Christmas is **'Rosalie'**. They are rather expensive, but five is enough for a smallish bowl of say 8ins across. They are pink Roman hyacinths, rather smaller than the usual hyacinth, but guaranteed to flower early and quite often have a second flower. 'Rosalie' are so reliable for Christmas that in a warm autumn they might have to be held back a little – in a cool sunny room if possible – before bringing them into the full warmth.

The earliest flowering hyacinths of the usual kind are white, then come blue, then pink. Do not buy the "exhibition" size, they are a nuisance indoors and out, as they flop and have to be staked; the "first-size" is quite big enough.

'L'Innocence' was the favourite white, but that too had a year or two when the flowers inexplicably got the 'bends', growing into strange shapes and are only just recovering. The blue ones I should recommend are **'Ostara'** or **'Delft Blue'**. **'King of the Blues'** is a marvellous strain but not always easy to obtain.

Pink are more difficult especially the reddish ones, which have a way of flowering low down in the leaves with hardly any stalk, which is maddening. Again it is a matter of knowing just when to bring them on and the first-timer is often very worried by it. If 'Rosalie' shows any signs of 'low-flowering' don't worry for they catch up in the end and the stalk will appear just in time. If the first-timer should be particularly fond of pink, **'Lady Derby'** is an easy one. Yellow and mauve are uncommon colours in a hyacinth and therefore more difficult. This too is the case with all unusual colours in any plant.

OUTDOOR HYACINTHS

Any of the hyacinths in the catalogue will grow outside, except the specially prepared ones. Hyacinthella hyacinths are midway in size between the Roman and the ordinary size, such as are sold for bowls. They come in an unusually good selection of colours which blend well together and a collection of these is very good value.

Tulips

There is a bewildering choice of tulips. The different kinds and times of flowering are well explained in the catalogue, but even so it is a help to know a few well-tried names.

Early single tulips are expensive, but a few planted amongst the earlier kind of daffodils look well and are worth the money. **'Brilliant Star'** is a favourite, a true red and reliably early. **'Keizerskroon'** is a very spectacular red and yellow which looks best on its own. It is early in a sunny spot, but can hang back in a shadier garden as mine have done. **'Peach Blossom'** is an early deep pink double tulip. It used to be my favourite but suffered a sad decline in the way of other overworked varieties, though has appeared again recently.

The species tulips with striped leaves are usually seen in the rockery. '**Red Riding Hood**' has a slightly larger flower than most of this kind and is a good choice in every way; easy to grow, with a pretty flower, shaped something like a lily-flowered tulip and with attractive striped leaves. They will flower quite reliably in their second year, which is not always the case nowadays.

'**Apricot Beauty**' is a most unusual early tulip and its cup-shaped flowers are more like the shorter May-flowering tulips. It too should be planted on its own and if possible where the light can shine through it and show off the delicate apricot-pink colour.

The later tulips, usually coming out towards the end of April, are the cottage tulips and like the taller later Darwin I prefer them on their own. These shorter-stalked tulips are best for an exposed windy garden. '**Spring Green**' which is green and creamy white and the mauve '**Shirley**' come into this category and will take over when the daffodils and hyacinths are fading. The lily-flowered tulips are of medium height, flowering about the same time. Of these I grew '**China Pink**' and '**White Triumphator**' most successfully in my first garden and '**Marilyn**', a striped white and strawberry red, is in the tubs in my present garden. A mixture of these lily-flowers is good because they flower over a longer period and their unusual looks are always admired.

The May flowering (or Darwin) tulips and the Darwin hybrids cannot be beaten as a show in the garden. If one was feeling really extravagant, a large flower-bed filled with these – rightly called majestic in the catalogue – would be the pride of any first-timer. Before he wastes his money though, we must say that Darwins or any similar tall tulip, must have light and sun or they will not stand up properly. They are late-flowering and are sometimes not finished by the end of May, which makes difficulties when wanting to replace them with the summer bedding plants.

Like roses, the old favourites in the Darwin tulips still go on and are still worth growing. '**Clara Butt**', the lovely pink which is planted with the forget-me-nots; '**Bleu Aimable**', another 'blue' which is a pretty mauve.

In a really large bed, a mixed collection of Darwins or Darwin hybrids would look very well and be less expensive bought this way – there is a big reduction on 50 bulbs, often almost half price.

Q My favourites are the parrot tulips, but I haven't seen many
of them lately. Can I still buy them?

A They do still appear in the bulb catalogue, but they do seem
to have gone out of favour; perhaps because they are inclined to
be floppy and easily spoiled by rough weather, which is the reason
I haven't mentioned them before.

Q I like their strange colours and the way they look different
from the ordinary tulip, which one sees plenty of in parks and
public gardens.

A What about '**Queen of the Night**'? To be found amongst
the Darwin or May flowerers, is nearly black and very striking –
when the light shines through the colour is a deep intense
purple; too sombre for some tastes, but a favourite of mine.

Then amongst the earlier *Viridiflora* tulips there are '**Artist**'
(green and pink) or '**Hummingbird**' (green and yellow). For
the later ones, the Rembrandt '**Union Jack**', cream and rich rasp-
berry red, is very effective and easy to grow. Another striking
Rembrandt tulip is '**San Marino**', red and yellow, a later and
taller version of 'Kaiserkroon'. Slightly more feathery and worth
risking is '**Fantasy**', a deep pink, which is a parrot tulip.

I have expanded a little on the unusual and striking tulips, no
more difficult to grow than any others, because so many Q's
suffer from feelings of inferiority about their gardens which are
totally unjustified. Go to a good bulb firm and your garden can
be as good as anyone else's.

Daffodils and Narcissi

We have already agreed to call daffodils the ones with the long
trumpet and narcissi the scented ones with the frilly cup. On reading the catalogue, the first-timer will find a great number of the
large-cupped narcissi. These are favoured because of their perfect
form with beautifully regular petals making an ideal frame for the
centres, much to our admiration as well as the bees'. From a practical point of view, I have found this category the best for going on
from year to year without deteriorating and if they do come up a
second year, it is always with a flower.

'**Soleil D'Or**', '**Paper White**', '**Tete-a-Tete**' and '**Minnow**'
are miniature daffodils for the rockery. Really tiny and almost fit
for bowls in the doll's house are **Minimus** or *N. asturiensis*. The

minute bulbs are fairly expensive but not difficult if not planted too deep. Plant them where they can be seen close-to and you will be rewarded by a doll's daffodil, trumpet and all.

Two more for the Alpine House and not for us are **N. triandus albus**, 'Angel's Tears' and the mis-named **N. bulbocodium conspicuus**. I know many expert amateur gardeners and not one has succeeded with either of these in the garden.

I visited the bulbfields with a great expert of long experience and I am afraid we were both delighted, amongst the splendours of the Keukenhof Park in Holland, to see the wretched little 'inconspicuus' doing its usual trick of producing a few spindly leaves and a bare patch where others should have been. To be fair, the Dutch growers had achieved one flower, which was more than we ever had, but that was rather a dreary little wind-sock shape and I only mention it because, along with 'Angel's Tears', it is so written up in the catalogues.

Daffodils and narcissi are remarkably tough when one thinks of the kind of spring weather they usually have to contend with – often indistinguishable from winter – and the only advice I would give is not to buy anything too expensive. It is quite safe to go by the pictures and to buy what you prefer, keeping an eye on the time they are coming into flower – mostly the end of March and into April, with the poetaz narcissi at the end. Pink narcissi and daffodils are no longer such a novelty and should not be too expensive. Do not be disappointed if they are orange to start off with (the pink bit is in the centre), they will turn quite a good pink in the end.

Q My mother used to grow 'Butter and Eggs', which I loved as a child.

A Yes, I remember them too. I suppose they were a kind of double narcissus; the cup was rather an untidy mixture of yellow and white, like a scrambled egg, hence the name. The old variety has gone as far as I can tell and the new double narcissi seems intended for shows and is very expensive.

'**Yellow Cheerfulness**' is pretty and has a double centre, like the older '**Cheerfulness**', but it is not what we mean.

Q The other one I never see which I remember is the **Jonquil**.

A They do exist and the old-fashioned one can be bought from the bulb catalogue and is always admired, but it has a habit of disappearing. I think it needs a fairly rich soil but is worth trying as it's not expensive.

SMALL BULBS

We have already come across crocuses for the rockery and edging and the smaller winter one is the species crocus. If one wants a crocus which is larger still, they will usually be described as 'jumbo size' and are intended for bowls indoors or for tubs or containers, but would be expensive if bought in large quantities. The best buy from any firm is a mixture of the large-flowering crocuses. Either get a mixture at random or ten of each variety, so that fifty will give you five distinct colours and you will know what you are getting. The latter naturally is more expensive than a 'collection' but is not too bad.

Grape Hyacinths – (Muscari)

These are another favourite and the 'Heavenly Blue' variety is the best value, but even for a small clump you will need at least 25.

Scilla – (Squill)

The little blue rockery flower is to be distinguished from the *Scilla nutons* which used to be the bluebell. **S. campanulata** now *Hyacinthoids hispanica*, is the cultivated coloured kind which you can get in pink and white as well as blue. For the small scilla, buy the **Scilla Siberica** and here again you will need 25 minimum.

The larger bluebell, the coloured kind, is rather a puzzle. It does not do all that well if planted from a bulb, but if one should seed itself in your garden it will increase all over the place as anyone will tell you.

It is entirely my own idea, but perhaps they are like snowdrops and should be lifted after flowering not kept as bulbs. I have no doubt that a friend who has a large number in his or her garden would be only too pleased to give away one or two clumps.

ADVANTAGES AND DISADVANTAGES OF ORDERING BY POST

After spending so long going through the catalogue, it seems only fair to point out some of the disadvantages of ordering by post.

We have already noted the high cost of postage and packing and alas, the postal service is not what it was and plants may be delayed on the way. When filling in the form, there is usually a section which says something like "special instructions". This is not for some learned comment only known to 'real' gardeners as I used to think, but a chance to say "not before the end of September" or "not at weekends", or whatever is useful to you and will prevent the parcels coming when you are away.

For a busy person however it is a great advantage to be able to order all the bulbs for the first garden without stirring from the house.

Q It needs a lot of thinking out.

A Why not take the catalogues away with you on holiday, I often do. One can get absolutely cross-eyed filling in these forms and a holiday provides some leisure and you will return with the form all ready to send. The sooner the better as orders are taken in rotation, but mid-September I have always found early enough.

TAKING CUTTINGS

Q I think taking cuttings would be quite beyond me, I am looking for something trouble-free.

A Cuttings are a sort of postscript to the month. It is usually the one recommended when plants will be mature and settled in, but still with plenty of new growth and not yet going over.

It would be absurd to expect someone who had just moved house to start taking cuttings, apart from the busy time in the house, there might not be much in the garden to take cuttings from. Equally, when the second garden is the holiday home, for many people the less to do the better. For the first-timer who has already been bitten by the (imaginary) garden bug, the second or third year will find him thinking how to get over the expense of bedding plants and wanting to feel like a 'real' gardener.

Also, there are the accidental cuttings. You might have used some hardy fuchsia prunings to stake difficult plants like carnations, only to find that left in the ground they are producing little shoots the next spring. I have already related how easy it is to break off the brittle new shoots of geraniums and it is the

AUGUST

work of a moment to put these in a jar of water on the kitchen window-sill (do not include ones with flower buds) and they will soon grow roots.

Garden pinks, the small relations of the carnation, are very easily rooted. In this case they are not so brittle and you will have to cut the little new tuft away from the parent stem; leave an inch or so of stem on the cutting and plant straight into a pot. The compost should be very light and if your own soil is sandy, mix it with a little seed compost and don't forget to water well.

The second stage is the tricky bit; the little roots look so strong and healthy and the leaves so cheerful, that it is a great disappointment to see them wilting once they have been transplanted. What they need is a gentle feeding tonic such as weak Liquinure which is what I use. I have no doubt though that a plant-tab of Phostrogen would do the trick and the tablets last from four to six weeks, which would be less trouble. Once the plants show signs of making new growth, the worst is over and they will be ready to plant out next year after the frosts, hopefully having made nice bushy little plants. If they are well grown but a little leggy, 'stop' them by pinching the top shoot off and this will encourage side shoots.

Pinks can be taken a little earlier and the pots can be left outside in a sheltered place, but keep an eye on them and water if at all dry. It is really the constant attention the little cuttings need, rather than actual skill, that is against 'striking' cuttings as it is called. Geraniums will need to be kept in a frost-proof fairly warm atmosphere, but they do not like too much heat. A verandah or similar is ideal in the winter.

THE COOL GREENHOUSE

Q We have found a little greenhouse in our new garden, but it is in a terrible state.
A It is very sad, so many greenhouses get neglected and then are beyond saving. The concrete base or foundation is expensive to make and pulling down the old house and putting a new one on the old foundation would be the cheapest way in the long run.

Of course the cool greenhouse is the best way of bringing on seeds and cuttings. It usually only needs heat in the very coldest part of the winter and this can be by an oil stove, sold for the purpose.

I only know the cool greenhouse from friends' gardens, but all are encouraging and say they are much simpler than they had imagined. They must be kept really clean and sprayed every now and then with disinfectant sold for the purpose. Put the plants under the benches for safety when you do this, but obviously the best time is when they have been planted out for the summer and you can really get at the little house.

The Chelsea Flower Show is the place to look for one, or 'small ads' in the gardening magazines.

TENDING THE AUGUST GARDEN

We were speaking of holidays and the idea is that August should be restful in the garden, so think ahead; stake your border, if any; plant out your bedding plants (early and late) in good time and leave the garden to get on with it. Keep the weeds down, but this is not the time when they are at their worst and the same applies to cutting the lawn, with any luck. Most plants have finished their main growth by now. Have a rest and enjoy your garden, for the busiest time is upon us!

September, a beautiful Autumn month, will be the end of the school holidays and probably the beginning of the end of a long stay at the 'second home'. In a dry year the leaves are beginning to fall and there will be a general tidying-up feeling. We do not want to spoil the last of summer by having too much to do in this way and as far as plants go, once they are staked they should not need any attention apart from the occasional dead-heading. In a wet year the weeds may have got out of hand and the lawn will still need cutting, but it is not nearly as impor-tant to get at all this as it is in the spring. The plants have made their growth and the time is not far off when they will begin to die down of their own accord; also, hopefully, the results of good plan-ning earlier will be bearing fruit – some literally. The dew at this time of year is heavy and saves watering leaves and also helps the grass to stay green.

Let us think of tending the garden and some later plants before going on to the actual planting which is now so near.

THE COUNTRY OR HOLIDAY GARDEN

You will have been there through the summer and can enjoy the early autumn without too much to do. It is worthwhile having **Chrysanthemums** and **Michaelmas Daisies** together with shrubs which have colourful berries such as **Cotoneaster**, **Berberis** or **Pyracantha**. All these will soon be making a show which is just when you want them, as the summer border plants are beginning to look past their best. Of course **Dahlias** are a great standby and are plants which like a wet summer.

None of the herbaceous or perennial border plants should be

244

cut down yet. Wait until the leaves are really dead (brown, withered and papery to touch) or you will injure the plant. Some people leave the dead leaves on all the winter to protect the plant from frost; if possible, for the weather can be difficult, I prefer to get the leaves cut down and a little mulch dug in. Use composted leaf-mould or well-rotted manure if available, but do not leave it lying on top of the ground for it harbours pests and causes diseases. Autumn weather can be very awkward for people with limited time and we will go into this more fully in October.

If you have been on holiday, the only job I would call at all urgent when you return to the garden is to look straightaway to see if any pests have got a hold while your back has been turned. It is no trouble to attack at once with Derris powder and one can leave the spraying (if necessary) until later on.

Very recently I returned after an unexpectedly dry spell to find the balcony window-box, which had looked so promising with its ivy-leaved geraniums a mass of buds only a fortnight before, now a mass of dry and yellowing leaves. I drenched it in Derris powder, then returned when I had the time to clear the leaves and spray and now a fortnight later it has recovered. It does not take much time to mix spray or scatter a few slug pellets and then the garden can be left while you attend to other things.

Q I am always in a fidget until the garden is tidy.

A Try and shut your eyes to it until you have sprayed or puffed, then no further damage will be done. The weeds and odd dead leaves will not hurt anything for a week or two and the grass does not grow so quickly either.

THE TOWN GARDEN

We have been considering the country garden which is the main or only garden. If there is a town house as well, I have always thought it too much of a good thing to have a proper garden at each end as it were – this is the great advantage of having a boat as a second home, no garden! Coming back to the town garden from the country, I would not expect to have to do more than sweep the patio, perhaps water a tub or two, then dead-heading and getting rid of weeds in a small way, but I still say that pest control is the most important.

Now to consider the town garden which is the main garden. I used to come back to my first town garden after a sailing holiday and perhaps had the inside of a week to catch up with everything inside and out, until we went away again for the weekend to tidy up on the boat. Most town gardens are not suitable for the later flowers; **Michaelmas daisies** get mildew and **Dahlias** straggle and do not flower well. Town gardeners usually end up by concentrating on spring bulbs, early border plants and such bedding plants as do well. These can only be found by trying them out, but one would expect to find such stalwarts as **Geraniums**, **Petunias** and **Lobelias** still in bloom.

The early annuals such as **Candytuft** and **Virginia stock** which we sowed in the spring will last to the end of the month, though they will be past their best and the late blooms of **Roses** (except ramblers) will go on until the frosts.

If a summer gale has made the whole border look a mess I have learned from experience that it does not hurt to leave it if you are busy elsewhere. It will not exactly pick itself up, but by this time plants will have often devised their own rather crooked way of growing, unnoticed when the plant was upright and the stems were supporting each other – trying to be too tidy is a waste of time and effort. A sort of first-aid is the best. Tie the plants back loosely to the stake and leave the stems the way they were growing before, otherwise you will get a bundled-up 'bunch of rhubarb' look. Replace the stakes if necessary, but usually it is only the string which has gone. If a stem is broken or straggling over something else, simply cut it away.

TUBS, BALCONIES AND ROOF GARDENS

If any reader is regretting his 'real' garden, this is when the concrete jungle comes into its own. When we had a roof garden I could not get over the way I could return after some weeks absence and in about half an hour restore things to their former tidiness. That and perhaps an evening or two when I watered with the hose, if it had been dry, was all. Once planted up the tubs are done for the season and one can get variety from different plantings in different tubs.

Q What about spraying?

A Yes, I had thought that a roof would be rather more free of pests than a garden at ground level, but they thrive – seemingly blown there by every breeze. However, the tubs are so much easier to get at, that one good spray, mostly against insect pests and mildew, will usually do the trick without having to bother when one gets back from holiday.

Q Can you mix the sprays?

A The trick is to buy from the same firm. Murphy's for instance will say on the bottle what can be used with their fungicide, but use one of their own products to be on the safe side. I use mine separately because I like to be able to gauge exactly what I am doing, but many gardeners always mix and save time.

THE FIRST-TIME GARDEN IN SEPTEMBER

We have not previously considered the possibility that the new house might need a lot of alteration and decoration and the new gardener might therefore have had some time to get at the garden before actually moving in. All we have already said about clearing and planning would apply if it would be easy to make frequent visits to the house, which of course depends a lot on its nearness to the old one. If one was able to be there when a firm was clearing, some kind of plan could be worked out for the autumn which is the main planting time.

Meanwhile it could be worthwhile planting later bedding plants. Do not embark on anything which will need more than occasional watering, having first made sure there is a garden tap. You will have plenty to do as it is, but it is pleasant to be greeted by a bit of colour when one moves in at last. Two plants which I am fond of, **Asters** and **Antirrhinums**, which we were discussing last month, are often left out of the small garden because one simply does not have the space to wait for them to flower in late July and August. Asters are even later and this would be their chance, also they are much less expensive than the more usual geraniums (pelargoniums).

Q Could one leave plants in like that without attention?

A It is worth trying. I have already described in August how successfully a neighbour leaves her bedding plants when she goes abroad. Of course there are a good many weeds, but these are soon cleared and the plants come to no harm. I would not think of planting out in a hot dry August, but July can be wet and thundery and if frequent visits to keep an eye on the builders are necessary, a lot could be done in a short time.

If you were buying a house around about Christmas and moving in in June which is the growing time, it would not be so practical. One knows only too well that occasional visits always seem to coincide with bad weather and planning and clearing would be the best thing, leaving established plants alone until the autumn planting.

SOME PLANTS AND QUERIES

Michaelmas Daisies

We have already noted that these are not for the town garden, unless it is unusually big and there is plenty of space for a wide border. Otherwise, they should not be overlooked, they are a cheerful addition to the waning summer and make one feel that there is still something to look forward to as the month goes on. They are tall, for the back of the border, but usually nice and compact and do not need staking. If you are looking them up in a catalogue, they are really called perennial asters, so do not go searching in vain under the letter 'M' as I have just done.

I was looking for the names of varieties, none of which I recognised and in the coloured bulb growers catalogue they are just shown as different colours. They come in pale and dark mauve, also pink like their annual cousins and there used to be a very good dark red variety which would be worth asking for. They are of the Novae Belgae (improved) strain, but not listed as such. They are probably taken for granted nowadays when the strain is not so 'noval' and is such an improvement on the old kinds.

Q   I found a row of them at the bottom of my new town garden. They went beautifully all through the summer, but the minute they started to flower the leaves were covered in mildew. I should like to keep them if I could.

A   It seems to be the mixture of a really warm, even hot day and cold nights which brings on the mildew. The experts say to try an anti-mildew spray about the end of August; it is difficult to do much once the leaves are badly affected. My own unprofessional advice is to try the spray anyhow and risk mixing it a little stronger than it says on the bottle. Leave for at least a week and then spray again at normal strength.

I had some dwarf michaelmas daisies given to me for my first garden. They only suffered from mildew in certain years and the spray certainly helped. I only got rid of them because in my North facing town garden they flowered too late, sometimes not until October.

Chrysanthemum

These are still cultivated to a great extent by professionals and specialist amateurs, who use heated glasshouses to bring them on for showing. Their enormous mop-heads are not for the out-door gardener, but the first-timer might like to have a try at the smaller outdoor kinds which have 'incurved' petals – like mop-heads but not so closely packed. There are smaller mop-heads, but I prefer the lighter effect of the 'incurved' and they mix in better with other border plants should one want them for a later display.

One of the pleasant effects of so much expertise amongst the specialist growers is that the plants are not expensive and a collection of five plants might be offered for under £4. As always with collections, the idea is to buy different kinds and see which does best in your garden. I was very successful with one described in the catalogue as "bronze-red and gold" called **'Mandarin'** (though I knew it under another name) and although it looks exotic it is very hardy and easy to grow.

Plants are grown from cuttings and sent out as nice little pot-grown plants from mid-April to June. As with all late flowerers, the earlier they can be planted out into the appointed spot, the better. The catalogue is always on the hopeful side, as even 'early' chrysanthemums don't flower much before August. When ordering by post, look carefully for the ones described as "garden" varieties – they should all be hardy except in the coldest winter and even then are not expensive to replace as we have seen.

Q Isn't there an awful lot of work disbudding and so on?
A I planted them in my first garden and they had to grow themselves. Getting a bomb site into some sort of a garden was no mean task and as far as I remember they had no fertiliser

except bonemeal, which was the only thing available. Even stakes were hard to buy and one had to make do with prunings from shrubs, but even so they made nice if rather straggly plants and flowered well. Single and spray chrysanthemums don't need disbudding and very little staking, so they might be better for you.

When the plants arrive, take them out of their pots and when planting add well-rotted manure to the soil, with as much material from the compost heap as is available. One can always add bonemeal at planting time, as it is a long-term fertiliser. We are hoping to get the little plants going as soon as possible, for if we 'stop' they will need extra time to come on again and make good bushy plants.

Q What if one has no manure or compost?

A I was unable to get these in my first garden, but nowadays one can buy good compost in bags such as Levington, Bio or the John Innes mixtures. I have found that although the John Innes formulas are numbered, most nurseries and garden centres will sell, not by the number, but by whatever purpose it is for; eg seedlings, seed compost, potting up plants and so on. Just tell them what you want the John Innes mixture for. Such composts are expensive and principally used for window-boxes and containers of all kinds. If you use them in the garden keep them concentrated, by putting some in the bottom of the hole and if possible, having enough so that the plant's first growth will be in the compost. Scattered about, it goes nowhere.

I will side-track briefly to discuss 'stopping' and 'disbudding'.

The quality of the plant is improved by simple stopping and disbudding, but if the little plant is looking bushy and putting out nice side shoots leave it alone. 'Stopping' is taking out the tip or growing shoot of the plant. It must be done early on, say a fortnight or so after you begin to see new growth. Keep an eye on it and if the plant is growing straight up with no side shoots, 'stop' at once before it has time to straggle. In this connection, stake straightaway so that it can be tied as soon as it begins to get taller. It is worth getting a friend to show you the first time.

'Disbudding' comes as soon as the plant has made good growth after stopping. This will take about a month and you should then start looking out for buds. Again get a friend to show you the first time.

Q It seems beyond me, but I am rather keen to try.

A If you have the chance and the distance isn't too great, why not go along to collect your plants from the actual nursery. You would get good advice and could be shown what to do.

Here are a few tips which may help.

Stopping. The growers advise mid-May for northern gardens and mid-June for South and sheltered gardens. In my North facing garden I would have tried to be earlier than mid-June, but all depends so much on the season and how the plant is growing.

Disbudding. Look on the new stems for the buds, which should have no stalk to them. There will be three buds, the main one from the tip of the flower stalk, the other two either side and a little lower. Rub off the two side ones gently.

Disbudding – the wrong way. The buds have been left until they are clear of the leaves and it is too late. If you take off the side buds (as I did) you will have one rather miserable flower on its own. This would be no better than if you had left it, though it would then have had the others to balance it. At this stage water with liquid manure fortnightly, or give a 'phos-tab' to each plant which lasts six weeks.

We will now go back to chrysanthemums and some of the different kinds.

Single and Spray Chrysanthemums

With single chrysanthemums one is back amongst the daisies, which will not please the daisyphobe. They need staking but not disbudding or stopping. Spray chrysanthemums grow very attractively and if one is content to let them·sprawl in a corner of the border they do not need staking either. They come in autumn colours which greatly appeal to me; buff yellow, dusky pink, deep yellow and a light and dark orange-red, which blend in beautifully with the others. They are hardy and flower over a long period, but are late – sometimes October or November. If there is room for them to have a bed to themselves they would be a lovely patch of colour to cheer up the fading garden.

Chrysanthemum leaves are pretty in themselves and some leaflets remain at the base all through the winter. I think that a bed of chrysanthemums never look dreary in the way some flowers or shrubs do when they are over or coming on, but obviously a small garden would not want its display to consist of something which waited until the autumn to show off at its best. If one can find a corner in the border where the summer plants will hide them until they start to bloom, they might still be fitted in.

Pompon chrysanthemums

Though not as attractive as their namesake in the dahlia family, these neat compact little plants with their button flowers, are very useful for window-boxes or containers if one wants something late-flowering and they do not need staking. They are only 18ins high and flower in August. If possible buy them as small plants before they come into flower. Ones bought from the garden centre are often fully out and though seemingly with plenty of buds coming along, somehow never do as well. Perhaps they are best as pot plants if the room is not too warm.

Dahlias

Called after the botanist Dahl, a great help when trying to remember the spelling for looking up purposes. (The botanist Fuchs is equally useful for fuchsias!)

Q Do you have to take dahlias up for the winter?

A This is so often the first question that anyone asks, that it is pleasant to be able to reassure them that though dahlias do need taking up, this is really no problem.

Q Gardening books seem to make such heavy weather of it.

A I can only say what I did in my first garden. At that time books were no easier to obtain than fertilisers, tools or anything else that one wanted and I had to rely on memories of my parents' garden. I remembered that one had to wait until the first sharp frosts had blackened the leaves and on as dry a day as possible cut them down. The point of waiting for a dry spell is that not much earth will come up with the tubers, which look like oval-shaped potatoes and what soil does come up can be easily shaken off.

To lift, put the big fork into the ground a little way away from the plant to avoid spiking the tuber and push it in hard; then one would hope to see the whole thing heaving up. Ease the tubers gently from the soil as there will be little roots coming from them, which have been holding the plant in place. Disentangle these rootlets from each other and the earth should fall away with a little shaking.

Q How far down should I cut?

A Right down, only leaving an inch or so at the bottom which you can hold on to.

Put the tubers away somewhere dry and frost-proof. They don't need heat and at my old home, they were put in a sack in the closed garden shed. I put them in the South attic, which was used as a boxroom and was unheated though it got plenty of sun. Keep them away from the light, wrap in something thick (old carpet felt is ideal) and place in a box. A good box is a shallow one with slats at the bottom, such as greengrocers still use. Look at the tubers after a week or two and get rid of any earth which is still there. Plant out when the frosts are over in the late spring.

PLANTING OUT TUBERS

When we were planning something to go in after late bulbs, such as Darwin tulips, we thought of dahlias. Dig a little bonemeal into the soil when you are tidying up after lifting the bulbs and plant the dahlias out with a little compost or manure beneath them. Put the stakes in at the same time; they need good strong ones, as with their hollow stalks and heavy heads they are very vulnerable to summer gales.

Before planting, cut off any tubers which have withered. If you find that what was one plant now seems to have come to bits – perhaps two or three – separate them gently and plant them separately and you have two new plants.

Q You don't think one could leave them in the ground?

A People do try, but frequently don't succeed; there are exceptions, for instance in a garden on a bank of the River Hamble. The owner had planted them when he bought a war-time MTB (Motor Torpedo Boat) to use as a house boat and these huge yellow dahlias, unstaked, came up year after year and I have never seen better. They came up through the grass of the bank which must have acted as a blanket and the mild climate in that part of Hampshire, where snow is a rarity helped. Part of the fascination of a garden is never being able to make any hard and fast rules. Another feature of the garden was that the high spring tides came up over the bank and must have left behind a fair amount of salt in the ground, not a thing which would be generally recommended, but the dahlias evidently flourished on it.

Dahlias need plenty of rain, but they need sun and an open position too. Readers may have admired them in gardens in Northern France where the climate is not all that different from ours and the rich soil of Normandy suits them perfectly. If the garden is too enclosed and the soil is poor they will straggle and not flower well. In the rambling thoughts on a wet summer, I might have quoted my sister's gardener who says dahlias are the only consolation; alas in a town garden this is not true, as they do worse than ever.

KINDS OF DAHLIAS

Single Bedding Dahlias

We will start with the little bedding dahlia, with its single flowers and small size. About 18ins each way, it is not at all the majestic plant which first comes to mind and is seen to such advantage in parks and public gardens These 'dwarf' dahlias are a very useful little bedding plant, rather less formal for those who prefer garden plants for their summer display and much less expensive if one is trying to fill large flower-beds in a country garden – say beds along the length of a terrace. Many large houses have been converted into flats and one can easily be faced with the problem of a stately home type-garden. If it has been laid out in formal beds, that will be the pattern imposed on the first-timer. The more ordinary bedding plants such as geraniums, petunias even busy Lizzies and the new varieties of *Impatiens* with the coloured leaves, come expensive on a large scale and do not do so well as in towns, liking the dry heat and shelter of a town garden.
Q I have bought little dahlias several times from the garden centre and they never seem to come to anything, neither making any new growth nor flowering well.
A This has been my experience too. For my first garden I

bought one red and one yellow dahlia from the pony cart which carried plants through the streets of London, before the advent of garden centres. They were the first ones I tucked up for the winter in their felt in the attic and they increased, so that I must have had a dozen or so before the new house was built next to us and they started to straggle and flower badly.

The small plants sold at garden centres are already in flower at a stage when the older kind would have been still in bud, so perhaps they are forced in to flower too soon.

Bedding dahlias can be ordered as pot plants from catalogues and will arrive the next spring. At the end of the season, though the tubers can be lifted as we have described, there is a danger that they will not stay small and in a year or two they will have lost their neat miniature look cultivated by the expert. They have a long flowering period, starting before the bigger dahlias and lasting right through the summer, needing no staking. They do occasionally fail, even in the garden where I have seen them flower so successfully. With everything which one buys from year to year, a cold sunless summer is a warning; bulbs, seeds and small plants are not going to be quite as good the next year, but one must take some risks!

Large Flowering Dahlias

It is obvious that if we are not going to plant them out before the end of May, that these Dahlias are late summer and autumn flowering. Considering the enormous variety which the specialist nurseries show, there seems to be rather a poor choice in the smaller coloured catalogue. If the reader is planning a large display bed, rather than some to plant out of sight for picking for the house, he would do well to visit a show such as the RHS Autumn Show, where the display from specialist nurseries has to be seen to be believed. Dahlias, like chrysanthemums, are still much grown by the specialist amateur and need watering and tending with liquid manure, according to the instructions from the growers.

If the first-timer is just thinking of adding one or two to the border to bring colour when the early plants are going over, I suggest the neater-petalled, large-flowered ones. These are the kind seen so much in French gardens, a particular favourite being

Dahlias
A late summer and autumn flowering, colourful plant

the red and white mixture, not much seen on this side of the Channel. As with chrysanthemums, choose the ones said to be "easy" or "vigorous" – none are hardy as we have been saying.

The coloured catalogues always have the advantage for the first-timer of showing a good picture. If you buy from the expert they will just give you a printed list and you must rely on memory for the ones you liked, therefore it is a good idea to make a brief note against their names.

Cactus Dahlias

These are only 'cactus' in the shape of the flowers and they need as much water as any other kind. They start off with curled petals and to my mind, especially after rain or wind, look too much as if they were beginning to wither before their time, but they have a novelty value and are useful for flower arrangements.

Pompon Dahlias

I mention these briefly, though they do not seem to have a place in the catalogues nowadays. They are a smaller version of the neater-petalled large-flowered ones, but the plant itself will often grow very tall and the small flowers with their long stalks can look out of proportion. One still sees them in flower-shops and indeed they are best grown out of sight with the ones for the house. All the same, I have a weakness for the clever compact way the petals fit so neatly into each other and the pompon makes a good foil to the more flamboyant kinds.

Q I must say dahlias sound an awful lot of bother.

A Perhaps they are more for the large garden with a gardener. I never watered or manured mine in my first garden, but as I have said they were single ones.

If we are speaking of adding one or two large flowered ones to a herbaceous border, there is no doubt that herbaceous borders in general are not for instant or time-saving gardens. One might get over the staking difficulty with the modern metal devices which vary slightly, but most take the form of making a firm ring round the plant so that it grows up through some kind of hoop. Anything with a thick hollow stalk like a dahlia would be safe with a stout stake put in early. Keep an eye on the string, so that it does not rot suddenly and let you down in a gale. I always keep a look-out at stately-home gardens and the RHS gardens at Wisley to see how things are staked, mostly to find that it is very simple.

Q If they have to be watered fortnightly in any case, it seems to me one might just as well add the liquid manure then, as it's the watering which takes the time.

A It's a point I hadn't really considered when advising on 'Phostabs' or similar. The dahlias would still have to be watered, unless it was a rainy summer when pellets might save one trouble.

EARWIGS

Q Then they get earwigs.

A Yes, we left earwigs out when we were thinking of pests because they are so much associated with dahlias. These pests eat the petals and the best way of dealing with them is still the old-fashioned flower-pot trap, which everyone tells me there is nothing to beat. Put a stake beside the plant with a small flower-pot up-ended on it, having filled the pot with dried grass or similar; the earwigs climb up the pole and get stuck in the hay. Drown them or stamp on them, but they are very nimble and it is really better to shake them into the water. The traps should be looked at frequently when the flowers are opening.

Q Would it be earwigs which are eating my pansies? Something is making holes in the petals.

A It's too late in the year for caterpillars which anyhow one can see under the leaves. It could be earwigs, but is more likely to be a very small leech-like kind of slug, which sticks to one's hands in the most unpleasant way. They don't leave a trail like snails or the bigger slugs, so look for them in the evening under the leaves.

Put out slug bait and if that fails try Derris dust. You need not spoil the look of the flowers if you sprinkle it round the plant lower down and on the ground and that will stop whatever pest it is from climbing up.

Q The more I hear the less I want them. They say that Chekov used to walk round the garden hitting the dahlia heads with his stick.

A Well it's your garden. Let's hope it was Chekov's too as it seems rather hard if he was a visitor.

SOME BERRIED SHRUBS

Q I can never tell those red-berried shrubs apart. In any case I can't see the point of growing something just for its berries. Suppose the birds get them or it's a bad year, one is left with nothing.

A It's true that the white flowers are not very special and one does get bad years without many berries.

Pyracantha

Of the three, the pyracantha is my favourite. It is a very strong and hardy grower and can be used as a barrier against the neighbour's cat, or even cattle in the country as it is very thorny. The red berries are reliable and pretty and usually last into the winter.

The first-timer will probably know it best as the climber which can be trained up a house with such good effect. It is the kind of shrub which sends out laterals (side shoots) from the main stem. It is pruned very hard so that only the climbing stem remains and only lateral shoots when they are wanted to go sideways. Say the main stem had climbed up the wall to above the first-floor window, the side shoots at this level would be trained to go between the first and second-floor windows, the lower ones having been cut away. Like wisteria, pruning needs a ladder and some skill for the shoots must not be let to get out of hand or it will not do well. Male Q's, particularly those connected with the armed forces, are very good at this kind of thing as there is something in the neat lines which seems to appeal.

Q When do you prune the pyracantha?

A There is no set time for pruning. 'After flowering' obviously does not apply as the flowers will turn into berries, but once the berries have gone in the winter one can think about tidying or hard pruning. The pyracantha or firethorn we want for climbing is the **P. coccinea**.

Q We do seem to have a very overgrown one by the porch. Can it be reclaimed?

A Sadly, if anything like full-grown (about 15ft), it has probably made such thick stems that it would never look right and besides, even the toughest plant cannot survive being cut right back in its old age. Though by all means consult an expert.

Cotoneaster

Perhaps the cotoneaster would be more the kind of thing you wanted. The one grown up against a house is **C. horizontalis**. It is a much neater grower, needs next to no pruning and will do well even if the house is facing North. Spreading its small neat leaves out like a fan it has rather a prim and proper look, which is disliked as 'suburban' by some. Rather unfairly I think for, having wrestled with town gardening for so long, I never despise a plant for being easy.

Q They say it attracts wasps.

A I believe they do produce a kind of honey-like substance which is attractive to insects, but not necessarily just wasps. Whatever the truth of it, it doesn't seem to prevent people from growing it. Personally, I think it looks pretty when the red berries come.

Berberis

The variety sold for hedging, though it can stand on its own, is **B. thunbergii**. It is deciduous and though it makes a thick thorny hedge, it is not quite as dense as an evergreen, is rather straighter growing and is not as exuberant as the pyracantha.

Q I thought berberis was evergreen.

A There are evergreen varieties and they are grown as much for their early yellow flowers as for berries.

B. thunbergii has an attractive variety, *atropurpurea*, with brownish-red leaves in the spring and summer turning a brighter red in the autumn, so that one gets autumn colour as well as berries until the leaves fall. It needs simple pruning; some smallish shoots will appear and have to be cut hard, but once thickened up into a hedge, it is not difficult to keep neat.

SOME MORE CLIMBERS

Honeysuckle – (Lonicrae)

Q I was thinking of having a honeysuckle by the front door.
A If we are thinking of the honeysuckle which grows wild in hedges, this is a real 'leaner' or twiner and needs help to start off. A piece of trellis-work against the wall of the house such as one often sees is fine. If it is to grow over a porch, this would do very well and once up there it will look after itself with a bit of trimming, but it will never make a neat shrub. For this you would have to choose an evergreen bush honeysuckle.

When we were trying to disentangle names of plants, we were speaking of some plants which always seem to be called by their Latin name and *Lonicera* for honeysuckle is one. As far as the smaller coloured catalogue is concerned, *Lonicera* is the climbing kind. The showy **L. x brownii** 'Dropmore Scarlet', with its spectacular scarlet trumpets is not scented like the others and sometimes the flowers disappoint.

For the first-timer, why not try our own wild woodbine, **L. periclymenum**. It flowers well, has a beautiful scent and it certainly does attract bees, wasps and every other kind of insect which likes honey. It is also very good for a high wall or tunnel pergola, mixed with other climbers. The bush honeysuckles are all evergreen and need a fairly rich soil. The one I saw growing in a garden in Hampshire, is a big shrub of 8ft or so each way, with pretty leaves and clusters of creamy, unusual looking flowers. It is very much the kind which makes one say "what's that?" which is always satisfactory for the new gardener. True the soil in that part of Hampshire is rich, but this garden had been much neglected and the honeysuckle had obviously managed quite successfully on its own, useful for the reader who has a big space to fill, but it is not for the border.

ANNUAL (sometimes perennial) CLIMBERS

Round about mid-June, the garden centres and nurseries will be selling half-hardy climbers which have been brought on in pots read to put out and start their climb up a wall or trellis. These are more ornamental than the ones we have been considering,

most are annuals and grown for their flowers, not as a permanent
screen or hedge.

Ipomoea

This is another name for the morning glory, the beautiful sky-blue
Convolvulus tricolor 'Heavenly Blue' which can make such a marvellous show in a sunny summer.

As soon as they appear, buy them if possible when they are
about 6ins tall and with signs of buds coming and do not move
them from their pots as you plant them out. The compost is
always very light and sandy and the roots tend to collapse as
one gets them out and then they do not transplant well. If already
in bud, or even in flower, they will have been forced on with too
much heat and are very liable to greenfly or worse, whitefly.
Whatever the weather they will not be at their best before
August, which is ideal for the holiday second home, or if one is
only away for a short time. They can climb as much as 8ft flowering all the time and are just the answer to those, and there are
many, who really only want a good bit of bright colour in the
garden for as long as possible. In hot weather they do fade
about midday, but as the sun gets lower in September they will
stay out well into the afternoon.

When growing from seed they need bringing on under glass.
Sow only two seeds in a pot (in case one should fail), then plant
them both out together pot and all. If the seeds are planted on
either side of the pot, they will not get in each other's way
when growing. Sun is needed to bring them on.

Convolvulus Major

These are hardy annuals so that they can be sown after the hard
spring frosts in the usual way, where they are intended to grow.
Being annuals they will only last the one year, so there is no
danger of their getting out of hand and twining round the
wrong plants like the beautiful white convolvulus, which is such
a menace in the border. Rightly called bindweed, it goes on
from year to year, the roots seeming to get stronger the more
they are pulled out. The Latin name for the wild white convolvu-

lus is *Calystegia sepum* and its cousin the equally lovely pink sea-bindweed, *Calystegia soldanella*.

Q Why aren't these last two called convolvulus? I thought that was their Latin name.

A Perhaps the botanists felt the two bindweeds should have a category on their own, to distinguish them from the garden plants we have been considering; we can't then make a mistake and plant the weed instead. The little pink convolvulus which grows by the roadside is called *Convolvulus arvensis*. There have been a lot of upheavals in the botanical mine-field as we were saying when trying to disentangle the names of plants.

If our hardy annual garden convolvulus had been sown in the spring, say at the end of April, it will start flowering mid-August in a small way and be at its best in September. The flowers are smaller than the big blue morning glory, but they make up for it in the pretty mixture of colours from palest pink to magenta and from purple to blue of all shades. Both types of morning glory need a good summer with plenty of sun to bring them on and the leaves of the annual convolvulus will wilt in the hot sun but recover as soon as the heat is off them.

I have said how a series of hot summers can lead one astray and during the sunny summers just after World War II, I had admired the colourful convolvulus growing up the makeshift wire fences round bombed gardens – timber was as difficult to get as everything else.

After a series of wet summers in the 1980's, we had an old-fashioned sunny summer again and the plants came out just when they should do.

Q I don't remember ever seeing any growing up fences.

A They are not much grown nowadays and fond though I am of them, I must admit that they are a dead loss in a bad summer and hardly get going at all. Look out for them in northern France, particularly in Brittany, where we saw them on a sheltered island in the Gulf of Morbihan many years ago.

Cobaea scandens and Passiflora caerulea

Although both these used to be considered indoor or verandah plants, these two flowering climbers which would be out at this time of year, do not need particularly good weather. They will be on sale about mid-June and will grow very quickly. Their best place is at the back of a border which has a low wall with a trellis, like so many town gardens. They make a pretty screen and background and can be treated as annuals, or one can chance it in a sheltered garden that they will survive the winter. They should have a West or South aspect and given this neither seems to mind a rainy summer and I have seen them both succeed when we have not had much sun.

The **Cobaea** has bell-shaped flowers of an unusual kind that look like a long tube in the bud and one feels they are never going to be fully out, but they do it in the end. They are listed as purple, but are much dependent on a fairly bright light, sun if possible, to show them up, otherwise they can look rather green and sombre.

The **Passion Flower** was named by the missionaries in its native land of South America, who likened the stamens to the five wounds of the Passion and the corona, or outer edge, to the Crown of Thorns. As a child, I could not separate it from this sad association and am not fond of purple; I have still never grown it, but just thought of as an unusual flower it is spectacular and will flower reliably.

If treated as perennials, both are vigorous and will need pruning in about March when the weather is picking up from the winter.

Q Things get so messy-looking in the winter on the trellis and I would rather get rid of them, though it seems a waste.

A At the time I was growing *Cobaea scandens*, they were treated as annuals; clean air was only just beginning to have an effect in the cities and like you I was only too glad to get rid of the dead-looking leaves in the autumn when tidying up the border. In any case these semi-evergreens simply hang on to their old leaves longer than most things and only get the new growth in the spring like everything else. If you want to get the trellis clear, as it is a risk in any case to keep this kind of tender plant outdoors through the winter, you are probably not going to lose by cutting it down in late autumn, as one would the Jackmanii type of clematis. With any luck, it should spring up again in late March or thereabouts. Alternatively, you could keep it in its pot when planting out and bring it indoors for the winter, first having cut it down to a manageable height.

Ivy – (Hedera) and Virginia Creeper – (Parthenocissus quinquefolia)

These are the two creepers which you are most likely to find growing up your house and if they are of any age they may both have
got rather out of hand. Your surveyor is not going to let you keep
the ivy, which can injure the brickwork by disturbing the mortar,
but he will probably spare the Virginia creeper if it is kept in hand
and does not cause damp by scattering leaves in the wrong places,
(for unlike ivy it is not evergreen). If you decide to prune it wait a
month or so, unless it is blocking up gutters or drains, for it will
turn a beautiful red before shedding its leaves for the winter. It
is self-clinging and I have always admired the neat way it puts
out its little suckers to grip the wall, unlike the ivy, which claws
into the mortar between the bricks.

Q I can't think why anyone should want to grow ivy up a house,
as it always gives trouble and is a great nuisance to keep trimmed.

A I think growing ivy up houses must have dated from the
romantic movement. People liked the idea of ivy-clad ruins and
the ivy was used to soften the hard outlines of a house. For
some time though, we have become frightened of its effect on a
brick-built house and the Virginia creeper is the one most often
planted.

It used to go by the name *Ampelopsis veitchii* and for years
garden writers ranted against this dreadful thing, so goodness
knows what I pictured, but found when I had my own garden
that it was the poor Virginia creeper. It does need keeping in
hand, but its great advantage of growing quickly to cover open
fences or an ugly shed, combined with its losing its leaves in
the winter, make it a very useful town plant and the reader will
undoubtedly see plenty in London where it must have been extensively planted about thirty years ago, when houses were
being built again.

Q I am sure we had one at home when I was a child, but it
didn't seem so rampant and I'm sure the leaves were smaller.

A There were a great many varieties that I remember, particularly one with pink heart-shaped leaves which grew up the wall of
my old school. They had a marvellous gardener who really lived
for the garden, so I daresay that it was something rather choice
and unusual, but it would be worth asking a specialist nursery
like Hilliers.

Sweet peas – Lathyrus

Before we go on to the annual which every one knows there is a perennial, **L. latifolius** the everlasting pea, which suffers from comparison with the showier sweet pea. It flowers at a useful time in the year, mid-June to July. It is a very easy plant, succeeding in all but the poorest soils and situations and there are some good modern varieties with larger pink and white flowers, instead of the usual reddish colour. It can often be found as a survivor if the 'new' garden has been cultivated and is worth keeping. Note however, that it is a 'leaner' and is happiest when it can find something like a tree stump or fence to climb up or lean against. Grown as a border plant it has to be staked and can look rather bunchy.

As anyone will tell you, annual sweet peas need cultivating. That is they need plenty of attention, frequent watering, with Liquinure or a similar preparation added fortnightly and as deep a trench as you have the energy to dig. Put as much compost and compost manure in the trench as you can lay your hands on. The compost heap will do even if unrotted and a reader wrote to The Independent newspaper to say he had grown a fine crop of (edible) peas using shredded newsprint from that paper. I have never tried it, but if compost material is scarce one has nothing to lose and it rots down in no time.

Garden centres sell little plants in May or thereabouts and the first-timer will probably be content with these to start off with. If he gets hooked, choosing colours and buying from a specialist firm like Suttons, will give him better and bigger flowers.

Q   Aren't they terribly difficult?

A   The best ones I ever saw were in a garden very near the tennis courts at Wimbledon. They like a bit of shelter as well as sun and a big garden a little bit out of town is just what suits them.

Q   I would feel very tempted just to put them into the ground and see what happened. Would they be a great failure?

A   The first thing to remember is that sweet peas have very long roots. That was probably why I had undeserved luck when I planted mine in a tub, as I related earlier on, the tub obviously had sufficient depth to accommodate the long roots. Also, the seedlings will need something to climb up. The tendrils are really only a nuisance, ten to one they will hang on to other plants or other sweet peas, anything but the stick or string planned for them until the whole thing is in a tangle. It does no harm to remove them and let the plant climb by twisting round the support. If the Sweet peas are out of sight they can grow up stakes cut from bushes, with the side twigs left on – these are the pea-sticks which the edible pea is usually grown on.

Q There is a space along a side wall where I thought they would look pretty.

A This would be perfectly suitable if they are not enclosed by other plants, as you will need to get at the bed to dig properly so that the roots are not cramped. Say your small plants are about 2ins high when you buy them in pots, the roots will be at least twice as long. Dig a hole deep enough to accommodate the roots plus a bit extra and put in any manure or compost which you have by you. For the top soil scatter over some Growmore and dig it in lightly, this is a great help when the seedlings are beginning to make growth. Use tall but fairly thin bamboo stakes, or if there are nails already in the wall where something has been growing, attach garden string to them securing with a small stick to start them off.

Never plant anything right up against a wall because of drying out and particularly sweet peas which need plenty of water. As we were saying earlier, water and fertilise as much as you have time for – the Growmore should help. When the flowers come always pick them, for if they are allowed to go to seed the plants will think their task is done and will not produce new buds in such quantities.

Q What about thinning the flowers?

A The really serious growers for shows and so on, do reduce the number of flowering stalks to get bigger flowers, but our garden centre ones are not going to be very big. In any case we are aiming at plenty of flowers to look at and pick.

If you ignore all this, simply putting the seedlings in a nice deep hole, you would probably get away with it in a rich soil, but in a poor town soil I fear they would not come to much, but even so they could produce a flower or two.

The other drawback in a small garden is that they may get mildew, leading on to some sort of 'die-back' virus. Plants do get infected in this way as we have seen with other annuals and there is nothing for it but to leave them for a year or two and then try them in a different place.

Q There seems no end to what plants can get.

A I have read in gardening articles that a lot of this sort of thing

comes from the mass production of plants for selling at the beginning of the summer. The demand is enormous and it is wonderful
really how well the plants do on the whole, added to which sunless
wet summers do not help this kind of thing. We will not go on
anymore about what can go wrong, for we are starting to plant
and plan our garden in earnest.

BULBS

Like all else in gardening, the time for planting bulbs depends a bit
on the weather. In general it will be the first two weeks in October. September often ends in gales and rain, then clears and we
get a sunny spell when the ground has cooled down a bit, perhaps
after one or two early frosts and this is the ideal weather for planting.

Q I find that the annuals are never over until the weather has
broken and then it's rather cold and late to plant.

A Exactly, the annuals will go flowering on in rather a half-
hearted way until nearly Christmas if there is a mild wet
autumn, so one has to be ruthless and just take them up.
Watch the professionals in the parks and public gardens, one
day a glorious end of summer display, the next, sadly nothing
and the bulbs going in.

Towards the end of the month, look out for the plump healthy
bulbs and never buy ones which have begun to sprout, for they
should make roots first. Rather unexpectedly, big stores such as
Harrods and Peter Jones have a very good selection of bulbs
and often less expensive than the garden centres. In fairness to
the latter, the big stores are able to buy in bulk and they have a
guarantee of quality, as no one is going to sell inferior bulbs to
such names.

PLANTING INDOOR BULBS

Q Is this the time for planting indoor bulbs too?

A Yes, they should be in their bowls by the end of September if
you want them for Christmas, so we might as well get down to
them now.

BULB FIBRE

You will probably be able to buy the fibre with the bulbs. Many hardware shops stock it at this time of year, but don't leave it too late, as they will only stock a certain amount for the planting season. A good average size for a bulb bowl would be about 8ins across and about 4–5ins deep. The secret of indoor bulbs is that they should make good roots and the bowls must be deep enough to accommodate them. More ornamental bowls which are used for cut flowers will probably be too shallow. Vegetable dishes from an old-fashioned dinner service are very good as they are beautifully deep, but of course if you use anything bigger you will need more fibre. A small bag will do your average bowl, but you will need all of the bigger bag for anything larger and if you have any over it will keep for next year – there is nothing more annoying than to want a small quantity, only to find all the shops have run out.

Soaking the Fibre

Fibre which stays damp is a help with root forming and saves a lot of watering and worry. If correctly soaked, it will last the six weeks the bulbs need to make roots and start sprouting from the top to form flowers.

Bulb fibre used to come in a cotton bag which one put unopened in a bucket of water and when it stopped floating and had sunk to the bottom, it was ready. The modern plastic bag has put a stop to this simple method of soaking, but I have found that by sticking holes in the bag with a meat skewer one can get the same result. It takes at least all day and often all night, but warm water is a help. Empty the water left in the bucket and leave the bag to drip for an hour or so. When you want to plant, open the bag and squeeze out the fibre so that it is damp all through, but not actually wringing wet.

Q Does one have to have bulb fibre?

A Your bowls have no drainage holes like a flower-pot, so you need something to keep the water from going bad and the fibre contains specially prepared charcoal for the purpose. If you have a large bowl of any kind which is filled with fibre and just needs topping up, you would be perfectly safe to add one of the bag composts, such as Levington or Bio, as the charcoal will already be there.

We went into indoor bulbs for Christmas when we were considering ordering from a catalogue last month.

Hyacinths are easiest for the first-timer and if we have managed to buy '**Rosalie**' we shall not be disappointed. Five will go nicely into our bowl and the bulbs can be planted quite close together but should not be touching.

The First Stage

Squeeze the soaked bulb fibre, put it into the bowl leaving about one inch at the top. Press the bulbs firmly down into the fibre, then cover until only the tips are showing. The fibre will sink a little as when one plants outdoors, so in the first place leave only about a quarter of an inch of the rim showing to allow for watering. While the bulbs are making roots they should be kept cool and in the dark. In my own case I had the ideal place, a North-facing attic which had a windowless section divided off where the cold-water tank lived. The tank had a wooden cover which made a perfect platform for the bowls. The next stage was in the North attic proper, which was light under the window but with no sun and finally they came into the sunny South attic until they were wanted. One would need some kind of a trestle table unless such windows had deeper sills than mine.

When the bulbs had had their first six weeks in the dark, there were signs of life from the tips, but with a specially early bulb they may show sooner, even after four weeks. If the fibre has been properly soaked they will have needed no watering, in fact drying fibre is a sign of growth. Try the fibre to see if it is damp underneath and if it is, just water the surface sufficiently to make it damp. Have a small watering can with a long spout, such as is sold for house-plants and water only the fibre, never the bulbs themselves, the tips particularly are liable to rot if water gets into them.

The Second Stage

The important stage comes once the tips are showing to make sure the flower bud is clear of the bulb. The tip at first will look just like

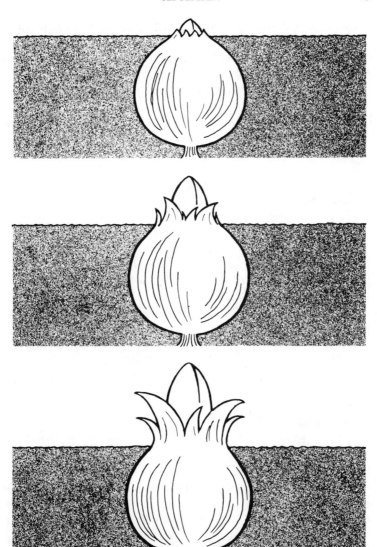

Hyacinth bulbs

Signs of life
1. Tip just showing. 2–3 weeks.
2. Tip starting to clear the fibre. 3–4 weeks.
3. Bud can be felt then seen. Leaves ... to show.
4. Hopefully long ... leaves are coming with the flower stem and buds tucked in them. Go on spraying (leaves and no flowers are a bad sign). 8 weeks.

two leaves joined together, then it starts getting fat. Feel gently in the fattest part and you can tell if the bud is there. At this stage it is safe to bring it into the light, but not bright light and the room should still be cool. The tips will be yellow after being in the dark, but they will soon go green even in a North light. When the tip of the bud can be plainly seen, we are probably between mid-November and the beginning of December and at the trickiest stage. Once the leaves are open and the buds really showing they are sure to be a success.

The Last Stage

When the bulbs are advanced enough to be in a sunny but still cool room, we are safe to bring them on or hold them back. Some are such early bulbs by nature that it is best to leave them in the cool sunny position until about a week before Christmas. Ideally they should have grown a bit of a stalk and be showing colour in their buds and a week will be plenty of time to have them out on Christmas Day.

'Rosalie' is a Roman hyacinth, but the usual ones will have to be specially prepared to reach the same stage at the same time. The last two stages should have been reached by mid-December.

Christmas Narcissi

As we were saying earlier on, though the large single flowered narcissi are late, the smaller bunch-flowered ones are early, even outdoors. The first-timer will probably know '**Soleil d'Or**' and '**Paperwhite**' from seeing them sold in the streets; they come from the South of France or the Scilly Isles and bring a breath of spring as early as January. Indoor ones meant to flower at Christmas will have to be bought specially prepared and planted directly they arrive, like hyacinths.

They are slightly more difficult as they must not be brought into the warm room until they are nearly out, or they will dry up and come to nothing. If they show any signs of drying when in the warmth, spraying with a 'mister' is a help – put them in the sink first of course, as the misting sprays shoot much further than one would think.

Tulips

I only mention them to say, that even if treated they are more difficult still, for they do not flower as early out of doors as hyacinths or narcissi. One walks a difficult tightrope between trying to have them out in time and not drying them up by bringing them into the warmth too soon.

In any case, even with our best endeavours, if there is a very cold spell in December the bulbs may be held back and it is not wise to try and hurry them. They will in any case be out early in January and much earlier than outside.

Q It seems hardly worth the bother unless they are out for Christmas.

A There is so much else at Christmas and you are quite likely to be given a plant as a present, a poinsettia for instance and then there is the holly and so on. After the New Year there is a blank with the coldest part of the year ahead and it's very pleasant having hyacinths coming on then without the worry of a deadline.

One can keep them in a garden shed for the first six weeks or so if it is frost-proof, then a cold window-sill or bedroom and on to a sunny window-sill or bedroom before coming into the real warmth. Some people leave the bowls outside and simply cover them with leaves until they are ready to come in; or plant them into a clay pot and bury them just below the surface. In this case the pot will have drainage holes so you are not obliged to use bulb-fibre.

Q My narcissi were just leaves with no flowers, except for one on an enormously long stalk.

A This is what they call being 'drawn up'. They were brought into the light too soon and even more than with other bulbs, tulips and narcissi must have the bud well clear of the bulb before leaving the dark.

Q What if they start growing without a stalk? My hyacinths did this.

A There is nothing for it but to bring them into the living room.

If just one bulb is doing it (pink are tricky in this way), look to see if it has made any roots as one can get a rogue bulb which fails to root even after all one's trouble. Remove it and move the other hyacinths to get them evenly spaced again; they are very accommodating.

Q All my pink hyacinths collapsed last year.

A Did they recover in the room? The stalk can grow quite well even when the flowers are very nearly out, but it is annoying as the flowers start at the top and that spoils the shape. An unusually mild winter or autumn can do this as it is impossible to keep the bulbs cool enough. Otherwise, if they do not grow well another year, the fault may be in the bulbs and I should try another firm or shop.

Q Do you think they were pre-cooled ones? The shop never said which kind they were.

A If a shop or store sells "bulbs for Christmas", I cannot think they are selling pre-cooled ones as it would be fatal to have them spread out or kept after they arrived. I guess they are just early varieties sold in the hopes they will be out in time. Plant them straightaway for you will need ten weeks at least.

The Christmas Amaryllis

Here we have something entirely different. A huge flower, in fact four trumpets go to make the one flower and as spectacular and Christmassy as anyone could wish. They are not grown in fibre and need to be in the warmth all the time. As the huge bulbs are a minimum of 12" round, you will need a big clay pot to plant them in and this time the mixture should be a rich loam, as for a lily. Either buy a rich compost specially sold for the purpose or use Bio or Levington, mixed with leaf-mould. You will need a little sand under the bulb for drainage and extra 'crocks' (broken clay pieces or large stones), over the drainage holes. Follow the excellent instructions which come with the amaryllis and you cannot go wrong.

As for 'bottom heat' which they need, I bring mine on on the floor of the heated linen cupboard and as soon as the tip appears, it is very easy to see the bud, I put it straight into the warm living room. They are expensive but one is plenty and in a warm centrally-heated house or flat they will get enough warmth without any difficulty. Some will even produce two flower stalks. They will need a stout stake, so it is worth buying a slightly larger pot than they would need just for themselves. Mine have sometimes been so huge that I have come into the room to see the whole thing keeled over. They should arrive at the end of October beginning of November and be planted at once.

Q I hate them. I saw them in Holland and they looked quite evil.

A Many people feel that way about them. There is something uncanny in the speed at which they grow once they start, getting on for an inch a day and not what we are used to in our climate. Originally they produced this long stalk without any leaves (they came after the flower) which added to the strange effect. The last two years the leaves have come quite normally with the buds, so the bulbs must have been improved. There is a pink and white variety, not quite so bold as the red, which I think pretty, but perhaps they are like orchids which people either love or hate.

The reader may be wondering what has happened to the outdoor bulbs – they are going in at the first opportunity in October, so we will move on without delay to that busy month.

October

The fine days at the end of September may extend into October, with one or two frosts at night and this is ideal weather for clearing, planning and for planting outdoor bulbs. Even more than in the spring there is no time to lose, the fine weather is often followed by wind and rain which makes gardening impossible for a time and alas, we are not going towards the better and sunnier months, but away from them into the frosts and cold of winter.

Q We have just moved in and I don't think I shall be able to get at the garden for a month or so, will it be too late?

A If you want bulbs for the spring, they should be in by the end of October if possible, but trees and shrubs (roses are counted amongst the shrubs) should be planted in November in any case. It's obvious that you will have to do some clearing unless your new garden is empty. It would be a shame to miss the best planting time and if you can get hold of a firm at once, they could do the work while you were busy in the house. Don't forget the short days – once British Summer Time (BST) ends at the end of the month, there will not be much light after four o'clock, particularly in a town garden.

If you succeed in getting a good garden firm they can probably supply bulbs and plant them. If you buy them yourself, remember it's getting late in the year and the choice will not be so great though they will be cheaper. There will also be more chance of bulbs having sprouted at the tips, reject these and anything which has lost its new shiny look. Leave the very early winter/spring bulbs until next year.

When I came to my present garden there was a lot to do in the house and none of my bulbs got planted until the end of October. We had a fairly mild winter so perhaps I was lucky, but I did not notice all that difference in the time they came up and flowered.

276

Bulbs have a way of regulating themselves even recovering from being planted upside-down, though of course I am not advising this. What can happen is that they may fall over sideways after being planted, whereupon the stalk bends round and comes up just the same.

Similarly they adapt themselves to changing seasons; until 1989 we had had a series of late cold springs and late fine autumns. I found myself expecting flowers much too early and clearing the garden later and later, sometimes not finishing until Christmas, if then. Meanwhile the bulbs flowered when it suited them and were just as good as ever.

SHAPES OF BULBS

Q I have bought a mixed collection of bulbs for the front garden of my new house and I don't even know which way up to plant them, or what kind of flowers they are.

A We mustn't lose our head and there is no need to emulate the ladies of my youth who were said in a dressmaking article not to be able to "cut out the simplest little garment without making the most appalling bloomers". First, take the bulbs and stand them the way they would balance naturally; the only ones which might present some difficulty are the flat-shaped ones which in a mixed collection are most likely to be crocuses. With a little commonsense all can be made simple and the shape most of us would expect in a bulb is something like an onion. They stand on a flattish bit which will be the root and the other end, the neck, will be the growing tip where the leaves and flower come from. Hyacinths and daffodils are the easiest, with hyacinths the shape most people expect a bulb to be and daffodils with their long neck, are both easy to plant the right way up. Hyacinths have the added advantage, if you have bought them in a collection, that they are coloured; red for pink and red, blue for dark or light blue and a greyish neutral colour for white. As for the daffodils, they will be either yellow, white or both, so you have a good idea of the colour scheme.

Q How do you mean coloured?

A The bulbs themselves look almost as if they have been dyed with the colour the flower will be and as far as I know no other bulb has this useful asset.

Anemones

While we are discussing the shapes of bulbs these should have a special mention, although they are not likely to have been included in a mixed collection. They are strange dried-up looking things which do not resemble anything else that I can think of. The growers sensibly recommend that they should be soaked overnight in tepid water before planting and though they do not look much different after the treatment, I feel it must do them some good. They are much smaller than the average bulb – if one can call them bulbs at all – and should have two to three inches of soil over them.

I have not recommended them to the first-timer because they are not particularly easy, especially in a town garden. Here is a short description in case the reader should be anxious to grow them and as they come very early are a change from daffodils and tulips.

The wild wood anemone which springs up almost by magic in the woods after a warm sunny day in spring has a cultivated cousin, **Anemone blanda**. Though said to be all colours, they are mostly blue and grow well under bushes and in clearings in the wild garden.

They need plenty of leaf-mould and if the soil is not rich, some bonemeal or manure should be added. They will do well the first year, but are inclined to disappear unless the soil and situation is exactly as they like it. In Kew gardens, little beds have been dug round the bushes or trees where they are planted and they grow very well. Kew is just far enough from the big city to have more of a country garden feel about it which they prefer.

St Brigid and De Caen anemones are the big coloured ones with the feathery leaves which are sold, often still in bud, early on in the year in flower shops. They are not particularly attractive as growing plants and most people grow them for picking, but they too are inclined to be difficult, coming up just as leaves. By all accounts the De Caen is the easiest and will do well in chalk; the St Brigid grows in milder climates such as the West Country. Their wild counterpart, **Anemone coronaria**, is the same but smaller and can be seen on the roadsides of Israel in February, which gives one some idea of the warm climate they come from.

FLAT BULBS

The flat, 'flying saucer' shaped bulb can be a little difficult. In the case of the small ones which will be crocuses, they often have a little shoot already appearing at the tip. This should not be, but if one has had to postpone planting it often happens. It is easy enough in that case to tell which way up it should go, but be careful not to damage the tip or you could lose the flower for the season. If no tip is showing, the flatter side is where the roots come from, but if you are re-planting old crocus bulbs, you might find a dead, withered piece on the underside, this is last year's old bulb and should be pulled off gently and discarded.

The Spring and Autumn Cyclamen

These little cyclamens are the outdoor kind, the large ones which people give so much as Christmas presents are greenhouse plants); the bulbs, or corms, are unexpectedly big and do present a real problem in planting. They do not have a flat or rounded end, each looking much like the other and the little whiskery bits left behind could be roots or leaves.

Q How on earth do you tell then?
A You could say that the remains of stems are longer and more wispy and that the root side is fractionally flatter. Of course, as we have said so many times before, if you can, ask someone. Luckily it is not such a problem nowadays as, like snowdrops, you can buy them growing in a pot. They are no more expensive, probably less if one considers the ones which fail to come up as can often be the case.

If you buy them now, they will be the winter/early spring **C. coum**. The easier **C. Neapolitanum**, which grow on the hills outside Naples, are the autumn flowering ones that will be out now. *C. coum* is very good as it is so early, even being out in real winter sometimes, but it tends to disappear in a bad winter. The small cyclamen like bonemeal and leaf-mould, a sunny summer and not too much shade.

Oval or Potato Shape.   If there are any small bulbs of this shape in a collection, they could be bluebells, but are most probably grape hyacinths. They are the exception and should not be planted the way they lie, which is lengthwise, but vertically. One end is more pointed than the other and is shaped towards a tip from where the leaves and flower will come. I am almost sure that in my first plantings I planted them all sideways and it never seemed to make any difference, but of course it is better to get it right in the first place.

PLANTING OUTDOOR BULBS

If the soil in the new garden has been prepared and dug over, with compost or peat added to difficult heavy soils, now is the time when the gardener will see the reward of his efforts. The bulbs can go in after the soil has cooled down, say after a frost or two and with a little rain to soften the ground, bulb-planting is not hard work. It can be a terrible labour with neglected soil, for a trowel is not much of an implement even to dig a comparatively shallow hole and 6ins can seem a lot; if you need to use the big fork, do that first. A busy person is not likely to have the time or energy to do both digging and planting in one go. If the soil remains sticky even after all your efforts, keep some builders' sand by you and fork or hoe it in as you plant and this will dry the soil up and make it easier to work.

Q How deep should one plant the bulbs?

A The general rule is to double the length of the bulb; a 2in bulb should have 4ins of soil over it. It is best to dig a 5in hole to allow for the soil to settle and put a little bonemeal at the bottom for nourishment.

Q Could one use Growmore?

A The general idea of the fertilizers made to a chemical formula – Toprose would be another – is that they are intended as boosters, to help the plants grow and flower through the growing season and to pick them up after it. They should be used twice a year, mostly spring and autumn, according to the directions. They are sprinkled on the surface and then forked and watered in. Bonemeal is a natural addition to the soil and acts as a long-term fertilizer. The flower-bud is already inside your bulbs, but they are not going to flower until March or April and want a steady growth-rate to make roots and then come into flower in the spring. Many professional gardeners do give a boost at this stage, particularly if 'real' liquid manure is available, but I find good bulbs and preparation will bring good results without further trouble.

Q What about flat bulbs though, how deep should they be planted?

A In their case, the measure is the height of the plant not the bulb. A tall thing like a gladiolus would need about 3ins of stalk to anchor it underground, so the hole should be 3-4ins. Daffodils too are inclined to flop if not planted deep enough. Include the neck of the bulb when measuring the depth.

Small bulbs of whatever shape should have about 2ins of soil above them and don't forget the hazards of cats, dogs, sparrows and above all blackbirds. The latter will come at once if the soil has been disturbed and the shallower planted bulbs suffer. You may have to re-plant and sometimes they are so persistent I have had to put defences of 'Dragons' Teeth' sticks round them (see Staking as a Protection).

Q Much the hardest work is planting bulbs in grass as there is no way of digging that first.

A When I offered to help plant bulbs in our local park, I was most interested to see the way the professionals did it. They had cut the turf and rolled it back, much as one would do if the turf was going to be taken away and planted elsewhere. Underneath of course was lovely moist soil and the grass was put back when the bulbs had gone in. They were planting crocuses to grow on a bank and sure enough they did appear in the grass next spring, but rather sparsely. The trouble may have been that we were a bit late in the season and they were not helped by the attentions of small children playing on the bank when the bulbs were coming out. They were better the second year.

Q I plant daffodils in grass and mostly just use a trowel.

A I have done it that way myself when I was younger and was pleased with the result, which is some consolation when battling away with the trowel.

Q I wonder if I planted my hyacinths badly last year, they came up all right but were ages in coming out.

A Not all bulbs are like the hyacinth. The early bulbs like snowdrops behave more like an alpine plant and the weather only has to let up a little and they will shoot up suddenly, leaves, bud and all and the flowers will appear seemingly overnight. People get very worried and even disappointed when they see hyacinth buds reach a certain stage – they can be seen quite plainly and

the leaves are opened out round them – but there they stay, sometimes for weeks. Hyacinths have often reached this stage by February and there they are, waiting for the warm sun of March to
bring them on and out. We should be glad that they have so
much sense, for this saves the flowers getting damaged by frost.

Q What would happen if I brought them indoors?

A They would come out in no time on a sunny window-sill protected from frost. If the windows aren't double-glazed the curtains
should be drawn behind, not in front, of them at night. They need
roughly the kind of heat they get in a cool greenhouse when being
'forced' for the house or for selling.

Q Is that all forcing means? It sounds more drastic somehow.

A Yes, because unless it's done fairly gently, the bulbs will dry
out or get drawn up and only produce leaves, as we were
saying last month with indoor bulbs.

Rhubarb for instance, in the kitchen gardens of my parents'
time, was simply forced by putting a wooden box over the rhubarb shoots.

Q You say that bulbs should go in now, but oughtn't one leave
tulips until later?

A The idea is that tulips are later flowering and more tender
than the other spring bulbs we have been discussing. If the
ground is too warm it might tempt them to grow too soon and
the frosts would injure them.

Perhaps because I have always had a sheltered town garden I
have never had any trouble in this way. The worst that has happened in the very cold weather of January or February is that the
tips are slightly damaged which is not noticeable when the plant is
fully grown. As far as I know, this applies to the country gardens in
the South, but I should not like to lay down the law in case it
should not apply to more exposed gardens and gardens further
North, about which I know very little.

Q Should one protect the tulips in some way?

A Later on in the autumn we will talk about Protecting Plants in
winter. To put it very briefly it is easy to do more harm than good,
for the trouble starts when the protection is taken away, the plants
can easily die and would have been better left alone.

Q My book says that if you have early tulips they should be
planted after the wallflowers.

A I should not like to burden any first-timer with the business of
dodging about between the wallflowers trying to plant tulips. The

best way would be to choose a sheltered spot, which wallflowers need anyway, like a narrow long-shaped bed and it would then be possible to plant tulips in between without too much trouble.

Q My bed in the front garden is more or less a triangle and is sheltered by the walls of the house.

A The walls would protect both tulips and wallflowers. After all early tulips come out in cold weather, not like the later Darwin tulips which do not bloom until more or less when the frosts are over.

In a bigger garden, if you are planning Darwin tulips after the dahlias there should be no difficulty. The dahlias will not be dug up and put away before the ground is cold enough and there will be a day or two at least, when you are getting the ground tidy and ready again for the tulips.

Q Should I always take the tulips up or will they do another year?

A No bulb does so well the second year and the ones gardeners of my age remember years ago were obviously prepared and brought on differently. My mother used to grow the old-fashioned Darwin tulips, 'Pride of Harlem', which were taken up after flowering and I can see them now, laid out in the garden shed ready to be re-planted in the autumn. Even nowadays tulips seem to flower well the second year, but one cannot rely on them. Of the narcissi, the large-cupped ones are the best for going on year after year and in grass, daffodils will flower well and increase without any trouble. The small species tulip in the rockery (the kind with striped leaves), can simply be left as the ones which come up again will flower, they are not like daffodils which often come up 'blind' (just leaves).

Q What about bonemeal? People say they should be fed after flowering.

A Yes and sometimes one reads that they should be fed while flowering. A lot depends on the bulb itself and what works with one doesn't work for another. Say you want the space for something else in the summer, my way of putting the bulbs in newspaper and leaving them in the compost heap until autumn works well, even in a wet year when one would expect the bulbs to have rotted. Take them out about September and leave them to dry in the shed or sheltered spot.

As you will have prepared the bed for the summer plants and probably given them a little boost later on, a sprinkle of bonemeal when the bulbs go in again should be enough.

I don't see a busy first-timer doing much more if as much. If one tries to be too careful in the first years and something happens to stop all the careful preparation, discouragement sets in, therefore we want the simplest and quickest method possible.

PLANTING BULBS IN THE ROCKERY

Q I find it very hard to plant even small bulbs in the rockery, as when I am digging a hole I strike rock all the time.

A We have to adopt a different method when the pockets are so shallow. Fork and weed the bit you are going to plant and put peat, leaf-mould compost, or the bagged compost to sufficient depth to allow for rooting, say 2ins. Scatter a handful of bonemeal and put the bulbs straight on to this pressing them down a little, but do not try to dig any further. Then give them 2ins of the compost to cover them. This is for small bulbs an inch or so high, bigger ones would want a little more above and below. Get the compost ready first and have the bonemeal to hand and it takes no more time than digging a hole.

Q I thought rockeries needed a lot of grit and stones.

A There are a great many kinds of rock plants. There are specialist plants which are true Alpines, such as one gets in the scree and rock of the high mountains. The first-timer's rockery is much more likely to be formed of ordinary garden soil. When an inconvenient mound of earth appears due to levelling a lawn or building an addition to the house, the surplus soil is often moved and turned into a rockery.

My own rockery consists of clay from the rest of the garden, which needs to be lightened with some sort of compost and sand, such as all bulbs and a lot of small plants like. As it's in the shade the heavy soil is not much problem as ferns and similar plants like something which holds the moisture.

Hopefully if your rockery soil is sandy, it will also have a sunny aspect and bulbs will do well with a bit of feeding, so all will benefit from the extra compost needed with a sandy soil.

OUTDOOR BULBS – Planting & Planning

The outdoor bulbs are only a part of the garden plan and at this point the reader might find it useful to have a summer of the bulbs we have been thinking about, bearing in mind when they flower and what size they will be. The small bulbs are nearly all early and will be planted in rockeries, along the front of beds and in containers of all kinds. The pockets of earth on low walls are notoriously shallow, usually a brick deep and small bulbs are useful for these.

The larger bulbs are later, i.e. spring and early summer. You will want these for a display in a front garden or formal bed, remembering that they will come out to make way for summer bedding plants. Daffodils and crocuses bought in large quantities are for growing naturally in the grass.

FLOWERING BULBS THROUGH THE MONTHS

1. Small bulbs for the rockery and front edgings

Winter Crocus	Species crocus, but these need sun or they will not open out fully.
Crocus tommasinianus	Mauve or purple – they have prominent yellow stamens which the birds love and should be protected by nylon strands.
Aconites	These are very attractive, yellow with a green frilly cup, but can disappear after the first year.
Scilla siberica	This is the small scilla – the birds will sometimes go for them if they appear early when nothing else is around.
Snowdrops	Not so good for edgings which often dry out – they like a really deep pocket of leaf-mould or a shady place to themselves; a clearing in the wild garden is good; a frost-proof hollow where the leaves collect better still.

All these can be expected in FEBRUARY or early MARCH – even earlier in a mild winter.

2. Later small bulbs – March onwards

Chionodoxa

This is a larger scilla, blue and white, a great favourite of mine and not so much seen as the smaller scilla. They are easier to grow and increase more readily in my experience.

Small early daffodils

'Tete-a-Tete', 'Minnow' and 'W.P. Milner', though bigger than the little early bulbs, should be planted on their own – in the front of a bed or on the rockery. 'February Gold' is almost the height of the full-sized daffodils.

Small early tulips

Species tulips, the smallest kind with striped leaves, are not always very good flowerers. 'Red Riding Hood' is the most reliable, but slightly bigger – for a small bed rather than a rockery.

Single early tulips

'Brilliant Star' is the best-known single, (the double earlies are slightly later).

Large flowering crocus

Best-known of all for an edging or under a tree – can be planted in grass as they do in the parks. A little later than the smaller species, but not much and the two kinds can be planted together.

Grape hyacinths or muscari

These come in blue and white – the latter are more expensive and do not increase well, but are worth buying all the same. Some people do not like their untidy habit of sending up leaves before the flowers come.

It sounds obvious, but do not have small bulbs too far away from the house and do not let them be smothered by other larger plants. Keep them to an edge and if you have them at a distance buy in quantity – there is no need to buy an expensive collection, what you need is for the colour to show up well.

3. Larger early bulbs

Narcissi

The two bunch-flowered narcissi '**Paper White**' and '**Soleil d'Or**', most often grown in bowls for Christmas, are still early outside, but they can look rather leggy. '**Cragford**' is later and suffers from the same fault. Grown out of sight, they are beautifully scented and ideal for picking. Left alone they will increase.

Early single tulip

'**Apricot Beauty**', though a little shorter than the later Darwins, has the same cup-shape. Grown in clumps they make an unusual sight, particularly with the sun shining through the petals.

Early double tulips

These are not particularly tall, but the flowers are large – they should be planted on their own. Making a comeback after an unexplained absence – probably a virus.

With the exception of the early narcissi, these can be expected in late MARCH or early APRIL.

4. Later outdoor bulbs

Hyacinthella

These are only slightly smaller than the usual size hyacinth. They can be as early as mid-March if a fine spell comes at the right time, but our spring weather has been so cold in the early part of the year that I should not like to promise them before April. A good mixture is effective and not so expensive as the full-sized ones.

Outdoor hyacinths

Sold under this description they will be full-size, but not so large that they flop in the rough winds and weather they can encounter. Most gardeners prefer to pick their favourite colour scheme, as they look well planted in blocks of the same colour.

The smaller **Cynthella** is better for window-boxes.

Hyacinths, good-tempered as always, can be lifted or if in bowls, left in their fibre to die down on a shelf in the garden shed. They will not force again, but do well if planted out in the garden.

Daffodils & Narcissi We have the whole range, from the end of March onwards. The first to come are the trumpet daffodils, then the large-cupped narcissi, then the scented single-flower poeticus narcissi. Faced with the bewildering choice, the first-timer might go for a collection – the kind which shows pictures of each flower and gives some idea of whether they are early or late. Something to take you through April is probably best.

Tulips **Lily-flowered tulips** flower late April-early May; **Cottage tulips**, with egg-shaped flowers and **Rembrandt tulips**, with colourful cup-shaped flowers, are both out in May with **Darwins** being the latest – mid to end of May.

PLANTING & PLANNING – Planting bulbs and plants together.

Q Though I have often had a mixed display, I have begun to think there is nothing like planting all of one kind and colour.

A I think a little depends on the design of the garden, but in general you are absolutely right. For a first-timer it takes a bit of resolution, as the temptation to try everything when one first has a garden is too strong and the result can be 'bitty' and disappointing. However, we have had a chance to see how things do and the failures can be written off to experience.

Most gardeners know a garden which they admire and envy; there is a front garden near my present house which I greatly covet. It is very simple with a lawn bordered by a narrow bed and surrounded by a hedge. The hedge is always kept clipped, the lawn is beautifully green and mown to perfection, in spring white hyacinths fill the narrow beds and in summer bedding plants, also white, take over. Such a display would not be cheap; the hyacinths always seem new, though for all I know they may be taken up and dried. The bedding plants for certain would have to be renewed each year, but the perfection is the secret.

Q I would rather have something which went on through the winter.

What about **Winter Primroses** or **Polyanthus**?

A In a fairly open position and given a little sun, the primroses would be a good bet and one should mix colours in this case to get the best display. October is rather late for wallflowers or forget-me-nots, as we have already said and like polyanthus they do not flower until early spring.

Q I have seen them flowering away in the South of France round about Christmas and the weather didn't seem all that warm.

A They say the secret is the hotter sun and more of it, also the cold winds never last and severe frost is almost unknown, though it can be cold at night. I daresay one could risk them in the West Country, though even in the South of France there is the occasional cold winter and umbrellas are hastily placed over them when the weather turns dirty.

ROCKERY PLANTS AND BULBS

Q Are **Winter Primroses** suitable for the rockery?

A The primrose family like heavy soils such as clay which retain moisture and the pockets would probably dry out too much. 'Wanda' primroses, the mauve early ones, did well on the flat part of my rockery, which was probably made when the kitchen was extended and consists of clay soil.

Q Last year I bought some **Iris reticulata** but they didn't flower well and some didn't come up at all.

A These small irises are very early and it's tempting to plant them for the spring, particularly when one has seen them in other people's gardens and nothing seems to be coming up in one's own. They need an open sunny position or they often fail to flower. They do not like a heavy town soil or a light sandy one (all bulb irises did badly in my parents' sandy garden), so I suppose the only thing is to find a sunny spot, put in plenty of rich humus (composted manure if possible) and see what luck you have.

Another kind of iris, developed from the little Greek iris such as one can see in the early spring in the ruins at Sunion, just outside Athens, is *Iris attiica* but it is not a bulb but a rhizome. The cultivated ones look like a small flag or bearded iris and not surprisingly they were flourishing in the sunny rock-gardens of an estate near Bognor, where the climate is proverbially mild. They don't do well in towns.

Q I can see quite a lot of small bulbs with mostly leaves, coming up. They are very scattered about and I should like to put them all together, would it do any harm to dig them up?

A One has to be a bit careful, particularly in a rockery where the soil is not deep, but at this time of year bulbs would not have made much growth. They are most likely to be grape hyacinths which do put up leaves months before they start to flower.

Crocuses, with small tufts of leaves, sometimes appear near the end of the month and I have often moved them to tidy them up. Wait until the ground is moist and get the trowel well under them; bring up plenty of soil so the roots are not touched and have their new home ready for them to drop into and they will hardly know anything has happened. It is worth trying, for a clump of bulbs in a bed or rockery looks much better than having them straggling about in ones and twos. To avoid root damage, always approach from underneath, never pull at them by the leaves.

PLANNING & PLANTING WINDOW-BOXES, ROOF GARDENS & CONTAINERS

Q How should I plan my window-box, if plan is the right word?

A Of course we must plan it, for if it is your only garden, you will be looking at it all the year through and we must make it a success. It will have an aspect just like any other garden and if it faces South or West it would be ideal for geraniums or petunias, but too sunny for the evergreens and ivy design which we were thinking of last month.

Q I really meant, could I plan it so that it would go on from year to year and I shouldn't have to replant it? I have read that one can plant at different levels, but would this be the right time of year?

A This is the time to plant your bulbs. To plant at different levels you would need tiny evergreens or a miniature shrub, say a small hebe. The bulbs go in first, deeper than the little shrubs' roots, then the shrubs themselves are planted at the top level and the bulbs will come up round them in the spring.

The drawback of trying to have a window-box going on and on, is the amount of space for intensive cultivation is so small, that the earth gets used up and your show deteriorates, particularly the bulbs and this is the main reason for the sad look of so many town window-boxes.

A trough-shaped container will be much deeper and is the sort of thing one could have resting on a low wall outside the front door. Filled with good compost, it will last for several years with the occasional watering. Geraniums would do well in such a box and some small bulbs could be added for the spring and left to die down. When needed it should be topped up with bagged compost or manure.

Q I had some bulbs in my window-box last year which I planted low down in the box and when they were over I planted bedding-plants on top of them. I am worried now, for the bulbs are coming up before the plants are over. It's my only garden and I don't want to spoil it, what shall I do?

A We have had some rather strange seasons, and unusually fine warm autumns which might make the bulbs come up early, or it might be a sign that they had become smaller. Bulbs can split up into little bulbs which don't flower and this happens quite often in a window-box if the soil is poor, or if a container has a bay tree or some such evergreen which is taking food from the bulbs planted round it.

As for the bedding plants in your box, I should leave them there in case they survive the winter and risk the bulbs coming up blind, i.e. flowerless. You can always replace them in the spring.

Q What makes bulbs come up blind?

A All sorts of reasons, but I should say mostly poor soil. Bulbs do seed themselves, which is a sign that they like where they are. In this case though, the original bulbs would flower just the same and the little bulbs with their tiny threads of leaves would scarcely be noticed until they came into flower a year or two later, so be careful when weeding.

Q I never realised bulbs had seeds.

A Naturally enough when we buy bulbs, ready-made as it were, we don't think of seeds, but you will see green lumps where the daffodils have flowered, which should be removed before you take them up. Lily seed-heads are so big that one can be deceived into thinking they are about to flower again. Leave the seed-heads and always supposing the lily likes where it's growing, you will see little thready leaves coming up the next year which will eventually become full-sized flowering bulbs.

The demand for something bigger and better has made the bulb firms vie with each other to produce ever bigger and richer-looking bulbs, but once away from the expert's hands the bulbs deteriorate. A reliable firm will not sell anything which is too small to flower and the medium-sized bulbs are the best buy if one is thinking of keeping them from year to year. In containers, however large, bulbs are not growing naturally.

Q Perhaps I could have some kind of evergreen that didn't mind the sun. What about hebes? They could be mixed with hyacinths.

A Hyacinths are certainly good lasters, in the sense that they go on year after year and are better than most bulbs in similar conditions. Hebes, the evergreen veronicas, have rather dark leaves and could look a bit drab on their own once the hyacinths have finished flowering. In June when the bedding plants are on sale, you could add some silver-leaved cinerarias (the kind grown for their leaves), which mix well with darker evergreens. They too are 'evergreen', keeping their leaves through the winter and only needing a little trimming when the spring comes.

To keep everything in good condition though, there is no escape from a little yearly or seasonal attention; fresh compost, a 'Phos-tab' for feeding, watering in a dry summer and weeding, though this is minimal.

Q I suppose it sounds terrible, but is there really nothing one can just plant and leave?

A I will not insult you by suggesting plastic flowers, but they do make a point, you mustn't expect to grow living things out of their real environment with no care at all. Of course you can get a firm to come and fix the box for you, as we were saying earlier on, but I have a feeling there is a tiny seed of the gardener in you or you would not be bothering to ask questions.

Q The fact is I don't know a thing about it but I shall have a try anyway.

A You may end up like Beth Chatto, the famous plantswoman, who declares she knew nothing when she started her garden.

URNS

These are the superior containers seen in stately homes and in that setting are probably antique and made of lead or stone. We shall most likely buy reproductions made in processed stone or composition, but even so they are not particularly cheap, though there is nothing to beat them in a formal setting. We have already thought of the first-timer who might find himself with a terrace or formal layout.

Urns are very useful too for giving a false perspective. They stand up on their stems and somehow give the impression that they must be leading on to a grand vista, even if it is really just the end of the garden concealed by shrubs, or anything else which can be made to look as if it goes on forever such as a wood.

The genuine article can be bought at firms such as T.E. Crowther & Sons, "Specialists in antique garden statues and ornaments".

Needless to say they are very costly, but I am a great believer when making a choice of this kind in going for the best and at least we have a yardstick to judge the others by. Crowther's address is: 289 North End Road, Fulham, London SW6 and they also show at the Syon House Garden Centre.

Q What about fibreglass? I feel very tempted, they look just like the real thing if one doesn't get too near and are much cheaper.

A On pillars such as we have been thinking about, they would be liable to be blown over in the wind, as fibreglass is altogether too light even when filled with earth. Some summers this would be happening the whole time and even if the urn escaped without damage, the plants would be ruined.

Q What about a trough then? I like the kind made to imitate lead.

A It would be sitting down flat so wind would not be a problem. If the site is at all exposed, fibreglass is not frost-proof, so you would have to wait until early summer to fill it with bedding plants.

FILLING THE URN

Q The urns in our new garden are on pillars, either side of steps leading down to the lawn and have been planted up with a conifer in each and are growing well. It seems a bit ungrateful to want more colour and it is a biggish garden. Should I leave them?

A The smaller conifers such as pencil-shaped cypresses or junipers, are very attractive and look appropriate in such a setting. They are not all that easy to grow well in containers and I should leave them. If the garden is fairly big you have plenty of room elsewhere, not like the very small patio dependent on containers for colour.

Q Why do they call them conifers? They don't seem to have any fir-cones.

A If they did have cones they would be different from the familiar fir-cone of the pine tree. I suppose they have been bred as miniatures and the cones got left out in the process. Interfering with nature always has consequences and we all know how difficult it is to get any flowers from the florist which smell like the ones in the old country gardens. I did see a mini one with cones at an RHS show at Vincent Square and regret not having bought it. I was not sure if it would do in the rockery at my present house and it was rather expensive.

For the summer planting we shall have to wait until about June next year. Fuchsias, which have become so popular, make a very good centre-piece and they can be used for trailing over the edge. They are sold as 'trailing' or 'upright', but the upright will need at least one stake to keep it nice and tall. '**Swingtime**' is a very good variety, with a lovely fat white centre and red sepals. Its only drawback is that it is inclined to flower rather late.

Q I suppose it would be worth the extra to buy it already in flower.

A If it's for the centre of the urn, you certainly want something nearly ready to flower and you also want a good well-grown plant, not just a cutting. The same applies to geraniums.

For the fillers round the centre, or packed in tight on their own, the new *Impatiens* is excellent. The flowers are slightly larger than the old Busy Lizzie, the plants more compact in growth and the leaves are very decorative.

Q I like the old kind which spread and hang over the edge. It saves having to plant something like lobelias which I am rather tired of.

A Surrounding something tall in the centre, the old-time *Impatiens* (the Busy Lizzie) packed in really tight, would take over and spread as much as you want and you would hardly notice the leaves for the mass of flowers.

Q What about something more unusual? Somehow an urn asks for special treatment.

A I have seen an all-white display looking most effective. In the centre was a really big fat geranium with white flowers and plenty of buds and the filling round it was of white petunias mixed with silver cinerarias. Get the very best and biggest as it is the sort of arrangement which needs to be rich-looking.

STATUES FOR THE GARDEN

Q What about statues? I should love to have one, but they say they are in danger of becoming the rich man's gnome.

A The same firm of Crowther's would have some beauties which would undoubtedly fill your need – at a price of course – and anyone who breathed the word 'gnome' would be suffering from a sad case of spite and envy.

At the Royal Academy's Summer Exhibition at Burlington House, Piccadilly, London, there are some sculptures specially intended for the garden, also others, which I imagine would be possible to have out of doors even in our climate. The artist would be able to tell you and advise on the most suitable material. Buying at Burlington House, you would have the advantage of your statue being one of an 'edition' of say nine, so you are not likely to see yours all over the place. They all come out of the same mould, whatever the material. Go early and if you are a Friend of the Royal Academy you can apply to go on a special day of viewing, which is confined to prospective buyers. Much less expensive would be the ones at garden centres, though some are dear enough, but there is nothing like looking round a bit. If all the garden centres have one particular statue one might think twice, but if you like it why not?

Naturally the gardens of the stately houses themselves show off this kind of thing to great advantage, but for practical purposes their statuary is too large to go with today's smaller gardens.

When all is said and done, why should a good copy of a good statue be any different from any other kind of reproduction?

Q I want a good statue because I intend to turn my tiny patio into a formal arbour. The only thing I found in it was a rather shaky archway with a dead rose. If I could strengthen the archway, I would have the statue in it with two tall thin evergreens either side.

A Some talented gardeners turn their tiny patios into a riot of flowers (all in pots), but this takes experience and they are often people who have given up a large country garden. There is a tremendous amount to be said for a formal setting such as you describe. The statue and its plinth, or whatever you could find to stand it on, would be all you need and the trees would look most classical. If you do buy a good statue, it is absolutely essential to get a builder to secure it really firmly, with a bolt if necessary to prevent it being stolen.

ROOF-GARDENS

These will be container-gardens and have the advantage over the 'real' garden, in that shrubs can go in now with no need to wait. The first-timer should see that, if his roof is exposed and windy, the plants are protected by some sort of fencing and that there is easy access to a water supply. If your roof has not been used as a garden before, consult your surveyor, tubs full of earth can be extremely heavy and you do not want to damage the roof.

SUITABLE SHRUBS FOR THE ROOF

The more sheltered type of roof-garden or large balcony will have railings or a balustrade already there. I have seen rambler roses growing over them with great success and the larger-leaved variegated ivy, though a slow starter, is a good choice too as it makes an excellent screen. When you buy an ivy, make sure the nursery understands that you want the outdoor kind.

Camellia

Q Could I grow a camellia? I have a very big tub on my roof-garden.
A Unfortunately they are very sensitive to cold winds and equally dislike anywhere too sunny and dry. I tried my camellia on the North side of my roof-garden, in what I hoped was a sheltered spot and although it got through the winter fairly well, the summer was too much for it. However hard I watered, the winds dried up the tub again and sadly the plant never came to anything.

A better choice was the dwarf lilac which was labelled *Syringa microphylla*, but it turned out to be the true lilac with full-sized purple flowers on a dwarf standard, not more than 3ft high. It went into the camellia's tub, placed more in the sun and did wonderfully. The second attempt to get the dwarf lilac resulted in a small-leaved lilac, very like the *microphylla*, but with long sprays of flowers instead of the miniature lilac heads. This version flowers twice and did well, but I was determined to get the one I had first tried for and succeeded at the third try. All three liked the open rather wind-swept but sunny aspect of the roof-garden.

Q What about trees? Some of the tubs are huge and one has a cherry tree already planted.
A In my case, none survived more than a year or so as they dry out very easily and do not take to the exposed position of a roof-garden. The experts tell me that no trees in tubs last more than four years so it seems hardly worth it.

Previously we have been thinking of the kind of shrubs so much favoured by developers for a windy or exposed roof-garden. Steer clear of two, **Senecio greyi** and the **Mahonia japonica**. The senecio is so easy to grow at ground level, that many country gardeners think of it as more or less a weed, so it is rather a shock to find it can be cut back quite severely if exposed to hard frosts. The mahonia (the evergreen berberis), the kind with long sprays of yellow flowers in early spring, is quite tough as a plant, but on a roof or in an exposed place the flowers will be spoilt every time.

As well as rambler roses the bush rose, in particular those of the 'Peace' family, do very well on a roof. I had just re-made a tub which had been filled with a rather ugly variegated euonymus. The euonymus is the spindleberry, but not at all like the wild one, with pink berries. When I was in the garden centre buying plants in June, I had meant to look for something like a fuchsia, but instead took a beautiful red rose which I saw called '**Grandpa Meilland**'. I had put manure at the bottom of the tub, to assist with moisture retention as much as anything and this proved quite enough for the rose to make very satisfactory growth.

Q I thought one planted roses next month.

A Yes indeed, November is their month, but we live in an age of instant gardening which one can take full advantage of when it comes to containers.

PLANTING, PLANNING & CLEARING

October in the 'real' garden, besides planting bulbs, sees the beginning of the clearing which so many people dread at this time of year.

Q I certainly dread it, there always seems so much work.

A I take it that you prefer what most people would call a proper garden, that is you do not want it all paved, with brick pergolas and other modern labour saving ways of garden planning?

Q Yes, I always think a paved garden of any size looks like a swimming bath with the water let out. I don't really mind what plants I have as long as the whole thing looks tidy.

A Once a garden is established, there is no difficulty in keeping it tidy if you make friends with a garden firm who will come, say in the spring and autumn. This is what I do myself now that I am getting on, as people say.

Q's who are doing their own clearing in the new garden should look out for the winter-flowering shrubs. **Winter jasmine** and **Forsythia** which will have already formed their flower buds can be pruned now, but beware of cutting away all the spring flowers. The **Japonica** or *Chaenomeles japonica* seems to be the exception, as the rather straggly growth it has made in the summer and autumn is nearly always flowerless. Flowers seem to come straight out of the main stem; actually they come in the angle of what was cut back the year before and the main stem. The professional gardeners in the park near where I live, cut right back in this way at this time of year.

Q The forsythia has grown tremendously in the summer and I can't keep it in hand.

A   The time to cut it is directly after it has flowered. Later on, if the new branches and leaves are overhanging something else, cut them back and tidy up stragglers, but leave it alone otherwise, for its beauty is all in the flowers and not the leaves. Never cut out old wood as it is there to protect the young shoots; I did just that and killed the plant, for the young shoots died in the spring frosts and the bush never recovered.

Whilst considering clearing, it goes without saying that you do not want to be left with all the debris of a cleared garden (with the exception of loose bricks which can be useful). If you do have room too, hang on to twiggy small branches, as they are very useful for staking things like pinks and outdoor carnations in a natural way. The main stem from which twiggy bits come should be fairly stout though, or it will not hold the plant firmly when you plant it in the ground. All the rest should be part of the bargain with the clearing firm and agreed beforehand. One may have to pay for them to drive it to a tip, but it is well worth the money.

Q   Will the weeds die once they have been uprooted?

A   No, they are incredibly tough and will live to fight another day. They should be pulled out by hand, taking care to look out for any roots which might get left behind. If this is too tedious use weed-killer, but that would mean leaving the ground unplanted until the spring. I forgot to include buttercups in my list of tough weeds; mine on the rockery, though greatly depleted, survived weed-killer.

I am so careful with weed-killer because the law keeps changing about what one can and cannot use and also in small gardens people naturally are worried about neighbouring cats and wild life in general. If a weed-killer is too mild though it seems to act like a tonic and encourage some things (this is the principle on which selective weed-killers work on lawns of course). If you mix the weed-killer yourself, buy a special can to spray with and never use it for anything else. However much one thinks one has cleared out the can, some can remain and one can find it killing not only ones own but a neighbour's roses, as happened to me on one frightful occasion.

Q   You are alarming me!

A   Well, have the firm to do it for you as I did, it can all be part of the contract.

Let's pretend now that our garden is simply needing the usual autumn clearing, tidying and planting.

SOME WAYS OF MAKING CLEARING EASIER

First leaves which we have made some sort of container for. A quick sweep of leaves takes very little time, the place looks less depressing in a moment and somehow the task does not seem so formidable. If you have a tree or trees anywhere near your garden, I can only say they have more leaves on them than anyone would believe possible. Some years the leaves will come down in two or three nights of frost which is much the best way. I do not favour waiting until all the leaves have come down and are lying about in heavy wet lumps. It is much less tiring keeping up with them as they fall, as far as one can.

In a bigger garden have a wheelbarrow; in a smaller one there are very good rot-proof bags sold nowadays, which are ingeniously wired so that they sit down flat and open and are easy to carry. Choose a still day to sweep otherwise the wind will always come round the corner and blow the leaves round in circles, even if you imagine you are sweeping with the wind. One of the most simple and effective labour savers ever invented, is two pieces of wood about 18ins long and 8ins wide, which you place either side of your pile of leaves, squashing them together and the whole lot will lift up into the wheelbarrow or bag without any trouble.

WARNING   Do not put woody things, diseased leaves or prunings, into the compost, they will have to be burned or disposed of on the dump. Luckily the modern machine dustcart (if one can call it that!) will deal with this kind of thing in small quantities. Bag it up securely and don't put too much out at once. Also, cutting into small pieces first makes it much easier to handle.

Q   Suppose a plant should have rust, how can one tell that from autumn colours?

A   Plants in general do not turn like trees and one should not expect autumn colours from them. If a rose does suffer from rust (a virus), it has probably had mildew earlier in the season and the plant will not be looking healthy. We shall have more to say in November when we come to pruning roses.

CUTTING DOWN THE BORDER

Here again I can speak from experience of past mistakes. Once the plants have stopped flowering, particularly in towns, the

leaves will soon look untidy and frankly ugly. It is a great temptation to cut them down and get rid of them, not only does this
harm the plant, but is a great deal more trouble. The small brittle
bunch of dead stalks and leaves, is unbelievably different from the
huge intractable bundle cut down too soon and of course takes up
much less room in the bin.

RE-MAKING THE BORDER

If you are thinking of re-making the border, do not try to do it all
at one time. Suppose you have a corner of late-flowering chrysanthemums, it is so easy to leave everything until they are over, then
Christmas is on you and nothing done. If you have an unexpected
hour or two, fine weather and the border ready except for the
later plants, start at one end and dig and clear as much as you
have time for. It is bad for the plants to lie about out of the
ground and the ideal is to get them back in at once, so do a
small bit at a time and it is not nearly such a labour. If this
isn't possible, always protect the plants' roots by leaving the soil
on them and wrap round with newspaper. You can heel them
in, but this makes extra labour.

Q How do I go about re-making the border? There are some
things I like but which are rather too big and can I leave the
rest alone if they are doing well?

A Yes, most people divide their border plants in the autumn
because they have become too big (hence the 'bits' given to
friends). There is no need to re-make the whole border. Re-
making is either because experience has shown one what does
well and the whole plan has been altered, or perhaps a neighbouring house has had a loft conversion or been re-built, thus
making the aspect shadier as happened to me after the war. If
the border has been neglected, it is a good idea to dig as
deep as you have the strength for, usually about a spade's
depth which is much harder than it sounds. Fill the hole with
anything you have cut down (chopped into small pieces), put
some of the earth back, tread down and put the rest of the
earth, incorporating bonemeal and composted manure, on top.
This is your platform for the re-planting. Border perennials do
not have deep roots on the whole, but the ones that do
should be left alone.

DIVIDING THE PLANTS

With the big fork, lift the plants out earth and all and lie them on sacking or newspaper. You will find that the plant seems to be growing in a circle round a dead or dying middle. The new growth is usually on the outside, so pull the best looking pieces away from the centre; they will separate quite easily and make plantlets, which should be kept and the old middle discarded. Plant two or three new pieces together to get a good show for the following summer. A day or two later, when the earth has settled, you may have to rake some more topsoil over them.

Q What plants ought not to be divided?

A Paeonies hate being disturbed. If they are very well established and you want to increase your plants, take from the side but do not dig the whole plant up.

Lupins make long tap roots so leave them alone and increase from seeds. They are very easy to grow that way and will often flower well after only a year. That is to say, if sown in the autumn, they will come up the next year and flower the following summer.

Just let **Japanese Anemones** increase on their own and they will make a nice clump. I have never succeeded in detaching their tough roots successfully and they take a long time to get established.

Of course, any shrub which is living alongside our border plants, should be left alone and only trimmed to keep it in shape. Never let them overgrow other plants.

Q I suppose one shouldn't divide a plant before its leaves have died down?

A No, the plant must be dormant in its winter resting state and besides anything else, there is nothing more tedious than dodging about through other plants trying not to damage them. Do not put compost down until all is ready, for the same reason, also it sticks to one's shoes or boots and makes a mess everywhere.

Q Is this the time for compost?

A It will be November before all is ready in most gardens. All plants benefit from a top dressing of well-rotted manure (compost is the easiest) and it is especially good for keeping bulbs in good trim. Dig it in.

Let us finish the month with a summary of some of the best-known and easy to grow Border plants.

RECOMMENDED BORDER PLANTS (All listed are "hardy")

Acanthus   Tall, about 4ft for the back of the border. The leaves are the ones used so much in classical design.

Achillea   The border yarrow. Go for the one with the flat yellow heads which is tall, about 3–4ft. Likes sun.

Japanese Anemone   Very useful. Late flowerer, end Aug. or Sept.

Aster   The perennial aster is the Michaelmas daisy, and the most commonly seen is the tall *A. novi-belgii*. The shorter ones for the front of the border are late in flowering and very prone to mildew.

Astilbe   This is more like the wild meadowsweet and likes the same kind of moisture. Astilbes are coloured hybrids and do well in shade.

Chrysanthemum   'Korean' chrysanthemums are the hardy spray kind. Late flowerers.

Coreopsis   Useful daisy plant because of its earlier flowering in June. Mid-border 2ft. Needs sun to do well.

Delphinium   Needs a rich soil. People are often disappointed when the huge spikes become smaller, but apart from this it is an easy plant and early – late June.

Echinops   Tall blue plant. The flowers are thistles, but globe shaped. Dries very well and easy to grow.

Achillea

Geranium

The true geranium (cranesbill) – choose the blue one – is for the front of the border.

Helenium

Very reliable mid-border plants, but not for those who don't like daisies. Easy to grow and good for picking – yellow and bronze.

Heliopsis

'**Golden Plume**' is a beautiful double flower. Tall, for the back of the border – daisy haters do not be put off.

Hollyhock

Very tall for the back of the border. It is best to leave them to seed themselves and renew at least every other year. Look untidy when over.

Hosta

H. sieboldiana is marvellous for a shady corner, which needs filling right up, but they grow HUGE leaves and the flower is small in comparison. '**Thomas Hogg**' is much smaller and has pretty green and white leaves, but it is more difficult to grow – for the front of the border. It is the giant cousin of the plantain weed of the lawn.

Lupin

The '**Russell**' strain went under for a bit, but is now back again – good plants for a new garden as they like untouched soil and will grow with no attention. Don't forget they hate lime (builder's dust, mortar dust etc).

Tree Lupin
Phlox paniculata

The one always recommended for the chalk garden. This is an old favourite – 3–4ft so middle to back of border. Grows well in light soil, but needs watering – not so good for a town garden. Needless to say, the easiest to grow is

Delphinium

not a particularly attractive colour, a sort of puce. Otherwise there are mauve, purple, brick red, pure white and white with a pink 'eye', which is very pretty and easy to grow.

Pyrethrum
These are pink and red daisies, with feathery leaves which rabbits like. For the front of the border, they come out in June just when the latest bulbs are over and the summer plants not yet in flower.

Sedum spectabile
'**Autumn Joy**' is a late flowering succulent, which makes a wonderful show after a fine summer with its mauve/pink flowers. Can be rather late in a bad summer.

Solidago
This is the golden rod which grew so easily in the old borders – it was more or less considered a weed. The modern plants are a great improvement, more compact and the flower is bigger. Not more than 2½–3ft. The older variety (you might be given some) is still worth growing and is 4–5ft.

Tradescantia
Much grown also in the old border, so again the reader may be given some. It makes a compact little clump, but produces flowers one after the other so that there never seems a real show. The flowers themselves are pretty, mauve or purple, with three petals arranged like a propeller.

Unless otherwise stated (as they say) border perennials tend to be mid-July or later, which is what makes the early ones so valuable. We have already considered chrysanthemums as late flowers and there is one more, **Rudbeckia**. It is rather a bold statement I suppose, but I really do think it will grow anywhere, however unpromising. It is very tall, 5ft or more and has a yellow daisy flower with a 'cone' for its middle. There is a smaller rudbeckia, known as Black-Eyed Susan.

The first-timer will probably have expected his garden to be nearly finished by the end of this month, but in reality the autumn weather lasts on until at least mid-November. More of Clearing and Planting next month.

The first-timer with a neglected garden which needs a lot of clearing should turn to November.

November

We should all pray that the weather will stay reasonably mild and will not be too wet, for this is *the* month for planting roses, ornamental trees and shrubs.

We are not speaking here of forest trees such as the oak, beech and elm which are, but sadly not as in the past, so much a part of our countryside. Anyone who plants one of these is unselfishly planning for the future and should be encouraged, but such trees need a great deal of room and are not for the small or town garden.

Q One does see forest trees in the big London gardens.

A Yes, we are lucky enough to look out on a row which includes, copper beech, acacia and chestnut trees and further on there is the remains of a lime walk, but these were part of the old estate planted many years earlier.

London is famous for its plane trees and there was the beautiful avenue of elms leading up to the Round Pond in Kensington Gardens, sadly killed by Dutch elm disease. None of them could be coped with in our kind of garden, only in parks and big open spaces. A great number of mistakes were made in the past and can be seen all over towns, where people planted trees such as poplars, acacias and the bigger flowering cherries in their front gardens, only to find that the roots interfered with the foundations and the trees had to be felled or mutilated.

THE NEGLECTED GARDEN

The difficulty will be to get your garden cleared in time for planting. If you plan to employ a firm do not delay, get them along to see the garden and at the same time order the plants you want.

Nowadays, firms will plant all through the winter provided it is mild enough, though it is not the ideal way because one can so easily be held up by snow and frost and even a mild winter has occasional cold spells.

Planting is possible in the spring, but there is danger of a spring drought and trees in particular need plenty of water their first year. Equally, the ground may be waterlogged and planting will be impossible until the late spring, which is rather too near the summer because most plants will have started growing.

Q I could get someone in to clear but I have no idea what to order.

A We are going on to a list of shrubs and flowering trees, most of which we have discussed in more detail as we went through the months.

Q Do any shrubs flower twice?

A Not as far as I know, though some do have a longish period of flowering. The **Winter Jasmine** and **Camellia** will flower over 2–3 months and **Hydrangeas** in the late summer will go on well into autumn, sometimes producing a few new blooms.

No one thinks of **Roses** as shrubs, but some of the 'perpetual' ones do flower nearly all the season and most have two flowering times, early and late summer. The exceptions, except for some modern varieties, are the shrub roses which are not for the small garden.

Q How about climbers?

A They count as climbing shrubs (the stems are woody) and can go in now.

Here is our list of shrubs and flowering trees according to the seasons. I have included some herbaceous plants which are often grown amongst shrubs.

Q Aren't all herbaceous plants border plants?

A Herbaceous just means that the stems are not woody. Most of them die down in the winter and some leave little rosettes of leaves behind them at the base. One gets used to thinking of herbaceous plants as border plants because of herbaceous borders. The ones we are mentioning now can go in anywhere, with shrubs if wanted and not necessarily as part of a border.

NAMES OF PLANTS – Shrubs, Ornamental Trees & Climbers (cl. shrubs)

Winter and Early Spring

Early Azaleas   Not evergreen and now called rhododendron. Not easy in a town garden.

Camellia   March is the great month for camellias. The **Camellia japonica** and the hybrid (mixture or cross) x **williamsii**, together with the **C. reticulata** (curved or hanging down slightly), all need the shelter of a wall for preference and not in full sun. Some people prefer the *C. reticulata*, as it drops petals when the flowers are over and there are no ugly dead flowers still on the bush – they take some time to drop.

Forsythia   Comes later than the jasmine, about the end of March and has a wonderful show of yellow. A very large tree-like bush. Can be trained against a sunny wall or even cut to make a hedge. Cut back the flowering stems when over to keep in order. Never cut out old wood, it protects the young growth.

Garrya elliptica   This is a tall shrub, 8ft. but not spready. It looks well by the side of a porch. Grown for its catkins – pale green – produced in February.

Jasmine nudiflorum   The winter jasmine – is also out in November in a mild year. Can be trained against a wall is very hardy, but needs a little sun to flower well.

Mahonia japonica   A spready shrub with pale yellow sprays of leaves produced in February or early

March. Can grow up rather suddenly and look ungainly, the 'topknot' can be cut off – prune after flowering back to the original bush. Evergreen, goes red in autumn.

Skimmia japonica

A small shrub which flowers early and is useful because it is so compact – say 2ft each way. Get *S. japonica reevesiana* which is both male and female and saves the trouble of buying separate m and f plants.

Viburnum tinus

The old-fashioned laurustinus. It will grow practically anywhere and flower all the winter. It is a big bush – say 8ft each way. When planning, don't forget that shrubs grow outwards as well as up-wards.

Hamamelis mollis

Best known of the witch hazels. Flower-ing from December to March, they have pretty if rather spidery little flowers and look best against a dark background. It is a TREE and needs 12ft or so head-room and similar spread.

Prunus

This Latin name covers all the flowering cherries as well as ornamental plums, peaches and almonds. Almond blossom is the first of all to come out, but is often spoiled by frost. The winter flower-ing cherry P. subhirtella 'Autumnalis' has leaves come after flowering, an attractive dark red.

Bergenia

Is a flat, rather straggly herbaceous plant, but is evergreen. Has early pink primula-like flowers and is at its best in a mild winter.

Passiflora
Popularly known as the passion flower

Winter Heather   Needs a bed on its own and not recom-
                            mended for a town garden, though they
                            do well on a windy roof-garden.

Helleborus corsicus   The green-flowered hellebore. Is taller
                            than **H. orientalis** and hardier. The
                            flowers of *H. orientalis* come out some-
                            times as early as January and can be
                            affected by frost. If held back by cold
                            weather, both will be out early in
                            April. *Corsicus* is the taller of the two at
                            2–3ft.

Late Spring and Early Summer

Azalea   These are the evergreen hardy kind
                            (cousins of the pot plant). They are diffi-
                            cult to grow in towns – like peat and leaf-
                            mould and do not like a hot dry summer.
                            They come out at a useful time, after the
                            late bulb display in May.

Buddleia   **B. globosa**, with mini-orange like
                            flowers is easy to grow and not quite so
                            strong-growing as the variety with the
                            long mauve spray flowers. Both are tall
                            bushes, however much they are pruned
                            or cut down and grow like weeds almost
                            anywhere.

Camellia   The bulk come out now – choose a
                            colour which appeals to you, but make
                            sure it is hardy.

Ceanothus   Trained against a wall, it has blue clus-
                            ters of flowers in May and is so vigorous
                            that it is a great shock when a cold
                            winter kills it, but is much grown all
                            the same. It does well in towns.

Choisya

An attractive shrub with evergreen leaves and white flowers in May. Grows to 4–5ft and the same round, is bushy and compact, but not quite hardy. It does well in towns.

Cytisus

This is part of the broom family, some are low growing and all need sun. Cut back after flowering – once they start to look like their name it is too late. Never cut right down or hard back as you will kill the plant.

Kerria japonica

It will grow in any soil, is not too big a shrub at 4–5ft and has pretty yellow flowers which are out with the leaves. Is good in town or country.

Lilac

The Latin name is *Syringa*. Unless it is bought as a standard it makes a really large bush. It needs as much space as a small tree.

Philadelphus

Also called mock orange or wrongly 'syringa'. It is a large shrub with fragrant white flowers in June and July, which is a good time. The double varieties are smaller shrubs but do not have the same show of flowers. Prune immediately after flowering.

Pieris

P. 'Forest Flame' is a lovely shrub, is slow growing to 4–6ft and though compact can be fanned out. The young growth in spring is red, fading to pink lily-of-the-valley like flowers later. The only drawback is that it is not quite hardy and an unseasonable frost can kill it – needs a sheltered position an acid soil and is good in towns.

Roses

All kinds are shrubs – although many what are called shrub roses are not for the small garden. One exception, **Rosa gallica**, the striped rose is worth growing, but only flowers once.

Viburnum

V. burkwoodii is one of the prettiest. It is a strong grower to 6ft or more, but is easy to control and can be kept low and fanned out if wanted. If the soil is acid, give a little lime now and then. It has large flat, scented flowers in April.

Weigela

It is a medium-sized quick growing shrub which needs keeping in hand. It grows well in towns and has clusters of pink or red trumpet flowers in May and June. The variegated-leaf variety is more compact.

Laburnum

Is always thought of with the lilac, though usually a shade later – end of May or early June when there is not much else. It is a real tree which again grows almost wild in towns or wasteland, but the modern varieties like *L. x waterii* 'vossii' are much superior.

Magnolia

This is a tree-shrub and can be as tall as 20ft but is more usually 10ft with a similar spread. It is very susceptible to the cold spring winds, as it is so early. The one most grown is **Magnolia soulangeana**, but **M. stellata** with narrow petals is said to be less tender. It is also much smaller. There is a deep mauve variety which is later, early May. If trimmed they can look like a large shrub.

Clematis   The earliest is **C. montana** which needs
                       plenty of room and the best variety is
                       'Elizabeth'. **C. alpina** is a beautiful
                       early one, but not so vigorous and will
                       do in towns.

Hydrangea   **H. petiolaris** is the climbing hydrangea
                       It needs plenty of room and a little sun to
                       flower well, but is otherwise good in
                       towns.

Lonicera   The Latin name for honeysuckle. It
                       needs sun and is often disappointing in
                       a town garden.

Wisteria   It is a really large May-flowering climber
                       which needs a whole wall or pergola –
                       some town neighbours join forces and
                       have it along two or three terrace
                       houses. Needs expert pruning back to
                       the wood to avoid it going to leaf and
                       not flowering well.

Later Summer to Autumn

Hibiscus   The non-tropical variety which grows
                       well over here can be blue, deep pink
                       or white. The white is the larger of the
                       two and grows to 6ft each way. It does
                       well in towns – will even grow on 'is-
                       lands' in roads!

Pampas Grass   The Victorian favourite now back in
                       fashion, but not for small children as
                       the leaves have sharp edges which can
                       cut them.

Yucca   Has a very spectacular flower, but not
                       every year and needs a longish hot
                       spell. Also not for small children, as it
                       has sharp thorns at the end of the leaves.

Clematis

The large-flowered ones come out in June and July. The easiest to grow are the **jackmanii** cultivars with *C. jackmanii* 'Jackmanii Superba' flowering from July to September and having larger flowers than the ordinary purple one. **'Ville de Lyon'** a dark red, is later and another good doer.

Cobaea

Another late-flowering climber, which is very useful for covering a fence quickly.

Passiflora

The passion flower, though so exotic-looking, is not difficult to grow and does well in towns. Flowers appear between June and September.

Autumn and Winter

Now come the trees and shrubs grown for their leaves or berries in the Autumn.

Acer

Many nurseries call a maple by its Latin name, but it's all the same. The Japanese maple is **A. palmatum** and the many varieties are grown mostly for their coloured foliage, particularly in autumn. Do check the size though. The sycamore tree is a maple, **Acer pseudo-platanus** and is a big tree – too big for most gardens unless one wants a screen, in which case it is a fast grower and very hardy. It would take too much light from a town garden.

Pyracantha and Cotoneaster

Very easy to confuse the two. The pyracantha is much grown as a wall climbing shrub and looks most handsome with its red berries in long lines on a house. It must be kept cut back, otherwise it is a

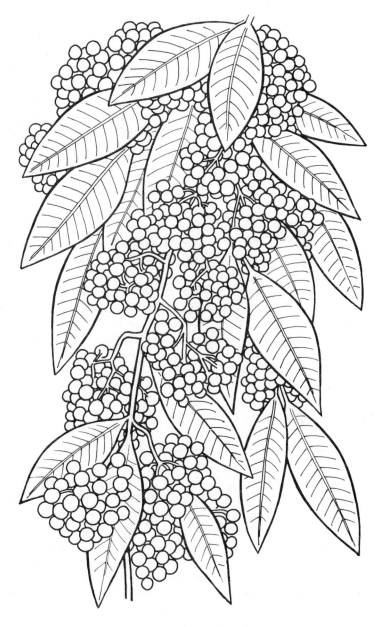

Cotoneaster
White flowers are followed by red berries

fair-sized shrub about 6ft each way, sometimes much more. The cotoneaster climbs on its own as it were, has smaller leaves and is easier to handle. Both have white flowers followed by red berries.

Sorbus avcuparia   Or mountain ash, has red or yellow berries. The whitebeam is *s. aria* and is often seen as a street tree.

Winter

We are back again to early spring!

As we have already said, there are many gardening books which describe plants in much greater detail and with much more knowledge. Make a start with some of the ones suggested and fill in gradually with the others of your own choice. Remember the choicer varieties are always more difficult to grow, which is no reason for not trying them, but a little experience is needed. As we said earlier on, some plants may be familiar from a remembered garden and it is a help to know whether they are likely to do in the new garden.

THE ESTABLISHED GARDEN

Q The garden is more or less straight, but I won't be there much in the winter. I mean to leave things mostly as they are, apart from a bit of tidying. Is there anything I should be doing?
A For the border, it does look tidier to get the plants cut down when the leaves die, but it is not necessary from the plants point of view. Get rid of any tough weeds which might take over such as, course tufty grass, ground ivy, docks and nettles. If you are short of time get help just for a day or two. Annual weeds, the small straggly ones, will come out easily with the hoe or weeding fork, for they should be stopped from scattering their seeds for next year as much as possible.

Don't let the leaves lie about on the beds or lawn all the winter. Collect them into a heap as we did when discussing compost. If you do have time to plant anything, dig an extra deep hole and get rid of some of the leaves this way; tread them down well, cover with earth and they will form humus for the plant. Climbers such as clematis do particularly well planted in this way. Many people say one should not include weeds as they come up again, but I have never had much trouble. Pounce on them early in the spring and they are gone before they can spread.

Q   What about pruning the roses?

A   Bush roses can be pruned in the spring but ramblers and climbers can be tidied up with the dead wood removed. We are going into this in more detail later in the month. If a bush is diseased cut it right down.

Through the summer we have been considering an imaginary border, with the idea of having continuous colour. We thought of climbing roses as a possibility up posts or a pergola, or if there is a path behind the border, climbing up a wall. As we were saying when thinking of forking in some compost or manure for the winter, if at all possible the border should be finished before we deal with the roses at the back. They can be very thorny and difficult if one is trying to get at them through a mass of border plants – there is no problem of course if there is a path at the back.

THE NEW GARDEN – A Problem Garden

Last month we were thinking of the first-timer who has a real problem garden, say perhaps part of a field with all the worst weeds, combined with builders' rubbish. So much depends on the weather, but I really feel that November is too late to expect to be able to plant anything for the winter. If the new gardener refers back to our Clearing and Planting section in the spring months, he'll have some idea what to plant for in the winter.

PLANTING TREES AND SHRUBS

Shrubs and particularly trees do not have shallow roots in the same way as the plants we have already discussed when planting our imaginary border and their hole should be as deep as one has the strength for. One should go over the spade's depth where, if the ground has been worked before, it will probably be fairly easy. You will then come to the hardest bit and a great help is to take the big fork and fork up the hard difficult earth, the sub soil before actually digging, removing any large stones at the same time. In a town garden, particularly a neglected one, some of the obstacles will turn out to be the inevitable builders' rubbish, which has been buried and must be got rid of even if not part of the actual hole. Lest this should sound too discouraging, the first-timer is not likely to find this in more than one or two places, but broken glass is often a great problem so wear gloves.

When your hole is dug, as we have just said, it is a great place for disposing of unwanted leaves, weeds etc, as long as they are not diseased. Put the earth back onto the leaves, leaving enough space plus a little to spare for your tree's or shrub's roots and add compost and well-rotted manure, as your tree will be there for a long time. A little bonemeal can always be incorporated when the tree is actually planted. Cut off any broken roots, otherwise a tree's roots should be left. Look for the mark of the soil on the stem and bury the tree to the same depth. Trees need watering for the first year or two and particularly in a dry spring, when they are starting to make their growth.

When ordering the trees, ask the nursery to supply stout stakes, as a young tree will need one for the first three or four years. The nursery will supply a band, rather like a dog collar, to prevent chafing and which can be loosened as the tree grows. Needless to say, with all the preparations involved, the sighting of your tree is very important. Have someone hold the tree where you want to plant it and by looking out of the window of your house you will get a completely different perspective.

The siting of shrubs is just as important. The great thing is to try and visualise the size they will be when full grown. Mixed in with border plants, they should be at the sides or back. However, with shrubs, unlike trees, they can be trimmed and kept in order and it is not a disaster if one has to replace them if a mistake has been made. In planting, we follow the same procedure as for trees, but the hole should be tailored to suit the individual shrub.

ROOTS

Roots, though they look so uninteresting are a vital part of the plant. It is they which will ensure if your newly planted trees or shrubs do well, though this applies to all plants.

Q How can you tell if the roots are healthy?
A They should look fresh, fat and not dried up. The main root of a tree usually grows from the stem in three main pieces. With some trees it is hard to tell where the trunk stops and the root starts, but your young tree will obviously have roots which have been underground. These are its holding roots which is why one should tread the earth down so firmly when planting. The outside small rootlets are the feeding roots.

If your tree has been delayed in transit, it's leaves may be dead. This is not fatal, but is a sign that the roots should be soaked at least overnight. They will be protected by sacking which should not be removed until you are ready to plant.

Q How can I tell what the roots are like then?
A Put them into a bucket of water, sacking and all, until you are ready, it can do no harm.

When we are thinking of fertilizers and saying that the dry kind always have to be watered in, this is because the feeding roots only take in nourishment in liquid form. A plant feels and feeds through its roots, boring though it may seem. Never leave roots exposed to a cold wind or hot sun – they should always be protected if for some reason the plant has to be left unplanted for a day or two. Wrap in newspaper and putting in the shelter of a shed or wall will be sufficient.

A good general rule if one is short of time is to make a plan, say by digging the hole well in advance. It can always be slightly enlarged to accommodate roots. One might be in the middle of planting, the telephone rings and it might then be too late to do anything that day, so have a simple plan ready to dispose safely of the unplanted bits. If you will not be back in the garden till the next weekend, just put the tree or shrub into the ground temporarily leaving the earth loose, and plant it when you get back.

PLANTING ROSES

Q I have found that roses will only lean in one way when being planted. They seem to have a sort of bias and just trimming the roots is no good.
A I think this is quite correct. There is the swelling where the graft is (where the cultivated rose is joined to the stock or root of briar or wild rose) and the balance will depend a lot on how

it is placed and as you say it will fall naturally one way. If the root has grown out very much one way it can be shortened without harm. When planting a whole bed of roses, provided they are all going to be the same height and habit, it is good to turn them about and see how they stand, but never force them if they don't sit down easily and naturally.

We need a sunny bed for preference, but if it is a shady town garden, allow for the fact that a rose on the wall will tend to be drawn upwards and grow bare lower down (nothing can be done, it is lack of sun and light generally), also bushes will lean forwards for the same reason. A sunny open bed has no such problems.

Q I have also found that mine will all grow out one way.

A Yes, often too the way you least want them to grow. I used to think the trouble was they were growing towards the light, but this isn't always the case. We have already seen that the root is the important part of the plants growth and that may have grown out to find fertilizer put down for another plant. Of course, as trees and shrubs grow older, the roots get tougher and go deeper.

You may find your rose, which you had planned to grow towards the left to cover a bare wall, will insist on growing all its new shoots on the right side. Leave the young shoots until they have lost their red colour then bend them over the way you want them to go. Luckily rose shoots are not brittle, so be firm but gentle. I know the problem as I have a rose that does just this. The experts who come and tidy my garden in the autumn are quite ruthless and will bend it much harder than I should dare.

Q Couldn't one replant it the other way?

A By the time a rose gets to this stage it is rather a gamble trying to move it. It is amazing how deep the roots can go in a comparatively short time. Sometimes I have tried to move roses which I have only just planted because of their unbalanced look, but they never settle down as it is obviously the wrong way for them and one must just let the rose grow as it chooses. With a bush rose, trimming or pruning is a great help.

When planting a rose follow the rules of planting. Roses, though their roots should not go straight into their compost manure need as much below them as we can spare, particularly in a poor soil. They too can do with water in a dry winter their first year. If the winter is cold leave the watering until the warmer weather starts again; the danger is a night frost which might cause ice to form and freeze the roots.

PRUNING ROSES

First of all, we can say that all new roses will have been pruned before being sent from the grower, so there is no problem for the first year.

Q When is the best time after that?

A The orthodox answer is: prune climbing and rambling roses in the autumn, that is to say about now. Prune bush roses in the spring, late March to early April, when the worst frosts are over and so as not to hold the flowering back too much. This involves cutting back lovely new shoots which is very hard for the beginner. Give the roses a little fertilizer after pruning (Toprose is a good one) and remember to water it in if the soil is dry.

Q Everyone round here seems to prune in the autumn and all the bush roses have been done.

A The unorthodox gardener will prune in the autumn and I am one, but I have always had a sheltered town garden. The fact is, at the end of the summer the leaves are usually very unsightly, sometimes diseased and the sensible thing seems to be to cut them off as soon as possible and not leave them lying around to infect the ground. The spores will stay there all the winter.

Q What's wrong with pruning them now then?

A The idea is that roses that have been pruned in the autumn may be encouraged to grow too soon and will be vulnerable to spring frosts. Badly damaged shoots should be cut away and if the plant has been pruned already this will weaken the whole plant and perhaps lead to disease and dying back.

In towns and sheltered spots, there is much less danger of a spring frost severe enough to do real damage and most people are willing to risk it and if the rose is not checked by spring pruning it will obviously flower earlier. In towns and enclosed spaces the sooner things flower the better. In a hot or dry summer the plants feel as exhausted as the humans and many of the later flowerers have a tendency to disease or mildew.

Q I really don't understand as they say to cut back to three buds, but all the buds on my rose seem to be at the top. Does it matter cutting all the buds off?

A If the rose is weak and spindly it should probably be replaced, otherwise a simpler way than counting buds is to aim at cutting the rose back till it is about half its present height. Find the nearest bud and cut there. The height of the stems should be as even as possible to improve the look of the rose. Cut near the bud with small secateurs which are easier to handle. If the bud is growing on the right side of the stem, cut very slightly to the right, there is no need to exaggerate. The idea of cutting close to the bud and following the way it grows is to prevent disease forming in the cut. Secateurs should always be clean for the same reason.

Q What do you clean them with?

A The ideal is to use a *very weak* disinfectant such as Jeyes Fluid, but rather than put them away dirty, wash them under the garden tap and dry them (it is a good idea to keep a cloth in the garden shed).

Q Is it necessary to have a tough pair of gloves too?

A Yes, one is inclined to skimp on things like really good gardening gloves which are expensive. I use the plastic ones for general gardening, but they do let the thorns in which are painful and can be poisonous, so a decent pair is a must really.

Q What does cutting back hard mean?

A Cutting back hard is usually recommended for producing prize roses at shows and not what we are after in a first garden. If your rose is a strong grower, it can be pruned harder than a more spindly one. As we have seen, the rose will arrive already cut back, so it will have its first flowering on shoots which grow out of the main stem it arrived with.

Roses should make good roots the first year and strong fat shoots from the base. Other smaller shoots branch out from these and will flower, but do not be disappointed if the rose does not make any new shoots the first autumn after flowering. It will probably make one or two the next year and one or more of the larger shoots it came with may die off – this is quite normal. How well it does afterwards depends on how strong a grower it is. If it doesn't produce any new shoots after a year or two, it either was a poor doer in the first place, or it doesn't like the aspect (usually not enough air and sun).

Q Mine must be some sort of a bush rose, as they are a much bigger sort of bush, with at least six or seven stalks coming up from the roots and they have a lot of flowers on the stem.

A The floribunda, or cluster roses as they are now called, have rather a different habit of growth and are pruned a bit differently.

The rule when pruning is always to cut out the shoots which have not come to anything, not flowered, died back or are too spindly and one has more of these on a floribunda. Some are really big bushes like '**Iceberg**', so often recommended for towns and quite rightly. Some such as '**Queen Elizabeth**' are huge very strong growers and in a class of their own and no amount of pruning will keep them low-growing.

Q People make them into hedges, but they never seem to flower well.

A I don't see how they can if one has to cut them back to such an extent. Of course, in the country they are useful for keeping out stray animals and make a nice dense hedge which is not unsightly, but it is different in a town when they are so often seen as overgrown monsters in someone's front garden.

Q My 'Iceberg' was flowering right up to Christmas last year.

A Of course this is a wonderful bonus and one wouldn't want to prune all the flowers away. Besides it is not good for the plant to be pruned when still going strong. When the time comes, cut the dead flowers off (taking in leaves as well) to the join on the bigger shoot, which will by then be further down than normal. Then wait till it starts losing its leaves, which will probably be in the cold weather in January and if any shoots or leaves look diseased remove them, otherwise leave to the spring.

The original floribundas such as '**Frensham**' needed very little cutting back, only the dead and spindly shoots removed, but the result is quite a big bush. If they are being grown altogether in a bed as a bedding display, the best way is to cut them in the autumn like ordinary bush roses. If the weather forces you to wait until the spring I should be inclined to leave them until the following autumn.

Those who have difficulty growing roses in a cold or exposed garden, will find the floribunda, particularly the older varieties will stand up better in those conditions. They would need less pruning and would probably be less straggly. When we are pruning, all that we have discussed must be considered.

Q I shall only have roses if I don't have to prune them.

A Choose your roses carefully and make sure they are suited to the site. There was a movement sometime ago to let roses grow 'naturally' into the shrubs they really are, but it didn't seem to catch on. Of course if you have any shrub roses they do not need pruning. They do need plenty of room though and the majority of them only flower once.

We have finished with bush roses and are now going on to the rather tiresome task of keeping rambler roses in order.

Q I dimly remember rambler roses growing over some sort of low fence or wall. They seemed to grow wild as I don't think anyone ever touched them.

A Pruning rambler roses is an awful business. One is supposed to cut out the old growth, that is the summer's flowering shoots and tie in the new, which will be getting in the way of everything. I can't really see why they shouldn't be treated like any other strong growing climber and just left alone, but they must have plenty of room and somehow kept a little in hand. It sounds as if the roses were growing over the iron railings which were so common when I was young. I am not sure if they can still be obtained easily, but they do exist. Their great merit is that they are strong enough to support the roses. A wooden fence is apt to collapse particularly if one tries to tidy up in any way.

A '**Mermaid**' rambler should be left alone as much as possible and never cut back the thick old wood, or it will die back. Climbing roses, such as '**Gloire de Dijon**', were great favourites and used to be left to climb all over a house and the only pruning was to cut off the dead flowers and occasionally dead wood.

CLIMBING ROSES

As we said in June, when thinking about the different types of roses, a climbing rose is not really a rambler, it is usually a climbing version of a HT bush rose, for instance '**Climbing Etoile d'Hollande**'. These are treated and pruned like a bush rose except that they are pruned in the autumn not the spring. Cut off the shoots which have flowered and tie the stems laterally to the wall. The rose will always try and grow straight up, which makes it look leggy. Sometimes this is lack of light and not much can be done about it.

BONFIRES

Bonfires follow on naturally from rose pruning, as it is safer to burn the prunings because of the risk of disease from the leaves. All other leaves can go on the compost heap. Cut all material for the fire into smaller and more manageable pieces and this helps especially with roses to avoid damage to oneself from the thorns. Make a heap where you intend to have the fire and leave it until the leaves have dropped off or withered and the stems have dried up a bit, as the fire lights more easily and makes less smoke. Start with paper, avoiding any liquid such as paraffin, but if things seem to be sluggish use one or two solid fire-lighters. A fine dry day with no wind is the best, but not so easy to come by at this time of year. If there is some wind remember the neighbours and watch very carefully that you are not too near a tree where the branches might catch fire. Also, a bonfire too near any plant will harm it as the heat is so intense. Rake out before going to bed and leave the ashes to weather down, as they make a very useful source of potash for flowers.

HEDGES

The reader who plants a hedge is more likely to live out of town, though one sees plenty of privet hedges in front of town gardens grown as a screen, which does save having to have net curtains in the window of what will probably be the dining room.

Q I loathe privet, isn't there anything else?

A The modern form of a rather despised plant is far less dreary and I have been most impressed by the speed with which the plants grow. A thin stem, not more than 2ft high, can make a nice bushy little hedge in two years flat. I have seen one do just this in a garden near our present house and as the plants looked no more than rooted cuttings I was amazed at how well they grew.

Q I don't care for any of those evergreen hedges and the conifer evergreens would be much too big, would a beech hedge be any good? People say they are very slow-growing though.

A I only know from seeing friends' hedges, but I would say they don't take more than five or six years to make quite a nice thick hedge, but if you want a tall one you would have to wait some time.

The old evergreen cypress which was so much planted, **Cupressus macrocarpa**, was rather dreary and liable to die in a cold winter just as the trees had reached a nice height. Lawson's cypress, *Chamaecyparis lawsoniana* is much more attractive and hardier. There is also a blue cultivar called *C. lawsoniana* 'Pembury Blue'. If one wants a change, the x *Cupressocyparis* *leylandii* 'Castlewellan' is golden. Of these I only know, by sight as it were, the ordinary green which I must say seems to me to make a very pretty hedge or screen. If one's garden is big enough, they make attractive trees planted on their own, but I do not think any evergreen of this kind does particularly well right in a town, as anything which does not shed its polluted leaves is at a disadvantage.

Go to a nursery rather than order by post and you will be able to see what height the hedge plants are already and it is worth it to pay a bit more for extra height. A reputable nurseryman will replace plants which die their first year, so make sure of this.

The wheel of fashion is turning almost as I write, for the Lawson Cypresses are now said to be difficult to keep in hand and people are getting tired of them. I know which I prefer, but of course the first-timer must make his own choice, always remembering the danger of losing the *Cupressus macrocarpa* in a very cold winter. We have already seen that the **Berberis Thunbergii** makes quite a dense hedge in spite of not being evergreen and also that the '**Queen Elizabeth**' **rose** and the **Forsythia** can be trained into attractive hedges.

PRUNING SHRUBS

The new gardener will have no difficulty in seeing the buds of the early-flowering shrubs. **Camellias** will be well-formed, indeed the earlier kinds may well produce actual flowers in November if the autumn is mild and I have even known a flower out before the end of October. The **Winter Jasmine** will be showing colour (yellow) very soon and the **Forsythia** probably sometime in early January. If any of these need tidying up it can be combined very well with a little winter decoration for the house, as if brought indoors they will soon be out and will not have been spoilt by bad weather.

Many readers will have childhood memories of bringing the sticky buds of the **Horse Chestnut** indoors. This is part of a large garden and it would be a great stroke of luck to find it already growing.

Q How can one tell the difference between horse chestnuts and the sort you eat?

A At this time of year the fruit will be falling. The 'conker' is a shiny brown, with a smooth shell and the eating chestnut is flatter, and the shell or husk is spiky. The Spanish or eating Chestnut is a much larger tree, with the trunk beautifully marked with ridges spiralling upwards round the trunk. The flowers in spring are rather dull yellow fingers and a nuisance to sweep up, whereas the horse chestnut, so often seen in rows in parks or along a road, has the beautiful red or pink candles.

Of course cutting a few sticky buds for the house is not going to prune a large tree and in any case, when the buds begin to swell the sap is rising and it is too late to prune a tree.

Q Can I cut back my **Mahonia** now? It has got completely out of hand and there is a thing, rather like a small tree, growing out of the original bush.

A You can cut back the leggy bit. The chances are that this year, it contained most of the flower buds, which in a mild year bloom in February in long sprays, but the following year the lower bit will produce the sprays. This is one instance when drastic cutting does work.

Fatsia is another plant which will grow to the height of a small tree in a sheltered spot. This too can be cut down to its original bushy bit. Both will grow again, as very strong growing shrubs are not easily deterred and a big bush remains a big bush whatever you do.

WARNING

The early laurustinus or **Viburnum tinus** will possibly also be in flower and can be picked, but the **V. burkwoodii** which flowers later, may look very dead at this time of year – it sheds most of its leaves and the ones it retains do not look up to much. It may have long trailing stems with dead-looking flowers at the end. Do not touch them for come April the new leaves will suddenly appear and at the end of the month the 'deadheads' will become proper buds and produce lovely scented flowers. Offhand, I can't think of any other shrub which is quite so deceptive! When it has finished flowering it is very easy to trim and keep in shape.

PROTECTING PLANTS IN WINTER

The worst kind of winter for tender plants is one like the winter of 1986–87, when quite reasonably warm spells as in January alternated with really cold ones, with the temperature at night well below freezing, 32 F. or 0 C., and with very cold winds in the day. Most unusually, there was no let-up during the cold weather and it remained freezing both day and night. With this sort of weather, particularly if the plants have been brought on too soon by a warm early winter which makes them more vulnerable, it would be worth putting up a temporary screen. If there is a draughty corner, like a passageway to the back door or an open part to the fence where cold winds can whistle through, move tubs to a more sheltered part and screen the ones that can't be moved.

Q I lost my **bay trees** and they are terribly expensive to replace. Should I cover them up during the winter?

A I never think one should cover something completely, thereby making it too tender, as the trouble comes when one takes the cover off. I should prefer, either moving them to a sheltered place in the very cold weather, or if this is not possible making a screen. Composted manure, dead leaves, bracken, straw, sacking, or even woollen material like bits of an old dressing gown, keep the roots warm, but do not use any material which will prevent the rain from reaching the roots.

Remember that snow is to be welcomed, it is a warm blanket for the plants and a marvellous fertilizer. In spite of the dreadful wet summer which followed that winter, everything flowered magnificently from the spring onwards.

Q What should I do with **Geraniums** or **Pelargoniums** as I shall call them, in winter?

A Much the best way in a sheltered town garden or window box, is to leave them where they are but not let them grow too tall. In a mild November they will be flowering still, but directly the frost comes the buds will be nipped or held back and you will not be sacrificing any flowers by trimming them down to a small neat bush.

In a South-facing balcony such as I had, with the protection of a glass screen half-way up the balcony, geraniums flowered all the winter.

Q What about bringing them into the house?

A If you have the plants in their pots when planting out, bring them in somewhere cool. The living room heat will be too warm for them; a verandah is ideal, or a sunny window-sill where the room does not get too much heat and a landing window-sill is fine provided it is not draughty, for though the heat from the house will come up to the landing it should not be too much. Do not put above a radiator.

Q How about watering?

A Geraniums do not mind being dry, but they do depend on a lot of rain in the winter, so keep them just damp as they would be in the garden.

Q People say they should be brought in and hung up in the garden shed to dry.

A I did try that once but without success. Only one or two survived and they came out so late it seems better to risk leaving them outside, when they will flower at the beginning to middle of June. This is not as early as the nurserymen get them to flower but earlier than the other way. Your indoor plants should be in bud by May, but do not put them out before the end of May, when the risk of frost is over. They will have become a bit soft at having been in all winter. If there is a very hot spell earlier in May, about 70 F. and it goes on for a day or two, they can go out then. Even if it does turn cold afterwards, my experience has been that the plant has settled by then and will be all right.

When we were discussing tender plants earlier on, we noted that there are many which will settle down in a garden and survive any but the exceptionally cold winter. Apart from the winter we were describing, it can sometimes happen that a particularly cold wind or two or three very hard frosts in January, will do the damage. Only a professional nursery gardener can guard against this kind of thing. The amateur must let his plants take their chance having chosen a sheltered spot for them in the first place. We have already noted how trees and hedges are planted as windbreaks and that the cold winds come from the North and East.

One or two plants grown in tubs, of which one of the best known the **Agapanthus**, the blue African lily, must be moved for the winter into a frost proof greenhouse and one may be able to make arrangements for a nursery to take them in. The house next door to my first home had several of these plants in the front and it was a sign of summer to see them out in the drive. So much were they associated with this house, that people coming for the first time to my own home, seeing tubs of agapanthus in the next door garden, were sure that I must live there and would ring the wrong bell.

The reader may remember the cold frame seen so much in gardens years ago, where things like Parma violets, such as were sold on the streets, were raised. They were very much the province of the professional gardener and can be compared to a cool greenhouse. It is very much more tricky than one would think to know when to open the frame and one can do far more harm by over-protecting than by leaving plants alone.

THE LAWN IN AUTUMN – Raking out Moss

The sort of moss one gets in a lawn is not the beautiful deep moss of the woods and forests, it has somehow adapted itself so that it grows quite happily in sun and shade. Even a hot summer, if there is sufficient rain, does not discourage it, but at this time of year it is less vigorous than when it starts growing in the spring. Try raking with a special lawn rake and sweeping up. If it has come right out there may be a great many bare patches.

People argue just as much about sowing lawn seed as they do about pruning roses. The old way was to sow in autumn so that the seed got the benefit of the winter rains and was fairly well grown by the spring. Others argue that the seed is best grown, like other seed, when the soil has warmed up in April. Specially treated seed can be bought so that the birds won't touch it and unless one is unlucky with a dry spell, April is probably the best month. If you leave your lawn unsown, put a little bonemeal on the bare patches as moss likes poor soil.

The best advice I was ever given about my London lawn, true only two strips of grass, was to leave the self-sown grass alone and sow with coarse grass seed. This self-sown grass is really a kind of weed, but it is not at all like the tufty meadow grass, it never grows too high and is evergreen. It has acclimatised itself so well that it comes under the name of 'London Grass'. In the end, when our garden became more shady, it was impossible to get rid of the moss and we changed to gravel.

Q Can I use a moss killer?
A Buy one which is only intended to kill moss. This can be done either in spring or autumn, but I feel it is better to get at it when it is already dying down a little.

If your lawn is in poor shape after the raking and you do not sow at once, another suggestion is to put down well sieved composted manure over the whole lawn and this should be done before the spring. Many people find that grass grows very well in a town garden and the moss need not spoil the look of it. We are not trying for the stately home look!

November is a very busy month. All gardeners have the now or never feeling. Although December might start off mild, we really are beginning the winter. The busy first-timer must not despair if he has to leave things undone, but just seize every opportunity as it comes.

December

Q I can't think what you find to write about in December.
A We can always move indoors. What about house plants? I also thought a section on the seasons with regard to weather would be useful.

Early December can be quite mild and work in the established garden not much different from late November, that is, tidying up generally as long as the weather permits. In a mild season, the later plants like chrysanthemums will stagger on and even roses will still be flowering in a subdued 'last rose of summer' sort of way. Picking the flowers with extra long stalks will tidy up the plants. Otherwise they should be left to die down like other border plants, until the frost blackens their leaves, when they can be cut down to where the small winter leaves will have formed at the base.

If roses are not diseased and are still flowering they should not be cut back, but pruned in the spring.

Leaves from the trees ought all to be down by now and can be put onto the compost heap or into the bin, with any small leafy prunings which are not diseased. Cut into small pieces as we did for the bonfire, which not only makes them easier to handle but will help them to rot down more quickly.

If there is an early fall of snow in December this is often a sign of a cold winter to come. Get any plants indoors which you mean to keep and place on a cool window-sill or verandah. Tidy up as soon as you are able after the thaw and then the garden can be left to the frosts of January and the sleet of February.

Q Is it too late to get manure down?
A No, just in time to keep the cold of winter from the roots of tender plants. Wait for 'open' weather when the ground is not frosty and spread it over the surface of the whole bed, or concen-

336

trate it round the roots if you are protecting something like a hydrangea. Fork it in lightly so that the compost does not get blown about and does not harbour pests or disease spores.

THE 'NEW' GARDEN – The Wild Garden

Not many people will move into their new house just before Christmas if they can help it and as for the garden, the winter months are better spent in planning rather then in planting. However, the wild garden, which we only touched on very briefly when considering gardens that do not need too much upkeep, is something of an exception. The wild flowers which one would hope to see, are nearly all spring or early summer ones and the first hot weather in May will see the end of the majority of them. If the winter should be mild enough a bit of clearing now is well worth doing. The reader might be surprised at a wild garden needing any upkeep.

Q   What is the point of its being wild in that case?

A   A wilderness of docks, nettles and ground elder for instance is hardly a garden, wild or otherwise and we have dealt with this problem in 'Clearing & Planting'. Let us now suppose that we have bought the kind of garden with trees and undergrowth, which we intend to leave more or less as it is for the benefit of children and animals, rather than grown-ups and flowers.

Let's pretend that the first clearing is over and that paths have appeared and the brambles have been cut back. Though it is an awful struggle to get brambles in hand, don't forget the welcome blackberries in the late summer.

Drawing the line between weeds and wild flowers is for the gardener to choose, but most people would be delighted to find such things as **Bluebells** and **Foxgloves** growing in a clearing and to see **Wood Anemones** springing up as if by magic in the early spring. Depending on the soil and the amount of light, there are many small plants which are found in woods such as **Herb Robert**, the small **Cranesbill** and the **Spurge** with its strange green flowers. The undergrowth might be mostly ivy or there could be a mass of what we now call 'ground cover', some interesting and some rather ordinary. If the wild garden is to look after itself, the first-timer could leave any such plant and see how things develop. If wild plants are suited to their environment they can grow together very happily.

The weeds of cultivation, such as dandelions, daisies and plantains come on mown or cropped grass for the most part; the odd one which seeds itself at the edge of a wood or coppice is not likely to do much harm and makes a nice patch of colour. Weeds such as nettles and thistles should be kept down, especially if there are children around. **Primroses** do well in a clay soil and **Cowslips** where the soil drains better, such as on chalk downs.

As we are nearing Christmas, a nice surprise for the first-timer would be some **Holly**. Small woods or coppices suit holly, it usually berries well and if a holly bush is going to have berries, they will be red by this time of year.

Of course a pond, or better still a stream, is a tremendous bonus. We have gone into the water plants when thinking of the Bog or Water Garden.

Buttercups are rather more a flower, or weed, of the cultivated fields. With their creeping roots, they are not a good idea grown too near anything else that you might be nurturing as they will soon take over. If the buttercups are there the early **Dog-violet** will not be far away.

Q Somehow I feel I should never have the luck to find anything worth having in my new garden, it is wild all right but only just out of town. What about those packets of seed you can buy, would it be worth sowing any?

A As we are hoping for a trouble free garden, why not sow some as you would other annuals and hope for the best. Wild flowers, given that they are immensely tough, have survived by adapting themselves to a particular environment and will stand being cut down year after year (think of alpine meadows).

Q They say on the packet what one should do and it does give some idea of what sort of situation they like. The only thing is that the wild garden at the Chelsea Flower Show, looks an absolute mess I think, not at all like an alpine meadow, or an English one for that matter.

A One should look at that display more to see the kind of flowers that would come up. It is hard, in fact impossible, to reproduce nature in such a short time and in such a small space. Only some will survive of the ones you sow and they will be the best adapted to your garden.

Q I suppose you could say that the alpine meadows were cultivated to some extent.

A Yes, it was cattle farming mostly and sadly this is not paying in modern times, so the meadows as we knew them might disappear, or be kept as a kind of natural park. The cows helped by eating down the grass and their manure was an extra fertilizer.

Most people with a wild garden compromise by planting, to a certain extent, in such a way that the plants can be left alone. If you are thinking of giving nature a hand, by sowing wild flower seed or planting bulbs, the wild bluebell is **Scilla nutans** (not the little *Scilla siberica* of the rockery). Foxgloves have **Digitalis** for their Latin name, the same as has been used as a heart drug for so long. They will come up easily and sow themselves for the next year. Choose a sunny clearing in the woods, the best being dappled shade, where the sunlight comes through the branches and the shade is not too dense. Primroses can be bought at garden centres, also cowslips and the nearest one would get to the wild wood anemone is the **Anemone Blanda**.

HOLLY

Hollies like a sunny and sheltered position, which is why they grow well in the shelter of a coppice of small trees and bushes; the shelter is there but no tall trees to blot out the sun.

Q My holly bush looks quite healthy but it never has any berries.

A Holly has separate male and female plants and they are not self-pollinating. The old advice was to plant a male variegated bush, a golden such as **Golden Queen**, along with two or three green bushes which were female and would have the berries, so that the bushes never looked too dull.

Q I have no idea which mine is, it never does anything. I believe it should have small white flowers but I never see any.

A Lots of gardens have these holly bushes refusing to produce anything except leaves. I suggest you buy a new bush altogether, checking at the same time that your old holly bush was planted in the right place.

There is a beautiful new variety which I have seen at a show called '**J.C. van Tol**', with shiny green leaves, nearly thornless and with the large red berries one wants for Christmas. It has the added advantage of being a hybrid and is therefore self-fertile so means that one needs only one bush. The old coloured variet-

ies, 'Golden King' and 'Golden Queen' are still obtainable and
note that the king is female and the queen male – the same
applies to 'Silver King' and 'Silver Queen'.

As Hollies are evergreen they drop their leaves gradually
throughout the year and the dead ones are very prickly indeed.
Small children should be warned and they are best not added to
the compost heap, but burnt with the rose cuttings.

IVY

After holly comes ivy and if we imagine the wild garden as a
small wood or coppice, there is bound to be ivy around. Looking
carefully at it, it is usually easy enough to pick up at least four
different kinds. Mark out the ones which seem to like to crawl
rather than climb, (they normally have smaller leaves) and keep
a check on the climbers before they get out of hand; for instance
climbing up trees, where they will be expensive and difficult to get
rid of.

Q They say now that ivy doesn't kill trees, it only climbs up
those which are already dead.

A It still might bring the tree down for, if left for a long time, it
can grow a stem which is almost a trunk in itself and must be
heavy.

If we need some ground cover, there are two plants which are
most usually recommended. Firstly, the little mauve **Periwinkle**,
Latin name *Vinca major* or *minor* according to the size of the plant.
This is disappointing on a poor soil producing very few flowers,
but in richer soil and a warm situation it is a beautiful little
plant. It grows wild in Gibraltar flowering through the winter, a
good clue to the kind of climate it prefers.

The other plant is the creeping **St John's Wort**, Latin name
Hypericum calycinum.

Q Is that the rose of Sharon?

A It is sometimes called that, but there is no agreement as to
which hypericum is called by this name, so ask for the creeping
one and say you need it for ground cover. It is rather prone to
rust, but possibly in a wild garden one would not notice this
and to my mind it is a waste of time trying to cure it. It will
flower quite well in most situations.

WEEDS AS FLOWERS

When we were describing the garden convolvulus, we had a word to say about the large wild convolvulus, which looks really beautiful with its white flowers in August. If your wild garden is at your holiday or second home it would therefore flower just when you wanted it to.

Q What is wrong with it? I have always loved it.

A It is the dreaded bindweed of the flower garden. Although it dies down in the winter the roots go on from year to year and it can become a very persistent weed, leaving behind strong wiry stalks, even when it has 'died', strangling the unfortunate plant it climbs round.

Like many other readers I have childhood memories of this plant. It grew over an evergreen bush in the grounds of my grandparents' garden and never did any harm. The fashion in those days was to have the vegetables and flowers in a walled kitchen garden quite separate from the lawns and trees. There should be plenty of space for it in a wild garden where it would not interfere with other plants.

The gardener should beware of another plant classified as a garden climber, **Polygonum baldschuanicum**, usually just called polygonum. Readers may remember the courtyard of the In and Out Club in Picadilly where, until quite recently, a wall which must have been every bit of 40ft was entirely covered by this plant, showing what it can do if given its head. It has recently been christened "The Russian Vine", but this does not stop it deserving its other 'pop' name of the "Mile-a-minute" creeper.

Some misguided person had planted it at the end of our first garden, which had been neglected all through World War II and we found what can only be called an enormous bird's nest. It was just a mass of dead wood, for the new shoots had grown over the last year's growth and so on in layers. When we made a bonfire of this in the adjoining bomb-site, it went up for all the world like the pictures of an atom bomb.

Underneath were the sad remains of a syringa, which had about two or three thin stalks left. Luckily, one of the toughest shrubs itself, it survived and flourished, so can be recommended for a wild garden provided it gets a certain amount of sun.

WEATHER

Of course, the weather is all important to the gardener and it would indeed be rash to try and predict our unpredictable weather, but with the help of certain milestones (i.e. one's own and family birthdays and public holidays), one can begin to see patterns recurring. How many white, even cold, Christmases can you remember? How many really fine and warm Easters? How many really bad Whitsuns, now called the Spring Bank Holiday? Is your own birthday like mine, always cold and sleety, or fine like my elder sister's, or thundery after a hot spell like my younger sister's? It is astonishing, variable as our weather is, how months do fall into patterns and trends, all of which is useful when planning ahead. The reader must be warned however, that most of what I say applies to the South of England where I have always lived.

Here goes an attempt to make some sort of sense of the seasons, month by month.

WINTER

December – It is impossible to write of December weather without having half an eye to Christmas at the end of the month. Whatever the Christmas cards say, the reader knows perfectly well that a white Christmas is the exception in the South. There will be frost at night almost certainly, but the coldest weather comes more towards the beginning of the month. If this spell is really severe and has been led up to by frosts earlier on and the snow only barely thaws before Christmas, this *is* the sign of a hard winter to come. The one I remember best, the winter of 1946–47, started with just such a spell which persisted; then a heavy snowfall, followed soon afterwards by frost, which really set in hard towards the end of January and which didn't let up until April. This is truly exceptional so I do not wish to frighten the reader and incidentally, it was followed by a beautiful summer.

Indeed, the ideal pattern which we have been following through the months, may well lead to a cold but fine and sunny winter, for it is the high pressure which brings both, hence the idea that a cold winter should be followed by a hot summer. However cold the early spell, more often than not it goes temporarily over the Christmas season and reappears early in January. When Pope Gregory reformed the calendar by introducing the Leap Year, eleven days were 'lost' in order to tidy things up. If we count eleven days from Christmas we come to January 6th, Twelfth Night, when the weather is often much more like the traditional Christmas, which may partly solve the riddle.

January – Even if Christmas has been cold or snowy for once, the more usual pattern is for late December to be warmish, then comes the old Christmas, on January 6th, when the weather invariably turns cold. If the winter is going to be severe, though the frost might have gone temporarily, the turning point is round about the 18th of January when a cold wind and a hard frost might come, which can last through February. The cold spells to look out for are the ones that come from Scandinavia (via Siberia). Plants hate cold winds as much as we do so if you can, move tubs into a sheltered spot.

February – In my opinion and that of the Q who shares my life, this month is the worst of the lot; no wonder the papers are full of advertisements for Caribbean Cruises. If January has been cold, the chances are February will be just as cold but more unpleasant, not dry and sunny but cold and sleety. Once in a blue moon it can be quite sunny and pleasant and one could at least walk round the garden and see what is happening. The reader can rely on the weather turning dirty on the 13th of the month and I can remember only one really fine sunny day in seventy years! The old name was 'February Filldyke', very appropriate, as the winter rains are important and almost everything seems to like a good soak. Also it is wonderful for Spring blossom and the later roses.

SPRING

March – We used to be told that "March winds and April showers bring forth May flowers". I was never clear exactly why, winds did not appear to have much effect on growing things, except to blow them down and the April rain always seemed to overdo it. If one is trying to make sense out of the growing year, one can see that after a wet February the drying winds of March would do good, especially as they are usually sunny days as well; then a warm wet April foretells a dry and sunny May, even if the nights are still cold. If such a weather pattern can be established, it is indeed a good sign for a sunny summer.

What do we get though? There has been a trend in recent years for very cold weather in the early part of the spring, to last right until the end of May. Fifty years ago, point-to-point races in March could be freezing cold, then too hot for winter clothes but the former never lasted and a warm spell in March could be relied on. Now we don't get the mild spring-like weather but go suddenly, whatever the weather, from winter to summer. A good thing is that, at last, the days are longer and one can spend more time outdoors.

April – There are frequently as many April showers in March these days and April is still winter, as we noted last month. An unusually mild winter will almost certainly produce a freakishly cold spell in mid-April, sometimes even with heavy snow. The best a gardener can do is to shake the snow off boughs which may be carrying blossom. Luckily, daffodils and hyacinths are much hardier than one would think and will survive. Our ideal pattern will produce the "showers and bright intervals" beloved of the weathermen, without any extremes. Easter day can fall as early as the 29th March or as late as April 22nd. An early Easter can often be cold and windy with sometimes a dusting of snow and a later one perfect, sunny and warm and everyone's idea of spring. Too warm a spell will produce cold winds and snow showers within a week or ten days, but do not be disappointed, it will not last. All you can do is get down to the garden when you have the chance.

May – A cold spell at the beginning of May can almost be guaranteed. The poor cricketers who are visiting us from warmer climates, huddle into their sweaters at Lord's and the old saying tells us not to cast a clout till May (month or flower) be out. The end of May has a reliably warm even hot spell and was the time when the coke boiler went off and the electric heater took over in our household. May in general is sunny but the cold nights mean that one should be careful of plants that are not completely hardy (see Tender Plants).

SUMMER

June – The weather is beginning to set into a pattern and there is no justice in it, with a horrid cold spring frequently setting the scene for a horrid wet and cold summer. 'Flaming June' is our ideal pattern. June is the month with the longest days, with the longest being June 21st and it should also be the sunniest month. A really fine June is the signal for an exceptionally good summer; look out for things getting dry, then settle down to enjoy it. If the reader doubts these two extremes, he has only to think of pictures of the Ascot Races, either brilliant sunshine and lovely clothes, or everyone cowering under umbrellas and macintoshes.

In a town garden, if the rainy weather is not too cold, the plants prefer something on the wet side to something on the dry side. Even in a bad year the end of June can be relied on for a warm sunny spell.

July – July is rather more consistent than other months, being predictably close, warm and thundery and with a rainfall to be relied on. In a year which follows our ideal pattern, it may not be very sunny, but there is a feeling of heat building up and fine sunny weather promised for August. There is often a brief really hot spell, even a freakish 90 F. – in a bad summer it is the equivalent to snow in April – then back to thunder near the 21st of the month, followed by quite cold weather.

August – Following our perfect summer pattern, we have had some rain from thunderstorms in July, so we are not too much troubled at the prospect of hot sun and dry weather in August. Nowadays we are used, if not exactly reconciled, to the main holiday month being cold, wet and windy, but although the weather pattern has undoubtedly changed hot weather does come along at this time of year, as 1989 showed. Whatever the summer, the weather is always bad over the old Bank Holiday at the beginning of August and sailing gardeners will think of the Cowes Week gales. Perhaps the 'greenhouse effect', or whatever it is, will bring us back our runs of hot dry summers.

Anyone who doubts the reality of the old summers should think of Edwardian times, when 'everyone' left London because the heat was excessive; the fashion followed the weather. We are also told that children have unreal memories of hot summers, yet there is a picture painted by the impressionist Alfred Sisley named 'The Road to Hampton Court' It is actually a picture of the lock-keepers cottage near the weir at Sunbury on Thames, dated 1874 and there is the sun blazing down upon the shadeless towpath, exactly as I remember it as a child in the 1920's. Furthermore, when I was growing up in the 1930's there were places called Roadhouses, where one could have supper after a dance and bathe out of doors in an unheated swimming pool; the one I remember best was just roped off from a small tributary of the River Wey.

AUTUMN

September – Like July, the weather pattern is more reliable than August. It is rare to get a bad September and a dreadful summer can be redeemed by two or three weeks of really good weather, just as most people have given up in despair. The days are getting shorter and the nights colder, the dew is heavy and will save watering if August has been dry.

We did not mention the Spring Equinox, the time when the nights and days are equal. March is such a blustery month anyway, that we do not notice a gale or two in the same way. The gales which so often follow the Equinox at the end of September, can come unexpectedly at the end of a long fine spell. This is the time of the spectacularly low tides, when sandbanks uncover and rocks appear. We are told that the moon has nothing to do with the weather, but many country weather prophets are convinced that the weather changes with the full moon. Keep an eye on anything that might blow down in an unexpected gale; sometimes a container can be blown over, the plants tipped out and broken.

October – The best possible summer that we have been imagining can fade away gently in October, with sunny days and nights still not too cold, then we get a sudden frost and that is that, with a fairly cold November to follow. September gales carry on into October and we can also experience the tail end of hurricanes which form the other side of the Atlantic. They very rarely reach us in the shape of a wind actually of hurricane force, like that which arrived on October 16th 1987 and did such terrible damage to trees.

Frosts are to be expected by mid-October, not severe or long-lasting, but enough to make us think of tidying up for the winter and bringing plants indoors. A maddening and fairly reliable pattern is for prolonged fine, almost summer weather, when it is too early to cut plants down and the leaves have hardly started to fall, to be followed by a sudden change into wet and windy weather which prevents one working outdoors. The reader must not be impatient, nature has to be lived round as it were and we must just be prepared, as soon as the weather recovers, to get on with the clearing.

November – Not the most pleasant of months, but greatly improved by clean-air policies which have put an end to the old 'pea-soup' fogs, so often the result of fine windless weather. The morning's heavy mist never dissolved in a town as it did in the country and it became overlaid by soot and general pollution in the air, thus giving November a worse name than it really deserves. The beginning of our ideal month would be a continuation of the fine autumn weather. With the end of Summer Time (BST), the days become suddenly shorter with no light in the evenings. A cold spell is to be expected round about the middle of the month but snow is unusual. If snow does fall it is depressing, for it seems that the winter has begun all too early, though strangely this is not usually the sign of a severe winter but rather the reverse.

Our less than perfect November is cold and wet, just as we are wanting to get the garden tidied up for the winter before it becomes too cold. Leaves sometimes hang on well into the month, then a sharp frost brings them down all together. The frosty weather brings the autumn colours to the country, but alas not so much in the towns. They are green one moment and then begin to go soggy and half dead rather than turn a good colour. Maples (Acers) and some flowering cherries are the exception.

WEATHER FORECASTING FOR THE GARDENER

The general forecasts from the Met. Office give a good idea of the weather as a whole and their bad reputation comes mainly from too great expectations. Weather is very local, some places are

A

WEATHER FORECAST

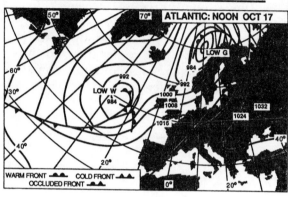

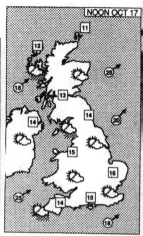

Low U is moving rapidly north and filling.
Low W will move north east.

B

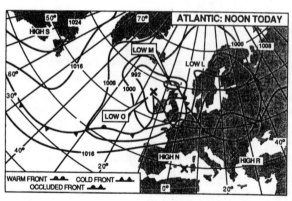

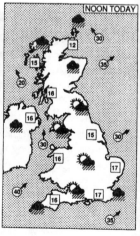

Low L moving east, filling slowly. Low M moving north-east.
Low O moving quickly north-east amalgamating with M.
High N re-established stationary. High R stationary. High
S moving east. Little change.

C

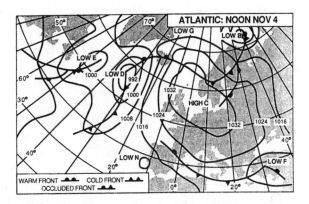

High C drifting very slowly east. Low B moving steadily east-
northeast. Low D moving steadily north. Low E moving southeast.
Low F moving east, little change. Low G filling. Low N drifting
north, filling slowly.

D

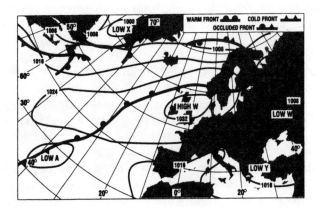

Lows W and Y will gradually drift north-east and fill. Low X will
move east north-east and fill slowly. Low A will edge eastward and
deepen slightly. High W will remain nearly stationary.

noted for thunderstorms and some, like the East Coast, noted for staying dry when rain has been foretold for all regions. Depressions stay away or are deflected, the promised shower becomes a downpour and what happened to the bright intervals? A friend may come back from a day at the seaside a short way away and have experienced sun all day.

If the gardener chooses, a supplementary weather forecast is not at all difficult. If for instance you want to plant out seedlings or small plants but you will be away all the week, it is important to know if it will rain, or if there will be a sudden hot spell. For future planning, if you are obliged to look two or three days ahead, the weather map is a great help. First think of the past week; has it been very unsettled; has the forecast been wrong most of the time; does it seem to be clearing steadily, not just clearing in the evening, only to rain again the next morning (one of the hallmarks of the rainy summer). Then take a look at the weather map.

'A' and 'B' take no explaining as they are obviously very bad with wet and windy weather. You could be sure of rain for a day or two. 'A' is actually a picture of the Hurricane (Low G) on the following day, October 17th, making its way across Scandinavia. Low W is going to move up and to the right (NE), so we are expecting more of the same, with the North probably faring worst. The aspect of a weather map is like any other, North at the top, West and East left and right (making WE) and South at the bottom, where the luckier Spain, Italy and N. Africa have an area of high pressure as usual. If however you are feeling envious, look at the spiky cold front already over the South of France – trouble is coming, probably thunder and even hail.

Low W is engaged in an interesting little struggle between a cold (spiky) and warm (rounded) front, signs of pretty strong winds still to come, as indeed they did for a day or two. It is the contrast between warm and cold fronts accompanied by an altering of pressure, which produces change.

'B' shows how things had worked out a day or two later. The little curl of hot and cold fronts is straightened out into an occluded front and as you see from the key and symbols, it is a mixture of hot and cold currents which is very unsettling. Looking to the right, you will see that High N has seen off the cold front, which is now poised over Italy and Greece. A really bad summer in the British Isles is usually paralleled by an exceptionally hot and dry summer round the shores of the Mediterranean. The 'Highs' get so well established that they take a bit of shifting. Cold weather as we know it, is rare in the Mediterranean winter, but the bad weather in the shape of depressions is a winter pattern of strong winds and rain. The famous 'mistral' coming off the ice and snow of the Alps can feel extremely wintry, so they do not escape altogether.

'C' has a picture of better weather for us. High C is obviously good news for the British Isles, but its centre is drifting East, which is away from us. Look to the left or West, where the depressions come from and the good news is that Low D is moving steadily North, away from us. Further North there will be a good deal of wind and rain, the lines (isobars) being so close together. Further into the Atlantic, just starting off from America, low E is preparing to come for us by going SE, down and along.

The weather may not do what is expected, as was seen when a sudden change in direction brought us the hurricane. Sometimes the miracle does happen and all the depressions get deflected further South and the Mediterranean area gets the bad weather for once. The barometer or 'glass' is a useful weather prophet.

HIGH AND LOW PRESSURE

You will have seen the numbers in the centres of the lows and highs, with the centre of Low G (the hurricane remains) at 984 which is very low and the centre of High C at 1032 which is very high. These numbers are millibars with 32 being very high and 29 very low. The barometer standing at 32 for several days means a really good fine spell setting in and the 'glass' dropping to below 29 means some sort of catastrophe – on the night of the hurricane it was reading 28.8. I only remember seeing it as low once before, when we experienced the tail end of another hurricane.

A barometer is a very useful weather guide and if it falls suddenly, expect a sharp storm probably with rain. If you are looking especially for rain, say you have just planted seedlings out and will have to leave them, low pressure is a good sign. Apart from the 'glass', the night before you leave, look for a watery moon its face partly obscured by mist or cloud and that is a sure sign of rain. A bad weather sign and not good for the garden, is a halo or ring round the sun which often appears about midday in the summer and can forecast a sudden violent thunderstorm or hail. The halo is formed by particles of ice caused by a cold front moving in.

On the other hand, you may be thinking of spraying the roses and do not want a shower for at least an hour or so and the weather may be damp, but somehow the rain is holding off. An infallible sign of rain coming soon, is when white clouds appear under the dull over all grey of the sky. The fluffy white clouds which look so pretty in the summer are a good sign, for when they begin to form the pressure is rising and high pressure is moving in.

Q What about red sunsets at night? I always thought they were a good weather sign, but we had a terrible storm once after a lovely sunset and the weather was bad for days.

A The fine sunset is an intense pink rather than red and it should spread onto the evening clouds, but not be too spread about so that it looks ragged and untidy. The calmer the whole thing the better. The very spectacular hard, stormy red sunsets, covering a more extensive area than usual, are a very bad sign. As you say, the weather can break up for a long time and often heralds the end of summer. The wet greenish sunsets are a bad sign too, they mean rain and unsettled weather.

A fine spell often sets in with the wind changing from the prevailing SW to E. If there has been a long rainy spell, the birds will suddenly start to sing as they feel the pressure lift. After a long fine spell, feathery clouds high up in the sky, are often the only sign of a gradual change in the weather. They too are crystals and the cold front is on its way, but it may be a week or so before any real change is felt.

Most people will have a few old wives tales which they remember from childhood and are more or less true I think, taken in conjunction with the other signs. Owls sounding very active and hooting more than usual at night, are a wet weather sign; also cows lying down, but be careful for it is the way they are lying which is important. Lying on their sides in the very hot weather and taking the weight off their hooves, does not count but pass their field on a lovely sunny day and see them lying down, front legs tucked in much as a cat tucks in its paws, having arranged themselves into a 'V' formation, presents a low profile to any bad weather and you will have rain by nightfall.

Q I must say I always thought cows lying down was an old wives tale and nothing else.

A No, many times I have wished it was all nonsense as the weather was so fine, but the cattle knew better. The fact is, they must feel the damp air coming up on the wind and make their dispositions accordingly.

HOUSE PLANTS

Florists always have a very tempting display of pot-plants, which we often buy or are given as presents in preference to cut flowers, only to find that they do not last much longer, which is always a source of disappointment.

Q The trouble about being given them as presents is that one feels so bad if they die.

A Yes, one prays that the donor will not see them sadly finishing their life on the compost heap or in the dustbin. I am inclined to think that they have been grown to tempt the buyer and are not really meant to last much longer than cut flowers, but I suppose that is defeatist and we must make an effort to keep them.

Q I find the ones sold as house plants are easier. For one thing they often have a label with instructions as to temperature etc.

A Naturally it is an advantage for a plant to have been grown specially for the house. The trouble with other kinds which are sold for their flowers, the indoor azalea for instance, is that they were brought up under glass with expert knowledge and really need a greenhouse to retreat into when they have finished flowering. They can sometimes be planted outside in the summer, but this is not always possible and the plant has to be discarded.

House plants are different altogether. Most of them are grown for their leaves and are much easier, though draughts and fluctuations of temperature are their main enemy. For many flat-dwellers house plants are their only garden and some of them become great experts, overcoming all the difficulties and this time the poet is right, they are like green thoughts in a green shade.

Q I always think watering is the worst part. I never get it right and there seem to be different rules for every plant.

A Watering worries everyone. Some plants can't have too much, some only need a little and then there are the kind which can be plunged into a bowl of water. Other kinds, mostly ones where the bulb or corm is on the surface, prefer to drink out of the saucer they are standing on.

Q How can one tell when the plant wants water and how much to give it?

A The earth in the pot feels dry, or the plant is drooping. As we are all busy it is very likely you have forgotten your plant, or have just come back from holiday and there it is drooping and looking half dead. Unless it is the kind which has the roots or bulb on the surface, plunge the pot into a small sink or deep basin of water. Hold it down or it may fall over when your back is turned, until it stops bubbling. You might have to leave it there all night and by the morning it will have picked up.

In a general way, feel the leaves gently and if they are healthy and springy to the touch they can be left, but if they are the least bit flabby they need watering. Plants need more water when they are growing and producing buds, but in between they can usually manage with little water.

Q I did water my primula when it was drooping but it died.

A The indoor primula plant is one of the easiest which the florist sells but, unlike other pot plants, it doesn't recover if it gets too dry as it cannot take up the water, so will drown and die. Feel the earth to see if it is damp and water regularly with a small can – the earth should be damp not wet.

If the plant is drooping it does not always need water and after a particularly cold night plants do flag, as they do outdoors, so leave them alone and let them recover in the warmth of the day. At night, be careful to move them well away from the window and out of draughts.

Q I was looking after a plant for a friend and it flopped completely. It didn't need watering, what should I have done?

A Looking after a friend's plant is very unnerving. Do ask what sort of aspect (sunny or shady) it is used to and whether the friend has central heating, as temperature is very important.

Some plants are particularly awkward to have in a room if the temperature fluctuates. An even temperature, say the kitchen, would probably suit it best.

Q Should I feed it?

A No, if the plant is past taking up water it could not absorb a 'pick-me-up'.

SPRAYING

Central heating causes a dry atmosphere and plants should be sprayed fairly often. Touch the leaves, they should never feel dry and papery, except those of course which may be dying off in the natural way. If you want to revive your plant with a really good spray, put it in the sink to avoid splashing polished furniture etc. Be careful when you put it back in its place that the leaves have stopped dripping.

SPRAYING INDOOR PLANTS AGAINST PESTS

There are two kinds of sprays. One a fairly large 'mister', almost as big as the garden plastic sprayer and the other much smaller, which should be used for the more delicate plants.

Q I must use something on my plant, it has a lot of little white flies.

A This wretched pest is a curse of the greenhouse and all indoor plants, as the warm conditions evidently suit it. It would be better to take the plant out of the room and use a special spray, such as Sprayday, which I hear good reports of. The trouble is the spray might be too mild for the white fly, which is resistant to almost everything and one has to be careful not to kill the plant instead of the fly. I have tried my old standby Derris powder, taking the plant right outside if the weather is at all suitable, then one can use a gentle spray to wash the powder off. What I would really advise is to discard the plant as it will affect the others.

FAMILIAR HOUSE PLANTS

I find myself in a little difficulty when writing about house plants for the beginner, for some of the most usual often given as presents, are by no means easy. The cyclamen and the African violet are such ones, so let us start off with one or two easy house plants.

Maranta

This is one of the easiest house plants to manage. The maranta family is grown for its leaves, which are green and attractively veined in red, although it has quite a pretty little flower and the best of them is **Maranta Tricolor**. Though it is said not to like direct sunlight, mine was perfectly happy standing on a table against a wall facing a large South picture window. This gets over the difficulty of needing a good light, but not direct sun. It wanted no feeding, only an occasional drink from the saucer it was standing on. Entirely through my own fault it died, because I put it out in the garden and did not bring it in early enough, which should be by the end of September.

Swiss-cheese Plant

This is the one with the big shiny leaves with bits cut out of them. One might almost think some pest had taken a few bites, but the leaves are meant to look like this and the plant has been given its name after the gruyere cheese which it resembles. It needs a warm room away from direct sunlight and is often grown most success-fully in centrally-heated flats. As long as it is kept away from draughts, the plant can stand on the floor, for it needs plenty of room to grow upwards, living up to its Latin name of *Monstera*.

Devoted owners tend their leaves with oil sold for the purpose, which gives them a beautiful sheen. Though this is not strictly necessary, the leaves do need to be kept free of dust. Spray occa-sionally, keep moist and they can drink out of a bowl or saucer; needing most water during the growing periods in spring and summer.

The Spider Plant – (Chlorophytum comosum)

This is the one which reproduces itself with lots of little hanging stems on which new plants form.

Q Do they ever have any flowers? We have one on the office window-sill which has little plants almost down to the floor. Is that all that happens?

A It doesn't have any flowers, but the plantlets are very attrac-tive. If they are getting in the way of anything, they can be deta-ched (cut from the main stem with a clean sharp knife) and planted out in potting compost to start all over again. The Spider plant is reckoned to be one of the easiest of all indoor plants, which is why it is so often seen in offices and waiting-rooms.

Philodendron

Here is another plant grown for its leaves. Besides offices and waiting-rooms, foyers of hotels which go in for troughs of plants often
have them, as they do not mind the doors constantly opening and
shutting in all weathers. Philodendrons deserve their reputation of
being easy and putting up with neglect, which will endear them to
the busy reader. The kind most usually seen is **P. scandens**, the
climbing variety, which needs a fairly stout stake to hold its mass
of leaves and stalks. Like most house plants it should not be in
direct sunlight.

Tradescantia

This is a small trailing plant with pointed leaves which friends
often give little cuttings of, rather like the 'bits' from the border.
T. albiflora is said to produce white flowers, which would be
an improvement on the more usual variety, **T. tricolor**. The
latter grows very easily but relies on its leaves for colour which
often revert to plain green. The experts say to grow it where
there is plenty of light and others have told me to cut out the
plain green shoots when they appear to stop them taking over
from the variegated, but both bits of advice are worth taking.
The tricolor should produce very effective green and white
leaves striped pink. It is meant to trail not climb and it is a
waste of time, as I have discovered myself, to try and get some
of it up a stake as people often do. It is a vigorous little plant,
very easy to grow and should be given plenty of room to trail.
Q Mine is far too long, can one cut it back?
A It comes to no harm if the trailers are shortened and the cuttings root easily in water if you want more plants. Choose one of
the side shoots which is just coming into growth and when it is
ready to be transferred to a pot, having rooted, see Cuttings.

The Umbrella Plant – (Peltiphyllum)

This must be an easy house plant for I had it in my first house
with its old-fashioned draughty sash windows, no central heating
at that time either. It has attractive cut leaves, almost like a

small palm arranged something like an open umbrella. It is a convenient height at about 18ins and likes plenty of water, which it
can drink out of the saucer. With these very thirsty plants, re-fill-
ing the shallow saucer when the earth feels dry is better than letting it droop. The plant takes up what it wants and any water left
in the saucer should be emptied away.

Q Aren't there any easy flowering house plants?

A House plants are mostly foliage plants, that is grown for their
leaves. These are the true house plants, born and bred for the purpose and as such will last for years if conditions suit them.

With flowering plants we are moving into the cool greenhouse,
where the plants are forced on gently to be flowering at special
times, making them more difficult, particularly when they have
finished flowering. Before going on to them, we will just mention
the ivies, listed under their Latin name of *Hedera*. All like cool conditions and can present difficulties in warm centrally heated
rooms.

The Ornamental Ivy

We have already noted that the ornamental ivies, such as one
would buy for the house, are hybrids of **Hedera helix**, our British ivy and **Hedera canariensis**, which originally came from the
Canary Isles. Both ivies started off a plain green but we are looking for the variegated kinds and the names are as variable as ever.
Look for gold, which means yellow and green or silver, which
means white and green. The best ones for the house, like *H.
canariensis*, are the ones from the warmer climates. Ivies like to
be cool, but these hybrids will do in ordinary room temperature
provided they are not in sunlight or allowed to get too dry.

Q I bought mine, a beautiful green and white with big leaves,
straight from a garden centre, but it hasn't done well and I am
rather disappointed as it was expensive.

A It sounds as if it came from the enclosed part of the garden
centre, run more or less as a greenhouse with some heat. Windows are sometimes slightly darkened so that the sun never
comes through in a harmful way, which would scorch the
plants. Often these houses have an overhead watering system so
that the leaves never become dry and this produces the familiar
greenhouse smell of damp earth and warmth combined.

Greenhouse conditions are not easy to imitate in an ordinary room, but we will not despair. Move your ivy well away from any sunny window and give it a North aspect if you can. If it came from a greenhouse it will not mind a little warmth. Now for spraying; move the ivy to the sink and give it a real soaking with the spray, letting it drink up from a bowl at the same time. What is better still, is to put it out in gentle rain in warm weather.

Your plant could be the variety of *H. canariensis* which is seen so often growing up walls in sheltered spots. It can be an outdoor plant, so a shady part of the garden where it still gets the natural rain is a good place to recuperate.

Q Friends say I might have over-watered it.

A This is a danger, for as soon as a plant looks poorly one rushes for the watering can. Spraying never does any harm, but if the earth feels damp leave watering alone at the root level.

Q I can never make up my mind when the earth is damp.

A Just touch it with a finger and if the earth sticks to it, the earth is damp enough.

The Indoor Primula

The two kinds most often grown are **P. sinensis** and **P. malacoides**. Both are easy to grow as long as they are kept moist and away from heat, such as fires or radiators. Like the ornamental ivies, they probably did better when grown in the older kind of house. Indeed my primula was given to me in the war and it must have had a fairly rough time what with fuel shortages and so on, but managed to survive. I remember its being always thirsty, which was remedied by plunging it into a bowl of water when it more or less collapsed. It did recover, but I do not recommend this rather rough treatment, so keep an eye on it and a once a week plunge should be enough. Like most indoor plants they like plenty of light, but not direct sun.

Q They must get sun if they are put out in summer, why doesn't it hurt them?

A There is so much more light out of doors, that one can afford to put such plants in a shady corner where they would not get direct sunlight. The one our American neighbour planted outside by mistake faced nearly due North – she was lucky and it was a mild winter!

The label most house or indoor plants come with will tell you the temperature the plants like. Something in the range of 60–70 F would like a warm room and could be placed outside in a tub in summer and the cooler range, 40–60 F would need a sheltered shady spot.

Q Some people get rashes from primulas, which kind are they?

A It is said to be *Primula obconica*, but I would not risk any kind if I suffered from that kind of allergy; it would only spoil one's enjoyment of the plant.

The Indoor Poinsettia

These are the plants brought on for the Christmas season and are red, white (very pale green) or pink. The red are the easiest to grow. They will do well in the warmth of an ordinary living room when wanted as a Christmas decoration and can retire after the festivities to any room which is reasonably warm and has plenty of light. The coloured petals are really bracts, like clematis and the true flower is the yellow in the middle. The real flower is more seen in pictures than in life and I have found that it seldom comes to anything, but as one buys for the coloured leaves this is not important. The red particularly, will last quite easily for a month or two and when they have dropped off, as they do about March or April, they can look very poorly especially as this is also the time the old green leaves fall. As long as new buds are coming to replace the old leaves, you can have quite a pretty little green bush, but it will not re-colour and the most one gets is red stalks on the new leaves, particularly near the top. They need no cosseting but water regularly by immersing them every week or so, according to the feel of the soil and do not leave water in the saucer.

Growers recommend that the plants should be cut back within an inch or so of the roots and put in the dark for the summer, watering only enough to keep them going. When they start growing again in the autumn (instead of spring), the hope is that they will be stimulated into producing the coloured bracts. It sounds rather a difficult task to me, but if the reader should want to try I advise a well-grown plant (for they vary in size) with red bracts. Cut back before the new growth has started.

The Indoor Cyclamen – (large-flowered)

Q What about cyclamens? Mine have always been disasters.

A Everyone has difficulties with these; they are really cool green-house plants and need somewhere like an enclosed verandah to recuperate if they start to droop. They are lovely flowers and a present at Christmas of a handsome plant, perhaps in a gold-painted wicker basket such as florists sell, simply cries out to be the ornament of someone's drawing-room and to suggest moving it to some cold window-sill is very little help.

These cultivated plants are hybrids from the different kind of **C. persicum**, which grow wild in the warmer parts of the Mediterranean. Readers may have seen them just coming out in the Greek Islands or Israel in the course of a winter holiday. Although the days can be quite warm and sunny, the nights are distinctly nippy, but the little wild flower is quite hardy.

The best way with the indoor cyclamen is to keep it away from any source of warmth. It can stay in the day in a warm room, but at night move it somewhere cooler. Do not immerse in water, but let it drink from a shallow saucer of not too cold water. If it droops, move it somewhere cool, do not water and let it pick up gradually.

Q Do the buds need anything to bring them on? A lot of mine came to nothing.

A The plant has had the feeding it needs to bring it on and the usual reason for buds not coming out in an indoor plant is that they have got too dry. Spray gently with the small spray but do not let the corm (which you can see on the surface) get wet or it will rot.

African Violets

Here is another tricky one which has had books written about it. Even keeping to all the advice one can still have failures. I daresay the very fact that it is known to be difficult makes one worry too much and a great many plants both indoors and out would be better with less tending, not more.

Most people find that once their plant has settled down in a place which suits it, the trouble is not so much that it won't grow, but that it won't flower. Though seemingly healthy and

happy, once it has finished with the flowers it came with (sometimes even buds come to nothing) it never flowers again.

Q   Where's the best place to grow them?

A   They seem to prefer the country to the town, flourishing on
window-sills as long as they are not too sunny. Here again a
North window is recommended.

If you buy one at an RHS show you can always ask for an easy
colour, but in general, blue and mauve are easier than the pink
and near-red. As always, choose a really healthy bushy little
plant for your first attempt. My plants are all together on a
West facing table, just a foot or so away from the window. The
company of other plants is an asset, for they like moisture.

Q   People always tell one to put them into the bathroom, is this a
good idea?

A   The idea is to produce the same kind of damp warm climate
that they come from originally, but I have never found the bathroom does any good. Perhaps the smell of soap and bath-salts
overcome the good effects of the steam.

When their first flowering is over, a Phostab every six weeks or
so is a good idea. Some kinds, especially the blue ones, will go on
flowering if encouraged in this way, but others have definite spring
and autumn seasons. If you notice the plant is looking unusually
healthy and growing strongly, particularly from the centre, this
is a good sign. Give it plenty of water and if it is producing
flower buds it will drink from the saucer in one gulp, almost as
though siphoned up. When the flowers begin to fade it will
need less water, sometimes only once a week. Let it drink what
it likes and any water left in the saucer after an hour or so
means it has had enough and do not water the next day.

These are plants which are worth keeping once they have finished flowering, provided your plant seems happy. If it didn't
do well and you have no other convenient place, buy another
in bud and try again, perhaps with an easier colour.

Indoor Azaleas

These are great favourites to give as presents and the great thing
to remember is not to let them get too dry. They are evergreen
and if you notice the leaves beginning to drop, take them to the
sink and give a good spray at the same time as a soaking in the

bowl. Leave at least until the bubbles of air have stopped coming from the pot and even overnight would not be too long.

Q Don't they need soft water?

A Yes, they hate the lime in hard town water, but softened water is all right. The best one can do otherwise is to use filtered water or to boil a kettle of water and let it cool, in the hopes that it will have deposited the lime into the kettle. Natural rain is best, if the weather is warm enough and the rain gentle and of course if it is not too difficult collect rain-water from the gutter. I have a feeling that the busy reader will do none of these things, but use water from the tap as I used to and hope for the best.

I had a problem room facing North and South just like the garden, with the South end too sunny and the North end too near the fire. Even so I somehow managed azaleas at the North end, hard water and all, by giving them an occasional spell in the garden, or in the kitchen away from the gas.

Cinerarias

In the case of the coloured daisy-flowered plant, so often seen in the windows of smart hotels, they are recognised as one of the most difficult of indoor plants. They very seldom flower a second time, even with buds coming on and are even more inclined to flop suddenly than the cyclamen. They can do with quite cool conditions being almost outdoor plants and one sees them coming out in the very early spring in window-boxes. If a friend has a verandah or somewhere more suitable and can take them, I should make a present of them.

If you should choose to struggle on, the usual rules apply; cool room but no draughts, light but no direct sun and above all no watering if the plant looks droopy and the soil damp.

Q Why do they do so well in window-boxes?

A I often wonder myself. Apart from the obvious fact that the hotel can afford to renew them if they fail, I have always thought it must be that any real indoor site is too warm for them.

CONSERVATORIES

Though I am no expert on the care of plants grown in this way, I thought I ought to mention conservatories, as they have come back so much into fashion.

Q   What is the difference between a greenhouse and a conservatory?

A   Both are for the same purpose; to protect tender plants from the frost and to bring them on with a certain amount of heat. Such a greenhouse would not drop below 45 F. at night and be about 60–65 F in the day, depending on its purpose. The commercial growers usually specialise in certain plants, say carnations, and adjust the temperature accordingly.

A conservatory would be more for displaying plants and for bringing them on for the house, for instance the enormous mop-head chrysanthemums, left in their pots and brought in to stand banked up in a corner of the room. Such conservatories are usually joined on to the wall of the house to give shelter and some heat, but would need heating as well in winter.

The garden greenhouse of the bigger kind, would be built on to the outbuildings of a walled garden and these have benches and also beds of earth where the greenhouse kinds of tomatoes are often grown. In a walled garden one might have peaches against the wall or vines in their special 'vineries'; the latter being the real hothouse variety, seldom seen nowadays. All have glass roofs which can be opened in summer.

Q   What about the ornamental conservatories they sell nowadays?

A   They are certainly very decorative and designed to be built on to the house in the old way. If you would like to use it as a summer or even winter room, which of course would have to be heated, then the plants would be in pots, house plants probably and of the kind which like a higher temperature.

Q   Could I grow any flowering plants?

A   You would have to consult an expert, as tending a conservatory is a professional gardener's job. The easy way out would be to enquire at the RHS Show, where there are growers who specialise in old-fashioned conservatory plants and see how his plants would do in pots. They would not die in a cool temperature but they need heat, specially sun in the summer, to bring them into flower.

SOME PLANTS FOR THE CONSERVATORY

Here are a few of the old-fashioned favourites which I would love to see in a friend's conservatory.

Plumbago

This is a lovely blue climber with small trumpet flowers born in a cluster of ten or a dozen blooms. Given its head it will climb up the wall of your conservatory, flowering continually. They grow out of doors on the houses in Provence, where the winters are fairly cold with snow on the mountains not so far away, but of course the secret is the hot sunny summer. Your plant would not die, but it might easily fail to flower even in what we think is a sunny summer. It would be better to try and get the 'white' (a very pale blue) which flowers out of doors in a sunny corner, but must be brought into the house in winter.

Q I thought I had a plumbago in the garden. It's a small bush and quite pretty, but mine doesn't flower well.

A I found exactly the same when I grew mine years ago. For looking-up purposes, it is described as a flower "with a shrubby habit"; this garden kind is hardy and though it can be cut by frost in the winter, it will recover the following summer. The flowers are a darker blue but the same shape as the greenhouse variety and they need a really sunny open position facing South or West to flower well.

The Latin names are **Plumbago capensis** for the conservatory or greenhouse, and **Ceratostigma plumbaginoides** for the garden.

Q What a pity to give such a lovely plant such a hideous name.

A It's done now, for if they were to change the name or give it a prettier English one, gardeners would continue to call it plumbago. Occasionally the garden kind is called ceratostigma, which is not much of an improvement.

Datura

Of all the plants I remember, in or out of the conservatory, this is the one I most admired. The conservatory at my grandparents' house was something of a hothouse and stood in the shelter of the house but free-standing. It was heated by water pipes along the floor and tended by a boiler in the basement of the little building.

The pony, wearing her special treading-on-grass galoshes, brought the coke for the boiler from wherever the coalman had left the sacks. The whole thing was wonderful to a child's eyes and somehow fitting for the wonderful trumpet-flowered plant which grew in the corner of the conservatory, by the special water tank which held the rain-water led in from the gutter.

The flowers were cream in the bud, with the trumpet two or three inches long finishing in a crumpled looking flower which, as it straightened out a little, turned white and produced the most wonderful scent. I was delighted to see them offered for sale again in Blom's catalogue, but I must warn that it is a big plant, the one I remember being 4–5ft tall and the same across.

The first time I saw one growing, since the one I remembered, was in a garden in what was then S. Rhodesia, but it had single flower and though beautiful didn't have the lovely scent. 'Out there' it is called the moonflower, but the catalogue says 'angel's trumpet' and I can be no help, since I never knew its name, except that it came from abroad, all of which added to its glamour.

Q If I bought a really big pot would it grow in that?

A It seems to me that it would be a wonderful ornament to the new-style conservatory that one sits in and grown in a corner it would have all the room it wanted. In fact it is actually recommended for this kind of situation, which would of course mean heating, but this would surely not be a problem as the people using the conservatory to sit in would need heat every bit as much as the plants.

Gardenia

This is an evergreen bush, very similar to a camellia, but with scented flowers. They were much favoured as sprays to be worn on grand occasions and as exotic as an orchid. They need 60 F. all the year round, which is not easy for an amateur to achieve and though the plant might survive at a lower temperature, no flower buds would form.

Bougainvillaea

Another climber which eventually reaches about 10ft. It grows extensively in Africa, but the most likely place for the reader to have seen it would be somewhere like Madeira, with its warm equable climate. There is a chasm in the centre of Funchal; it must be a dried up water course, which fills at certain times and is covered in with bougainvillea. It is of that red which is so hard to describe, not exactly rose or maroon, but somewhere in between.

Q They sell it in the garden centres, can it be the same plant?

A I had not realised this. It is possible that it has been specially treated like the poinsettia, so that it never gets too big, or perhaps it is meant to be pruned and to climb up the sort of ladder-like stakes which one can buy at these centres. The easy one is **B. glabra**, which I have certainly seen in greenhouses growing up to the ceiling and making a good contrast with the plumbago. People do grow very tall plants in their 'plant room', for this is what it amounts to with the real enthusiast, but I do think somewhere like that is its proper home.

Q It would be lovely to have those exotic kind of plants, but I could never afford the heating, let alone the expert help.

A Further back in the year, I have said a little about the unheated greenhouse or frame. The sole worry is keeping the really cold frosts out, which means an oil stove at night through the coldest part of the year, no great expense and some winters would not even need that. These are excellent places for growing seeds as they can be sown as early as January and though slow to germinate, they will be way ahead of the ones sown outdoors. Bulbs can be brought on and plants, which like it cooler than the ordinary living-room, can recuperate. Half-hardy seeds will be safe if covered with a plastic sheet or glass and put near the oil stove or heater. If you raise seeds, far from being an expense it will be a great saver, bedding plants being so expensive as we have noted before.

TWO CHRISTMAS SPECIALS

The Norfolk Island Pine – Araucaria excelsa

This is a true indoor plant grown without any trouble at all, with the only worry being that the miniature pine, which was growing so prettily in its pot, suddenly turns into a real tree. My other grandmother had such a one many years ago in her drawing-room which, when I first saw it, was a tree about 3–4ft. It had been bought as an ornament for a small occasional table and soon had to be moved from there to the ground, where it gave no trouble only continuing to grow rather too fast. To the best of my recollection it never reached more than 6ft.

It needed shade and plenty of room and could be put out in a shady part of the garden for some light rain and a change of air. The room would have been cold by to-day's standards, almost exactly 45–65 F. which is its preferred range of temperature.

It is a very pretty little tree, the branches arranged so neatly in layers that it cries out to be a Christmas tree. I suppose the ideal would be to have it locked away in a cool room until it burst upon the family in all its decorated splendour, but not many readers will have such a spare room. A day or two of warmth at Christmas time should not be too much and it could go back to where it usually grew afterwards.

The Christmas Cactus – Schlumbergera bridgesii

The first thing to know about the Christmas cactus is that it is not a cactus and needs leaf-mould with a little bonemeal or other nourishment, such as is sold for pot plants. Once potted it can be more or less neglected and in this way it is more like a cactus, which it resembles; the kind with one leaf growing out of another in long sprays.

Q   All I know is that it should never be moved.
A   Yes, it cannot grip with its roots in the same way as other plants and is easily upset. It is usually very happy in the kitchen if not too near the gas, on a nice light window-sill. Water sparingly with a can, spray when the buds appear and do not leave water in the saucer.

Q   Mine came out in November, was that early or is it a different kind?
A   Most probably it was a different kind. There is one called **S. truncata** which is much earlier, sometimes even October.

Q   I have been told to put mine out in the garden in the summer.
A   Yes, the other school of thought only says not to move it when the buds appear. Something like a light frost is needed to stimulate it into flower and by mistake I left mine out in the October hurricane and it produced buds soon after, but died the next year. Pro-

vided it likes where it is growing I agree with the people who advise that one should keep it in the same place. It will grow into a nice bushy plant you can be proud of and likes the shade wherever it is. Give it a little nourishment, liquid or a tablet, round about October.

INDOOR BULBS

Have a look at the bulbs which are being grown for Christmas. They should be in a cool room in the house with the bud well visible (see Planting Indoor Bulbs). About a week before Christmas if they show signs of colour in the buds, they can be brought into the warmth. If the bulbs have not reached the right stage within ten days or so of Christmas, leave them in the cool and do not try to hurry them, or the flower bud will sit down without a proper stalk or the leaves will get drawn up leaving the stunted flower behind. In the case of narcissi, they can dry up and never flower at all. Keep them for January, a dreary month when flowers are expensive and let them take their own pace. Buy a poinsettia for Christmas instead.

We have now completed December and therefore the year. To sum up I am going to discuss achieving colour in the garden over a long period.

SUMMARY

COLOUR OVER A LONG PERIOD

Q I feel my garden is much too small to have colour there all the time.

A Never say die, for if you are certain that this is what you want, it can be achieved in quite a small space. Everything is a compromise though and there is no doubt that the really spectacular show of colour, comes from having your bed filled with only two or at the most three kinds of plants which will all flower together. There is nothing to beat this for effect, simple though it sounds.

Q I know what you mean, but I leave that sort of gardening for the public parks. I like things coming on all through the season as for me that is the interest.

A That too is my kind of gardening. The main drawback though to this sort of garden and getting a succession of colour, is that the weather can let one down. Plants which should be coming on hang back and one seems to have nothing but green leaves.

Q I have also found this and it is infuriating. What is the best way round it?

A For the first timer we have tried to recommend only those plants which are reliable flowerers. We have gone into these in some detail and the best way of explaining, is to show three pictures of three real gardens, where the plants are situated and what time of year they come out; all these I have tried myself some time or another.

OUR PRESENT GARDEN

The Back Garden

The little back garden is more or less as we found it and the huge heavy stones in the rockery would not have been easily done away

370

with. The beautiful flowering **Camellia** bushes were then about 8ft each way and the little **Maple**, though suffering from neglect, was so lovely with its spring growth that we would not have parted with it either. On the other hand, if the reader is only thinking of plenty of colour, it did not leave much of the garden free for other planting.

The two **Bay Trees** came with us from the balcony in the flat. The one in the shelter of the house, survived the sudden late cold and strong northerly wind of 1987, but the one in a less sheltered position, sadly did not. Many other gardens suffered in the same way and the second tub now has in it the compact **Viburnum 'Eve Price'**, which flowers all the winter and so in this way brings more colour. The small border on the right is intensely cultivated; the most usual pattern being the early **Daffodil 'February Gold'** followed by a later **'Thalia'** and the early **Tulip 'Keizerskroon'**. The later **Darwin Tulips** are for the two tubs outside the window, as I found they came out rather too late for the little border. At present they are planted up very effectively with lily-flowering tulips. The camellias are a joy from January onwards and take over from the pink **Chaenomeles japonica**, which is never tempted to come out too early however mild the weather.

Q The trouble with the camellias is that they are lovely in the winter and early spring, but then there is nothing for the rest of the summer.

A It has defeated me for eight years. The fact is that the garden is so shaded from the house on one side and the trees on the other, that I have not persuaded anything to make a show in the deep shade. At the moment we have an ornamental **Ivy**, the small one with variegated leaves which I planted out from the remains of an indoor garden bowl. I am trying a hydrangea in a pot, which can be moved out into the sun to bring it into flower and then back again, where I hope it will continue to flower. When we have planted out the little border for the summer and facing as it does nearly due South, almost any bedding plant will grow.

The Front Garden

Starting with the earliest flowerers. The small rockery could be planted with the early mauve **Crocus tommasinianus,**

Snowdrops or **Aconitum** or even all three and they will come out in late January or early February. In the front crocuses of the larger varieties which come on later in February or early March, make a fine and reliable show. These are followed along the edge by **Dog's-tooth violets**, which having flowered leave behind them useful green edging to keep the earth in place. Another good 'edger' to come later on is the small **Campanula carpatica**, which is very reliable and neat as long as it has a certain amount of sun.

In the corner is a clump of **Iris stylosa** (or *Unguicularis*), which will flower in January and even sometimes in December in time for Christmas. The **Forsythia** is fully out by March and provides as much colour as anyone could wish for. The evergreen **Azaleas** take over in April, with something like the early tulip 'Apricot Beauty' which can be lifted in the summer. The next early shrub is the **Viburnum burkwoodii**, with its sweet-smelling flowers in late March or early April. The **Viburnum tinus** on its right should flower from November right through the winter. May is always a difficult month if one is trying to have a long sequence of flowering and unless the April plants hang on as it were, we have nothing specially planned. The roses will come very soon in June and the ones we have here are **'Iceberg'** and **'Peace'**, neither of which mind a certain amount of shade and then there is **'Grandpa Meiland'**, which gets more sun. The smaller bushes for the front are **Garnette Roses**.

As we get into July the **Hydrangea** will be starting to flower and will make a magnificent display until the end of the summer. Towards the end of the month the **Fuchsias** will be flowering and will continue to do so until the frosts. The large *F. riccartonii* which grows almost wild in Cornwall was here when we arrived, together with the hardy red and purple 'Tom Thumb'. Last of all comes the **Andromeda** and though this is now classed as a pieris, it is hardier. It does not have the red spring growth of the pieris but the evergreen leaves are very attractive and the long lily-of-the-valley like flowers come just as everything else is beginning to fade in late September.

It is essential to fertilize the ground well where there is a long sequence of flowering plants. Leaf-mould and manure or bone-meal dug in in the spring and autumn will keep things healthy and the roses may need a little tonic such as dried blood as they come into flower.

The Rockery

We have noted the difficulty of rockeries tending to have just the one season, usually spring and when that is over they can look rather forlorn. Ours has two seasons, the early spring bulbs and the later blue and white **Campanula** and is so small that it can at least look tidy. The campanula stays neat and compact throughout the winter and then suddenly grows, spreading over the bare patches and flowering beautifully. Small **Roses, London Pride**, some **Primulas** and **Auricula** are what make up the rest of the rockery, except for the very successful **Ferns** and **Ivy** at the shady North end, which in the late spring have some **Solomon's Seal** appearing amongst them. The little evergreens, though not exactly coloured, keep the pattern interesting through the year. The rockery is part of the back garden.

Behind the rockery the climbing **Hydrangea petiolaris** is out in the early summer with its huge flowers lasting several weeks. The **Rose 'Prima Ballerina'**, after struggling in a dark corner, was transplanted to its present spot and makes a long and colourful display just where it is needed. In the middle, the **Pieris 'Forest Flame'** is a marvellous little one-man band when it comes to colour throughout the seasons. The pale green winter shoots are followed by bright red spring growth, which fades to a pinker shade. These are then followed by lily-of-the-valley flowers and so back again to the pale green shoots of winter. One hardly has a chance to see its ordinary leaves which are very neat and pretty and but for the fact it is not completely hardy and must have an acid soil, one could not wish for a prettier more useful shrub.

The little narrow bed right up against the house has proved stony and difficult and as such beds do, they always tend to dry out, with mulching seemingly to have very little effect. However, **Lily-of-the-valley** grow well there, coming out at a good time in May and as they can't be seen from the house they are good for picking. The end of this bed where it sticks out from the wall gets sun and herbs such as chives, parsley, sage and thyme, bought in pots and planted annually, all do well here. Rosemary, further along, is the only permanent bush. The small bed where the *Chaenomeles japonica* was growing when we came, also proved to have **Snowdrops** and we have planted Winter and Autumn **Cyclamen**. The **Winter Jasmine** planted in the narrow bed will train along the wall and take the place of *C. japonica* which was a victim of a cold winter.

OUR FIRST GARDEN *(see illustration on page 13)*

We arrived here immediately after the end of the war in 1947 and in this garden we are going to consider colour with aspect.

On the West side was a bombed site where three houses had been, with gardens the same length but slightly wider than our own. This not only let in the sun but allowed more air to circulate. The point about this in considering colour, is that with plenty of sun and air in a town garden, plants will behave more or less as they do in the country and flower when they are expected to. Bedding plants do well because they like really hot sun and a certain amount of shelter which a walled garden gives them. The right-hand house was still standing, with two acacia trees at the bottom of the garden and one tall sycamore on the East side. None of this mattered much as the sun soon moved round and I have pictures of the whole garden bathed in sunshine, which I can hardly believe when I think of the difference made by houses being built. Rather a sad contrast, but I hope it will encourage readers who have North-facing gardens.

Q I am told that my tree is a false **Acacia**. What does a real one look like?

A I'm sure your tree is what everyone would call a real acacia and often seen in towns, it has white flowers like laburnum, but it is a real forest tree whose Latin name is *Robinia pseudoacacia*. The true acacia is what we call a mimosa and in Australia a wattle and is the one with the tiny fluffy balls of yellow flowers, which is out in the winter in the South of France and sold on the streets to remind us of spring.

To go back to our own garden, the shady part had **Japanese Anemones** which must have been planted before the war and once established are practically impossible to uproot, but they came in very handy when the garden became more shady. It was in the very hot summer of 1947 that they nearly died, as I had removed the huge leaves they had grown, not knowing that they do this to protect their roots from the hot sun and one should leave them alone. From the colour point of view they were rather a dead loss as they only come out at the end of the